Escape from the Pit

A Woman's Resistance in Nazi-Occupied Poland, 1939–1943

RENIA KUKIELKA

EXCELSIOR
EDITIONS

Cover Credit: Renya Kukielka in Palestine, c. 1944–1945. Courtesy of Yfat Barkan-Pinto, Israel/ private archive.

Published by State University of New York Press, Albany

Escape from the Pit was originally published in the British Mandate for Palestine, in Hebrew and under the title *Bindudim Uvamahteret* in 1944 by Hakibbutz Hameuchad. An unauthorized English-language edition was published in the United States bearing an assertion of Copyright 1947 by Sharon Books, Inc.

Published in association with the United States Holocaust Memorial Museum.

The translation to Hebrew from the manuscript in Polish was done by H. Sh. Ben-Avram.

Printed in the United States of America

Excelsior Editions is an imprint of State University of New York Press

For information, contact State University of New York Press, Albany, NY
www.sunypress.edu

Library of Congress Cataloging-in-Publication Data

Name: Kukielka, Renya, 1924– author.
Title: Escape from the pit : one woman's resistance in Nazi-occupied Poland, 1939–1944 / Renya Kukielka.
Other titles: Bi-nedudim uva-maḥteret. English | One woman's resistance in Nazi-occupied Poland, 1939–1944
Description: Albany : State University of New York Press, [2023] | Includes bibliographical references and index.
Identifiers: LCCN 2022059322 | ISBN 9781438494784 (hardcover : alk. paper) | ISBN 9781438494791 (ebook) | ISBN 9781438494777 (pbk. : alk. paper)
Subjects: LCSH: Kukielka, Renya, 1924– | Holocaust, Jewish (1939–1945)—Poland—Będzin—Biography. | Jewish ghettos—Poland—Będzin—Biography. | World War, 1939–1945—Jewish resistance—Poland—Będzin—Biography. | Holocaust survivors—Israel—Biography. | Wodzisław (Poland)—Biography.
Classification: LCC DS134.72.K85 A3 2023 | DDC 940.5318092 [B]—dc23/eng/20230523
LC record available at https://lccn.loc.gov/2022059322

10 9 8 7 6 5 4 3 2 1

Escape from the Pit

Contents

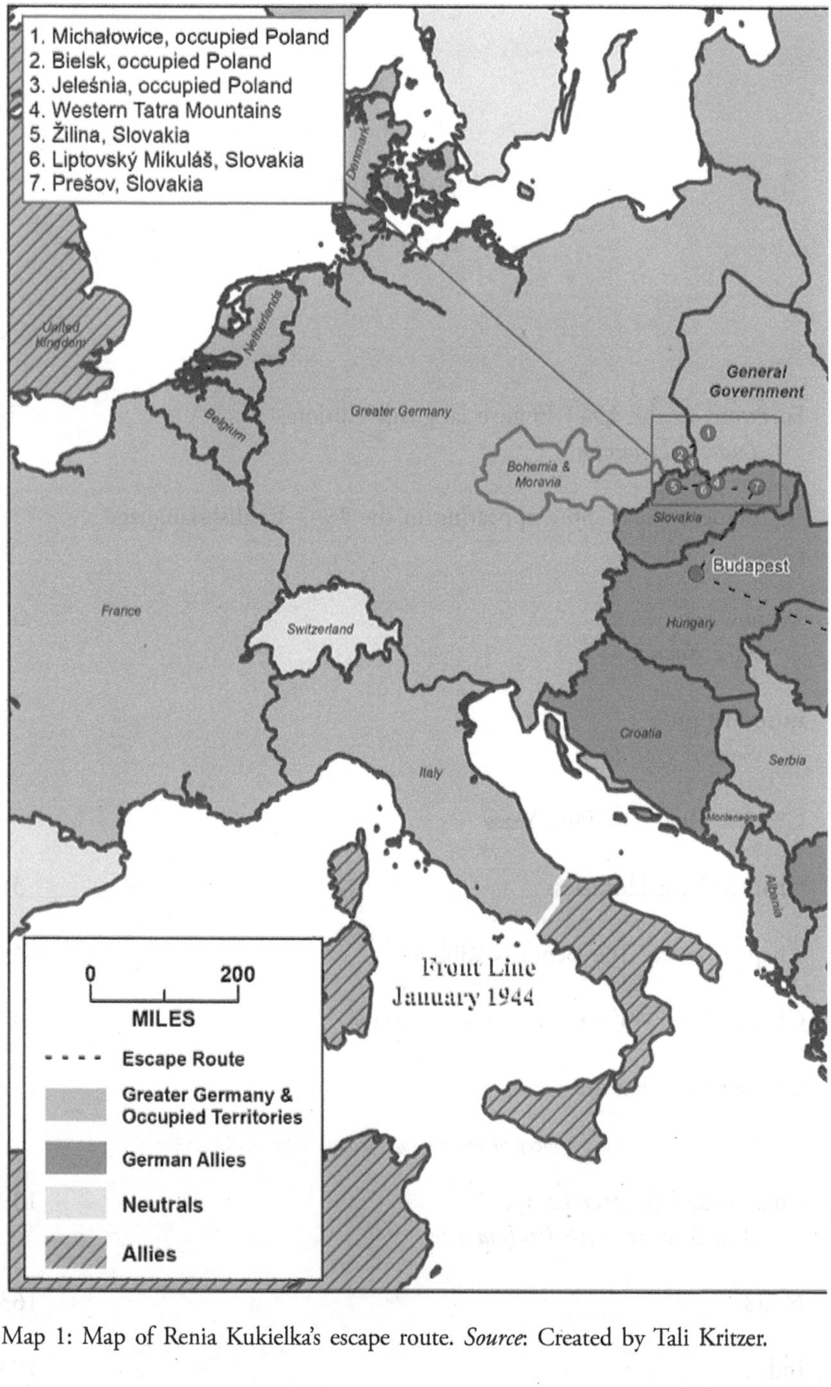

Map 1: Map of Renia Kukielka's escape route. *Source*: Created by Tali Kritzer.

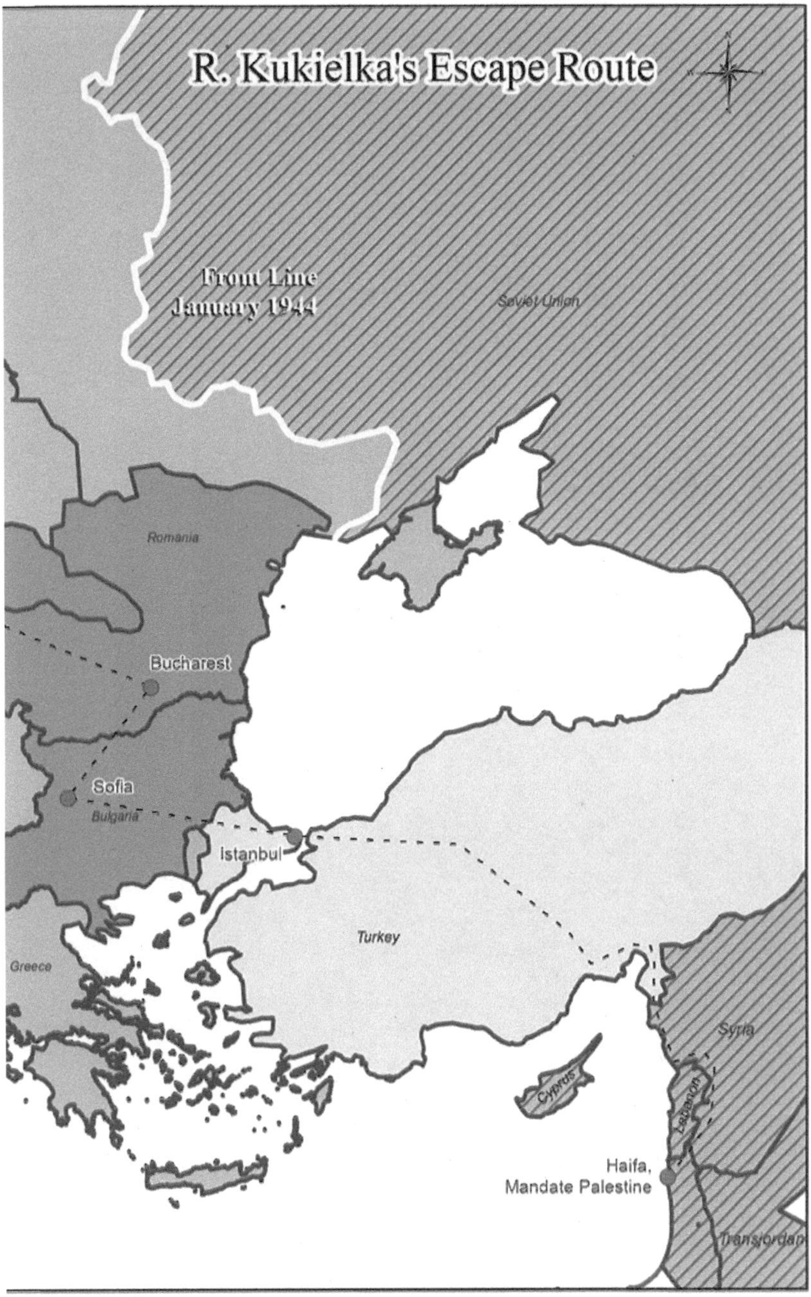
R. Kukielka's Escape Route
Front Line
January 1944
Soviet Union
Romania
Bucharest
Sofia
Bulgaria
Istanbul
Turkey
Greece
Syria
Cyprus
Lebanon
Haifa,
Mandate Palestine
Transjordan

Foreword to the 1947 English-Language Edition

Jewish literature is not poor in the chronicles of martyrs. We have the memorial books of the First Crusade; we have the *Scepter of Judah*, the *Shevet Yehudah* of Shlomo ibn Verga; and we have Joseph Ha-Cohen's *Emek Habakha* (The Valley of Tears). These chronicles pierce the heart and cry out their necessary implicit accusation against Christendom. But the subjective note they strike is one of passive suffering and their conclusion is always akin to Joseph Ha-Cohen's: "Behold, O my God, and consider and sustain their cause!"

The Enlightenment came and the Emancipation and, except by a few scholars, these books were forgotten. It was thought, for a decade or two at least, that a great change had come over the world. But soon—as history goes—the change was seen to be in its essence no change at all and at the very height of what the fools of time and circumstance regarded as an age of progress, the old, old martyrdom of scattered Israel set in again with fiercer horrors and more scorching shame for its perpetrators than any known in the long roll of history.

It was not strange, then, that a new literature of martyrdom should arise. But this new literature, despite the enormity of the sufferings and the crimes it chronicled, was different from the old. It was, it is, an heroic literature; it *is* the literature of a people that has a great, a burning, a triumphant will to survive—to survive not only in the body, but by its survival to cause goodness and justice and the free spirit of man to triumph over all the foul fury of the powers and principalities of earth.

The books of this literature are written not by writers, by artists. They are written by young men and women, by boys and girls who, from the depths of mankind's degradation, saved themselves and as many of their fellows as they could and who, by what they are and suffered and survived, vindicated—they alone of all the people of this age—the immortal spirit of man. They are *ours*, ours first and foremost. But unless civilization slides wholly back into the jungle they will also become exemplars and symbols of the heroic life in the spirit to world generations that are yet unborn.

Such is that girl named Renia Kukielka who wrote in her artless but searing fashion this *Escape from the Pit.* She was fathoms deep in that pit; she is now in the land of our redemption; she tells of the unimaginable bridge between that pit and that land. There is no comment to be made that is or can be worthy of that telling. The tribute we can pay to her and her comrades is one and one only: to read her story, to let it penetrate us to the marrow; to let it change all Jewish lives that have not yet undergone the great and cleaving change; to see to it that the sufferings and the vast heroism of herself and her comrades bear the right fruit of the total dedication of all Israel to its redemption in the land that is its own.

Ludwig Lewisohn, 1947

"Autobiographical" Note to the 1947 English-Language Edition[1]

I was born in Jedrzejow[2] (government of Kielce) in 1924. My father was a small businessman. As far back as my memory takes me, I recall that his main thought for the future was to move the whole family to Palestine. My father was an ardent Zionist. My education ended when I completed public school. Because of prevailing antisemitism, it was impossible for me to enter high school. Instead, I took an evening course for a year, studying various subjects, including stenography. When I was fourteen I began working in an office as a typist, but the job did not last long. When I turned fifteen the war broke out and brought an end to the peaceful days with my family. Days of horror followed. In 1942 the Germans murdered my father, two sisters and a brother.

In 1944 my third sister, Sarah, who was active in the rescue of Jews from the ghetto of Bendzin, was caught in the Aryan sector of the city together with a group of Jewish children she was escorting and was taken away to an unknown destination.

Of the seven children in the house, only three have survived—myself and two brothers. The brothers, who have suffered much, have been in a DP camp in Germany for more than a year now. They think of nothing but getting to Palestine to join their only surviving sister.

I had dreams of going to Palestine from my childhood days. I finally realized that dream on March 14, 1944. As soon as I came, I turned to a kibbutz. Only here, in the collective, I thought, would I find solace. Here I would find warmth and the opportunity to forget the pain of the past.

During my first days at Kibbutz Dafna things were quite difficult for me. I found it hard to work in the field, especially on account of the climate, but by now I am used to it and find no trouble in keeping up with the others, who have been here many years.

During my two years in Palestine I have always worked at agriculture, in the orchard. In the evenings, when the work is done, I find an opportunity to read and study and catch up on what I missed.

These last two years have taught me that I was not wrong when I chose to go to the kibbutz. Here is a place where one feels the pulse of building a homeland. Here is a home for those who are still wandering, and whose eyes are turning toward us to build their future together with us.

Renia Kukielka
KIBBUTZ DAFNA
Summer, 1946

Acknowledgments

The long process for republication of Renia Kukielka's forgotten 1947 memoir *Escape from the Pit* involved many people, all of whom were moved by her book. Since Renia is no longer among us, as Renia's literary agent, who carried out her wish to revive her book, I would like to express my deepest gratitude on Renia's behalf to all of the people who helped in this process.

First and foremost, I am grateful to Benton Arnovitz, the former director of publications at the United States Holocaust Memorial Museum (USHMM) in Washington, DC, for making the initial decision to republish Renia's memoir and for signing an additional contract with State University of New York (SUNY) Press. I was fortunate to have had his wise counsel over the years, assisting me in my search for a publishing house and giving me invaluable suggestions during the development of this project. It was a privilege to work with him until his retirement.

Equally importantly, special gratitude goes to James Peltz, editor-in-chief of State University of New York Press, for taking the decision to publish the memoir. During many years of working on this project, he has proven to be extraordinarily patient and attentive. I am also very grateful for his sensitive editing of my afterword.

This new edition of the memoir also owes its publication to Dr. Severin Hochberg, a now retired staff historian of the USHMM, who was the first to recommend the book's republication. His gratifying and fruitful collaboration over the years has helped to bring the republication process to completion.

Many thanks also to Professor Doris Bergen, an outstanding Holocaust historian, the Chancellor Rose and Ray Wolfe Professor of Holocaust Studies at the University of Toronto. I deeply appreciate her encouragement of the idea of publication of the memoir and her personal warm support, as she provided me with ideas and explanations. Following her invitations to Holocaust conferences and seminars, I was fortunate to be exposed to the newest research. She also popularized the memoir through her own publications and through a seminar.

And, very significantly, my heartfelt thanks goes to my beautiful daughter, Dr. Paulina Ezer, who was involved in the project from the beginning, being enthusiastic about my work and efforts to republish this forgotten memoir. With caring love, support, and inspiration, she patiently helped me with the research and editing of my afterword. She stood by me faithfully during the many challenges and successes. I am forever indebted to her!

Yifat Barkan-Pinto, in Israel, provided me with the very valuable book *I Was Ordered to Live*, written by her grandmother, Chavka Lenchner-Robinovitz, who was Renia's comrade in arms in Poland. Yifat also offered important photographs of Renia that were taken soon after her escape from Poland. Additionally, I am very grateful to Yifat for connecting me with a Holocaust historian in Israel.

I also want to thank Naomi Shimshi, an Israeli Holocaust historian, for gifting me the invaluable seminal work by Israeli historian Rivka Perlis about the Polish Zionist youth movement during World War II and for providing me with relevant parts of her master's thesis on the same topic.

Tali Kritzer, a professional cartographer, was very graceful in volunteering her work. In meticulous cooperation with Benton Arnovitz, she thoroughly created the map of Renia's escape from Poland.

The Ghetto Fighters' House Archives in Israel made a significant contribution to my research. In particular, many thanks go to Lior Inbal, a researcher at the Archives, for helpful suggestions regarding the Hebrew literature on the Zionist youth movement in Poland and for connecting me with Israeli Holocaust historian Zvika Dror and with the Israeli poet laureate Haim Gouri, who interviewed Renia Kukielka and wrote about her.

I am very thankful to Steven Feldman, the Emerging Scholars Program Officer, National Academic Programs at USHMM, for stepping up and bringing the publication project to completion in a receptive and attentive manner.

I would also like to acknowledge Sandy Bloom and Avril Hilevitz, the Israeli certified translators from Hebrew.

Finally, a number of people demonstrated cooperation throughout this project, and I would like to express my deep gratitude to them:

Cindy Cohen, a Toronto lawyer, offered to work pro bono at the initial stages of preparation of the memoir for republication.

Renette Bergman manually transferred the 1947 English-edition book to a CD, which enabled me to send the book to historians for their review and opinions, and to prospective publishers.

Meera Ezer provided committed and friendly help in translation of my interviews with Renia and others from Hebrew to English and in typing them.

Nancy Lawson, a volunteer at USHMM, retyped the newly expanded manuscript of the memoir, painstakingly inserting the newly translated-to-English omissions from the original Hebrew text.

Merav Waldman, Renia's granddaughter, a lawyer, who enthusiastically assisted Renia in signing the legal contract with me as her literary agent, later provided me with Renia's photographs for this republication.

Nathan Baker, an editor, gave sensitive and useful comments and suggestions for the final draft of my afterword.

Patricia Patchet-Golubev, my very good friend and a professor at Trinity College Writing Centre of the University of Toronto, provided loving professional support during the final stages of this republication.

Irina Liubanski, a former editor and a caring close friend, inspired me to begin this republication project, giving me valuable suggestions.

Lastly, I would like to acknowledge with loving gratitude my sister and her husband, Dorit and Haim Koren, who live in Israel. Given that I live in Canada, they were instrumental with various undertakings in Israel to support my archival research and deal with Israeli translators. They also video-recorded some pertinent interviews. Also, many thanks to my cousin, Aharon Kovnat, for his help with translation.

This project is dedicated to the memory of my father, Peisach Kovnat, who was a concentration camp survivor and a hero in his own right.

I cannot possibly list all people involved in this project. It was a labor of love for me in so many ways, made possible by the generous contribution of so many.

Asya Kovnat
November 14, 2022

Introduction

SEVERIN HOCHBERG

Shortly after her arrival in Palestine in March 1944, Renia Kukielka wrote down this memoir of her experiences as a survivor of the Holocaust in Poland. One of the earliest survivor accounts, it is startling and quite unique in its directness, raw power, and unprocessed immediacy. This is especially so because it was written by a teenager. *Escape from the Pit* is a personal chronicle, but Renia seems to have been aware that she was a witness to important historical events, and was writing to tell the people of the world about what she had experienced. Her account therefore constitutes an important primary source that sheds light on a number of historical issues. The topics upon which she reports include the brutality of the German seizure of her native southern Poland, the extent of antisemitism and other aspects of Polish–Jewish relations, the Zionist youth movements and their attempt to mount resistance in the ghettos, and the rescue network that existed during 1943–44 to facilitate escape across the Carpathian Mountains into Slovakia, Hungary, Romania, Bulgaria, Turkey, and Palestine, the so-called eastern land route.

German Invasion

Renia gives a vivid description of the chaos, violence, and destruction that she encountered in the immediate aftermath of the German takeover of southwestern Poland in the early days of September 1939, bearing testimony to the cruelty against civilians committed in the Kielce region during the initial stages of the invasion. These atrocities are not as well-known as are the later measures inflicted on Jews in Poland and the USSR. Southwestern Poland and Eastern Upper Silesia were heavily attacked during the first two weeks of the German assault on Poland by powerful German military forces, including armor and aircraft. The region was strategically located and included Poland's Central Industrial Zone, the largest industrial area in the country and thus of special importance to the Germans, who planned to annex part of the region and use its infrastructure to support an attack on the Soviet Union. Once the invasion began, the Germans were met with ferocious (and largely unexpected) resistance by Polish Army units as well as civilian militia. In order to deal with that opposition, the Wehrmacht units were augmented by formations of the Waffen-SS, by Einsatzgruppen, and by armed Volksdeutsche units made up of ethnic Germans who had fled the region between the wars. This combination of forces, backed by Hitler's order to the military to cooperate in SS operations, gave license to the violence against civilians, including the execution of thousands of Poles and the atrocities committed against Jews. Whatever the initial reservations that some German commanders may have had, the more conventional military forces very rapidly moved to assist the SS in crushing civilians. Kielce was the headquarters of Army Group South and for a time the Wehrmacht Tenth Army was led by the notorious General (later Field Marshal) Walther von Reichenau, who allowed SS Death's Head units to carry out "special actions" against Poles and Jews in Kielce province. Himmler's September 3 order that "insurgents be shot on the spot," directed against Polish civilians, gave bureaucratic sanction to this form of "antipartisan" action, while his September 8 order to spread "fear and terror in the population" was directed largely against the Jewish population and aimed at forcing Jews to flee the area before its annexation to the Reich on October 8. On September 10, Kielce had been "pacified" enough so that Hitler was able to visit the city. The following day in Krakow, Heydrich transmitted Himmler's orders to the Einsatzgruppen commanders in southern Poland and urged them to "expel Jews to the East," over the San River, which became the demarcation line between German- and Soviet-occupied Poland. From September 6 to September 11, a series of atrocities against Jews were perpetrated in the cities of east Upper Silesia.[3] This was the backdrop to the frantic efforts of Renia, her family, and her fellow Jews desperately running from town to town in order to find some measure of safety. She describes these attempts in her opening chapters.

Polish Antisemitism

The book sheds light on the controversial issue of Polish–Jewish relations, especially in southern Poland.

Renia's encounters with indigenous antisemitism are vividly described. While she is emphatic about her hatred of the Germans and her desire for vengeance against them, a desire that seems to motivate her actions and her will to survive, her attitude toward her Polish neighbors and countrymen is one of anger, mixed with a feeling of betrayal. Those experiences bring out the great paradox of Polish–Jewish relations. In her personal account, Poles help the Germans uncover Jewish hiding places; Poles attack and kill escaping Jews in the forest. Poles are blackmailers and thieves who hand over Jews to win German favor. She bitterly describes how Poles rejoice at the catastrophes visited upon the Jews. At the same time she notes the suffering of Poles at the hands of the Germans, vividly describing the deliberate strafing of Polish civilians by German aircraft. She also mentions the fact that some Poles hid Jewish children, smuggled food into the ghettos, and were sentenced to death for helping Jews. She tends to attribute most obliging actions by Poles to bribery rather than altruism, yet she clearly is aware that her own survival and escape would not have been possible without Polish help.

In 1940, Emanuel Ringelblum noted that Kielce province, where Renia was born, "was known for its exuberant anti-Semitism." In Kielce city, known as a "holy city" because of its fervent Catholicism, the Narodowa Democracy (ND) Party cofounded by Roman Dmowski (August 1864–January 1939) had a strong following and significant influence, with many Catholic clergymen among its members. This nationalist antisemitic group organized economic boycotts against Jewish-owned shops, sponsored mass demonstrations, and occasionally indulged in violence. Well before the famous postwar pogrom of July 4, 1946, which set in motion a westward movement of Jews from Poland, Kielce, on November 11, 1918, witnessed a pogrom in which ten Jews were killed and several hundred wounded. In Jędrzejów, Renia's hometown, local police prevented an ND-organized pogrom in September 1939. Boycotts of Jewish-owned stores and destruction of Jewish-owned property were fairly common during the 1920s and 1930s, as were random attacks on Jews. There were many instances of such antisemitic violence in this region. Renia wrote that "because of prevailing antisemitism, it was impossible for me to enter high school." This was not an uncommon experience for Jewish children, especially in the decade before the Second World War when relations between Jews and Poles deteriorated, and anti-Jewish actions increased following the death of Marshal Josef Pilsudski in May 1935.[4]

Youth Groups and Resistance

Renia's account illuminates the role of Zionist youth groups in occupied Poland. Divided by ideology and goals, they nevertheless managed to achieve remarkable unity by the spring of 1943, when it became clear that the German aim was completely to destroy the Jewish population. That youth-group members were aware of the extent of the catastrophe earlier than were most Jews in Poland is well documented in this memoir.

Because of their organization and activities and their ability, despite great risks, to keep open lines of communication between the ghettos, the organized youth groups were less isolated and had greater access to information. This helps explain Renia's references to Chelmno, Treblinka, and Auschwitz. While some of this knowledge may have been acquired after her arrival in Palestine and the exact details may not be entirely accurate, it is clear that a lot of the basic information was known to her while still in Poland because of her connections to the leadership of the youth groups.

Renia arrived in Bendzin, where she joined her sister, in November 1942, and became a member of its "kibbutz," a socialist-Zionist collective preparing for emigration to Palestine. After the horrors she had previously witnessed, she described the Bendzin "kibbutz" as "a paradise to me . . . Jews who lived like human beings, people of vision who looked forward to the future [in Palestine]."[5] The community of thirty-seven individuals belonging to various Zionist youth groups clearly became, for Renia and the others, a kind of substitute family.[6]

The situation in Bendzin, which was annexed to Germany on October 8, 1939, was relatively better than in some other ghettos, at least for a while. Until March 1943 it was an "open" ghetto, allowing for more movement in and out than at other locations. Initially, by July 1940, thirty thousand Jews had been concentrated in Bendzin and more than seven thousand of them worked in factories producing uniforms for the Wehrmacht, many in a factory run by Alfred Rossner, a sympathetic German. The head of the Zaglembie regional "Jewish Council" or Judenrat, Moshe "Moszek" Merin, was based in Sosnowiec and was in charge of thirty-two ghettos in Reich-annexed territory; Bendzin was among them. Merin more or less shared the philosophy and strategy of Mordechai Rumkowski, leader of the Lodz Judenrat, believing in active cooperation with the Germans in order to save "productive" Jews while sacrificing the rest if necessary. Ultimately, as in the case of Lodz, the remaining Jews of Bendzin were sent to Auschwitz.

Renia's respite in Bendzin was to be short-lived. In February 1943 the members of the youth groups in Bendzin, under the guidance of the Warsaw underground, made the decision to prepare for resistance against the Germans. Mordechai Anielewicz, who would become the leader of the Warsaw Ghetto Uprising, had visited the Zaglembie region, including Bendzin, in June 1942 and organized the local resistance movement, establishing ties to the Warsaw underground. Despite great difficulties, something resembling a national underground was created, and the Bendzin group, like those in other ghettos, received its directives from Warsaw. Renia documents the many difficulties in carrying out armed resistance in Bendzin: harassment by the Judenrat and Jewish police, insufficient weapons, and the hostility of the local Polish underground, which did not welcome Jews and gave them little assistance. There was also the fear of savage German reprisals against the remaining Jews in the Bendzin Ghetto, for whom the youth-group members felt compassion and a great deal of solidarity. There was the continuing capture of Renia's comrades, killed off one after another.

Contact between the underground organizations was maintained mostly by a group of young Jewish female couriers who could pass as Christian Poles. Renia's account of her activities as a courier for the underground are among the most gripping ever written. Like most of the couriers, Renia was young, spoke Polish well, did not appear stereotypically Jewish, and because she was female, aroused less suspicion. Using forged identification papers under the name Wanda Biduchowska, she made several trips to Warsaw, crossing the border into German-occupied Poland and back to Bendzin, in Reich territory. She carried money, forged passports and identification documents, and revolvers acquired in Warsaw. She witnessed and described the atrocities committed against Jews in Warsaw during the uprising and escaped from the Bendzin Ghetto during its liquidation. On her last trip to Warsaw, in late August 1943, she was caught near Katowice, tortured in the Gestapo prison during her two weeks there, then transferred to Myslowice prison as a political prisoner. She was spared the fate of ending up in Auschwitz probably because her German captors believed she was Polish and might be able to provide information about the Polish underground.

In the face of certain catastrophe, youth-group members were faced with the choice of attempting to escape or resisting to the very end. Representatives of the Yishuv (the Jewish community in Palestine), who managed to establish contact with the Bendzin group from Istanbul and Geneva, urged escape. The Zionist leadership in Palestine, while profoundly sympathetic to Polish Jews and heart-stricken by their massacre, regarded them as doomed. They did what their resources permitted as they were opposed to the martyrdom of highly motivated youth-group members who might be rescued and could play a key role in the building of a Jewish state after the war. Their emissaries urged *tiyul* (excursion), that is, escape via the "eastern route" through Slovakia, Hungary, and the Balkans to Palestine and were willing to facilitate the rescue of as many young people as could leave. Most youth-group members in Poland insisted on staying until the bitter end, alongside their fellow Jews, and favored armed struggle wherever possible. Renia describes the resolve of Frumka Plotnicka, a leader of the Warsaw underground, who after organizing resistance in a number of ghettos joined the Bendzin group. The Zionist leaders in Istanbul and the Warsaw ZOB (Jewish Combat Organization) offered to facilitate her escape to Palestine or to The Hague, but she declined, writing: "If it is decreed that we must die, let us all die together; but insofar as possible, let it be an honorable death."[7] The Bendzin Ghetto was among the last to be destroyed, and the armed uprising finally took place on August 1–3, 1943, during the last deportation of Bendzin Jews to Auschwitz. A few Germans were killed. Most of the remaining members of the underground were killed in the uprising.

Renia escaped from Myslowice prison on November 12, 1943, with the help of her sister Sarah and a woman named Halina[8] sent from Warsaw. There was nowhere for her to go at that point and, after a period in hiding, she joined a group undertaking an escape across the Tatra Mountains to Slovakia.

Escape to Slovakia

Among the Zionist leadership in Palestine the rescue of Polish Jewish youth, as important as it was, was nevertheless referred to as a "minor rescue plan" compared to the larger Transnistria and "Europa" rescue plans that were being contemplated in 1943. Yet it was determined that priority be given, wherever possible, to rescuing children and Zionist youth who had survived annihilation. In addition to the natural affinity felt toward the young Zionists in Poland and admiration for their astonishing courage, it was considered that these young people might inform the world about the mass slaughter that they had witnessed firsthand, and would be most valuable in the coming struggle for the creation of a Jewish state. Scarce resources were therefore allocated, on a modest basis, to saving members of Zionist youth groups.[9] In order to carry out this particular form of rescue, money and an organized support network were crucial. Money was needed to pay smugglers and to bribe officials, to forge documents, and to pay for food and transportation. Much of this work was done by the clandestine Section for Special Operations of the Jewish Agency Political Department (Lishkat Hakesher) based in Istanbul, which reported to David Ben-Gurion, Eliezer Kaplan, and Moshe Sharett. Ben-Gurion was the de facto leader of the Jewish community in British Mandate Palestine; Kaplan was the treasurer of the Jewish Agency and Sharett was the head of its Political Department. Part of the costs were borne by the American Jewish Joint Distribution Committee.[10]

Only a small number of individuals were able to escape from occupied Poland via the exact eastern land route used by Renia and to arrive legally in Palestine.[11] Small groups of Polish Jews had escaped to Slovakia beginning in 1941. These crossings were suspended during the period of deportations from Slovakia and resumed during the latter half of 1943. Although this was a difficult and dangerous journey, especially for someone in Renia's condition following her incarceration, she was fortunate in the timing of her clandestine journey to Slovakia and then on to Palestine via Hungary, Romania, Bulgaria, and Turkey. She happened to be close to the Polish–Slovak border and crossed the mountains along a route where contacts already had been established. Smugglers and guides on both sides of the border were well paid to facilitate the journey. Once in Slovakia, Renia was in a country that had stopped deporting Jews in autumn 1942 and many of its officials were willing to look the other way in exchange for bribes as long as Jews from Poland were en route to Hungary. "We were all amazed at the efficiency with which every step of the trip had been planned. Each detail had been attended to," wrote Renia about her crossing into Slovakia.[12]

Renia and other members of her group arrived in Hungary, officially passing as Poles, a few months before the German invasion of that country in March 1944. Her stay in Budapest would have been impossible a few months later; she got out in late February, a step ahead of the Germans. The Jewish Agency's Palestine Office in Budapest provided passports and Turkish visas and her group registered at the Budapest consulate of the Polish government-in-exile. After affirming that they were Roman Catholics, adherents of Sikorski (prime minister of the government-in-exile) and not members of the PPR (Polish communists), they received identification certificates. The officials at the consulate almost certainly knew they were Jews, but had been heavily bribed with money from the Joint Distribution Committee.

The situation in Romania and Bulgaria during her journey through those countries was equally propitious, since both nations were in the midst of talks with the Allies and increasingly unreliable in their support for Nazi Germany. Once in neutral Turkey, where there was a strong Jewish Agency presence, the group received precious Palestine immigration certificates from the British Mandatory authorities and were able to make their way legally by train through Syria to Palestine, where Renia arrived on March 6, 1944, and began writing this powerful memoir.

CHAPTER ONE

The First Years

War Begins

SEPTEMBER 1939

The war has begun. It appears that the Germans have already crossed the Polish border at every point. People do not know what to do. There are rumors that the Germans are burning, plundering, strangling, gouging out eyes, cutting off tongues and women's breasts wherever they come. Especially do they make a sport of tormenting Jews. There is no pity in their hearts for Jews.

All the Jews, and Gentiles as well, shut up their homes and flee, not knowing whither. They trail on foot from one village to another, from one city to another. People are jammed together along all the highways—a great, countless mass of human beings. Only dust rises above them. All march on foot—men, women, and children; civilians as well as soldiers already retreating from the front. Trains are not running. Railway lines have been demolished.

In a few days the Germans will reach our town, Jędrzejów. We have not much time left in which to consider matters. We, too, are forced to flee. We can think of no better place to go to than Chmielnik,[1] a town on the other side of the Nida River.

Everybody else is headed that way, for it is believed that the Polish Army will make its stand at the river and stop the enemy. We have relatives in Chmielnik.

Leaving everything we own behind, we set out for Chmielnik. On the highways we stumble over the bodies of men and cattle killed by bombs. There are villages going up in flames. Planes dropping bombs swoop down repeatedly, driving us prone into the fields. Now a bomb crashes nearby. In the quiet that follows, groans are heard. We run over and find a cluster of severely wounded people. Again a plane approaches. It flies low, spraying machine-gun bullets. Then nothing is heard but a whistling sound in the air. Rows of running people have fallen. One notes various oddities: mothers holding their babies in their arms have been killed, while the little children remain alive and cry out with heaven-rending voices; little children are killed while the mothers protecting them are only wounded. The sun shines. Along the road the stench of dead people and cattle is suffocating, unbearable.

After a day and a night of marching, we arrive at Chmielnik. The houses are destroyed. Here and there bare walls of brick stand out, with the people beside them, weeping for their kin who still lie under the wreckage. Seared and scorched survivors are being carried out from one burnt house, its flames still flickering.

The people are confused, completely at a loss. While we hastened to Chmielnik, they were planning to take refuge with us, or to flee to the town of Staszów for safety. All of us together flee from the frying pan into the fire.

After some days a report reaches us that the Germans are already in control of Jędrzejów. They are shooting on sight in the streets. They have seized ten boys, shot them in the marketplace, and have announced that anyone daring to speak or do anything against them will be killed in the same way.

We expect the arrival of the Germans in Chmielnik at any moment. The men decide to go on so as to keep as far as possible from the Germans. The weeping and wailing of the women is unbearable. It is difficult to part from husband or father. Most of the men flee to the other side of the Bug River, for the Soviet armies have arrived there.

Houses stand empty of their dwellers. The well-to-do families have hired horses and carts and taken their valuables along with them to the other side of the Bug, for, one hears, life is more secure with the Russians.

One evening, German tanks appeared in the distance. The first to go down was a Jewish lad, who had been appointed by the police as a militiaman. He happened to be there when the tanks entered the town. Since he had a rifle in his hand, he started shooting at the enemy. Many bullets struck him and tore him apart. He behaved more bravely than did the Poles; these, seeing the German tanks, hid in their holes.

Ten minutes later German soldiers walked about the streets of the town, entered homes, brought out pails and washbowls, then washed themselves and their horses. They were hungry and took away all the food they found in the restaurants. They did not pay for anything; instead of money, they left scrip. They also entered houses and took with them anything they liked. Soon enough, there were Poles who made friends with them and called themselves Volksdeutsche.[2]

Night fell, the first night after the arrival of the Germans. Gates and shutters were closed and barred. It was expected that on this night the Germans would surely massacre the Jews. We assembled in cellars and garrets. Throughout the night we heard machinegun fire and the crash of falling brick walls. From every direction came moans, cries, and wails. The night seemed to last a year. I peered through a crack in the garret, and saw the whole town lit up with the fires of burning houses. One part of the town was completely in flames.

And now they pound at the gate of *our* house. It is an iron gate, well bolstered with iron bars. But the Germans do not hesitate long. They smash the windows looking out toward the street and enter. But they miss the garret completely. They examine everything, take whatever strikes their fancy, and leave.

The night is endless. The continual shooting, the cries—there is no end to these.

Persons afflicted with heart disease expire from fear, weak persons faint.

Finally, the dawn. At nine o'clock in the morning the doors are slowly opened. A horrible spectacle indeed. . . . Stealthily, one person comes to another, goes from gate to gate. Everyone is pale, fearful.

The events of the night are recounted. High-ranking officers, guided by Polish men and boys, entered the home of every Jew. When they had their fill of robbery and plunder, they marched the fathers and sons of every family out into the yard, and shot them by their gates. The wealthiest Jews were herded together in the synagogue, which was then locked and barred, sprayed with gasoline and put to the torch. Likewise, they surrounded the small Jewish street, shut up all the houses, and, after spraying them with gasoline, set them afire. Women and children, realizing that they were doomed to die in the flames, started to leap out of the houses. Those who did not die immediately were shot dead by the Germans standing about. Nearly a quarter of the inhabitants were thus burned alive or shot during the first night.

Thenceforth, to be seen in the street was a crime punishable by death. To go out to fetch some water meant to risk one's life; but there was no alternative. Corpses lay in front of houses for two or three days—since it was forbidden to go out, it was impossible to give the dead decent burial. At nightfall, no one was sure he would see the light of day on the morrow. Poles would point out where well-to-do Jewish families were still to be found, and these were liquidated immediately.

So passed more than ten days. At last the Germans called upon the populace to return to its normal way of life. They gave assurances that, if the people obeyed orders, they, the Germans, would harm no one. Life and work were resumed, for man needs bread as long as there is breath in him. But even though people had money to spend, the first signs of hunger appeared. The bakeries had to supply the army first; the civilian populace got only what was left. Every slice of bread was precious. People rose early so as to be among the first in the bread queue. The Germans, policing these queues, pushed the Jews to the end of the line.

We stayed in Chmielnik until Father, who had fled, returned. Together with some other men, he had reached Staszów. But the Germans came there too. The refugees then realized that it was useless to flee from place to place, and they returned to their families. We now decided to go back home to Jędrzejów. Again, a full twenty-four-hour stretch of walking was before us.

Before, we had met on the road hungry, tattered, miserable Polish soldiers. Now we met a proud and haughty German soldiery, smug and exuberantly singing: for they had conquered almost all of Poland.

In Jędrzejów, too, the Germans had carried out a massacre of Jews after capturing the town. This was their practice in almost every settlement and village.

Not many days passed before we learned to know the Germans very well. They gathered all the Jewish professionals and sent them out of town—ostensibly as hostages: not one ever returned. One day they marched fourteen young Jews charged with possession of weapons to the marketplace and shot them in public. Another time, they planted a revolver in a large building almost entirely occupied by Jews, and then came to search for weapons. Of course, they found the revolver immediately. One man out of every apartment in that house was condemned to death. They then announced that all Jews, regardless of age, must assemble to witness the hanging of these men. The condemned were hanged from trees in the main street, where they remained for a day and a night. Only at daybreak could the Jews take them down for burial. There were many similar incidents.

Early in 1940 the Germans issued the following decree: All Jews are obliged to wear on their garments white ribbons with blue stars.[3] If a ribbon is soiled, or its width is not as prescribed, or it is not found in its proper position on the sleeve, the guilty man is to be shot. All possessions, estates, and houses were taken away from Jews and turned over to the Volksdeutsche. Overnight, some of the poorest of these quasi-Germans were transformed into millionaires. The Volksdeutsche became the masters of Jewish property, and the Jew—a servant on his own estate.

The Ghetto

Decree followed decree. Jews were compelled to be janitors in their own house, and pay rent to the authorities. Storekeepers were forced to serve their customers for a small wage paid them by newly appointed commissioners, who now received the profits. Jewish estate owners had to install a Volksdeutsch in their estates and instruct him in its management. For this service, the Jew got a small room for himself and his family, and a ration of bread, potatoes, groats, and flour—everything weighed in decagrams. It did not take the Germans long to discover that the Jews found even these arrangements tolerable. They therefore expropriated the Jews completely. The Jew was then compelled to pack his bag and leave for the city together with his children, to beg for alms.

All the possessions Jews had acquired during a lifetime of work fell in a single day into the grasp of Poles or Volksdeutsche. The Poles, in the overwhelming majority of cases, were highly pleased. They would walk about the streets, pointing out houses with their fingers, as if to say: "Shortly this or that house will be mine." And so indeed it turned out.

In April 1940, the Germans issued a decree according to which certain streets were to be set apart as living quarters for the Jews. Forty-eight hours later, no Jew was permitted to appear on any other street. They were forced to abandon their houses, possessions, and furniture, take sacks and bedding upon their shoulders and "move." Even in cases where the Germans did allow some persons to take their furniture along, it proved useless. There was no place to move the furniture into. A number of narrow, dirty side streets, previously inhabited by Poles of the most extreme poverty, were turned over to the Jews. Each small apartment was occupied by several families. Living-room furniture was chopped up for fuel. The main thing was to find a way to stay alive another day.

The Germans established a Jewish Council and a so-called militia. The council received its orders and was compelled to meet German demands.

The militia too was but a tool used by the Germans. Soon Jews were forbidden to go outside certain specified Jewish districts without obtaining a pass from the council. However, the Poles were as yet not forbidden to enter the Jewish districts. This, too, was useful in keeping us alive; the Gentiles would smuggle in food in exchange for the goods they wanted.

At the beginning of 1941, new edicts were issued. The entrance of "Aryans" into the Jewish district was strictly forbidden. A wall was built surrounding the Jewish district on every side and Jews were thenceforth confined behind barred gates. Jews received bread-ration cards at the rate of ten decagrams[4] per person daily. Selling bread or any other commodity in larger quantities than fixed by law, or at a price higher than that established, was punishable by death. Walking one step beyond the limits of the district was punishable by death. Travel by train was allowed only in urgent cases of illness, and even then only upon a physician's certification. For hiding in order to evade forced labor, the entire family of the offender was liable to the death penalty. All persons from fourteen to sixty-five years of age had to work practically without compensation; for the slightest shortcoming in work a man was sent off to an undisclosed destination.

The Jewish Council consisted of a number of men called supervisors. Heading them was the president of the council, "elected" by the Jewish population. The council's function was to carry out the orders of the German authorities and the Gestapo in the ghetto. If the Germans needed anything—furniture or any other objects—they would demand it of the council. The council was obliged to satisfy these demands and the Germans were not at all concerned where it obtained the things required.

The council was thus compelled to provide German families newly settled in Poland with clothing, underwear, bedding, and furniture. The goods were simply taken from the Jews, not paid for. The council was required to provide the Germans with tailors, seamstresses, carpenters, and other craftsmen. These artisans received no compensation for their work, except, from time to time, a little food. If the Germans failed to obtain a set number of men for labor, the SS or Gestapo men would beat the council supervisors murderously.

The Jewish militia had its own particular duties: to assist the Wehrmacht in guarding the boundaries of the ghetto, so that no one dared go one step beyond them; to find men in hiding, evaders of forced labor, who were sought by the Gestapo; to aid the German and Polish police in their own searches; to maintain order and take part in the liquidation of the Jews. Only men of the meanest sort obtained employment in the militia, for who else could undertake to help beat, murder, and make sport of their own townsfolk? There were very few men in the militia who had any humanity in them. Most behaved like beasts of prey, some even worse than the Germans. They wore boots and white hats and were armed with rubber truncheons.

Life in the ghetto was very arduous. Men and women were forced to work all day at various kinds of hard labor outside the ghetto. They were occupied in the demolition of houses wrecked by bombs, the repair of highways and railways, and in clearing the streets of filth in the summer and of snow in the winter. Many persons were engaged in loading and unloading bombs at the train depot. The Germans would stand at a distance and watch them work. At times a bomb exploded and all persons nearby were killed. The Germans showed no concern; the people were buried in the field and the thing was over with.

The laborers were marched to work on foot, a distance of many kilometers. When they arrived at their place of work, they were already sorely tired. Gendarmes stood guard over them as they broke rocks with heavy sledges. If one of the laborers asked for a moment's respite, they would beat him mercilessly. Even when a man was injured at work, he did not dare show his wound for fear of blows, but kept on working. As a result, Jews injured at work died of blood poisoning. Even in the most intense cold, in stormy weather, the police would march them all to work on foot. The people tramped in the snow up to their knees, and behind them the gendarmes rode on their horses. The Jews' garments were torn, their faces thin, emaciated with hunger; they walked on, always on the watch for a German knee or fist in their sides. Many returned home with hands, feet, or noses frozen. The German Army guards, and policemen who supervised the workers, were able to watch them through the windows of warm shelters.

The children, remaining at home while their parents were at work, had to prepare their food themselves and take care of all their needs. The wealthy made as good arrangements as they could: they bribed the Jewish Council and the militia so that the poor might be sent in their stead, or they simply hired some poor Jews to work for them.

Because of insufficient nourishment, and the difficult housing situation with its overcrowding, typhus was rampant in the ghetto. Stricken houses were immediately shut off from all sides and warning signs were posted. The sick were brought to a Jewish hospital, specially set up to receive them. Most of the sick died in the hospital for lack of medical supplies and proper care. Rumors were heard, moreover, that the Germans had deliberately forbidden any aid to those stricken with typhus and that, in fact, an order had been issued to poison them. Special bathhouses were set aside for disinfection of persons, bedding, and garments. The immediate effect was that after such disinfections, not a garment was left for the people to cover their bodies with. Conditions grew worse from day to day, and many entirely lost the will to live.

Early in 1941 the Jewish Council was ordered to deliver up, on a certain day, 220 young fellows for work out of town. The strongest and healthiest boys were assembled, among them my fifteen-year-old brother. At first the family tried to induce my brother, a mere boy as he then was, not to allow himself to be sent from the city for labor. But my brother would not listen. It was well-known that if anyone called did not appear, his entire family would receive the death penalty; and my brother did not want to cause our death.

All through the night those about to depart sat in the firemen's hall outside the ghetto. During that time they were examined by a doctor, who had to certify that they did not bear any contagious disease and were in a sufficiently sound state of health. The Gestapo men who guarded them did not allow them to sleep and made sport of them in a variety of ways. They forced them to sing Jewish songs; anyone reluctant to do so, or who did not have a pleasant enough voice, was severely beaten. Afterward they were ordered to dance Jewish dances, made to hit each other until they drew blood, while the Gestapo men stood about watching and laughing.

At the break of day trucks arrived. The boys started leaving the hall. At both sides of the door stood Gestapo men. Each boy, upon going out, was clubbed repeatedly with a rubber hose. If anyone stopped, afraid to pass, or uttered a cry, he was hauled out of the line and the Gestapo men gave him a beating, blaming his cowardice for the blows. These boys could no longer enter that truck unaided, and the others lifted them in their arms. To each vehicle were detailed four Gestapo men, with a machinegun and a dog.

My brother's first letter reached us a month later from a town near Lwów. It was very bad for them there, he wrote. They worked from early morning until late in the evening. They slept in stables and barns. They suffered cruelly from hunger, and even more from cold. If we wished to see him return home alive, we must send him frequent food packages and warm garments. From others, even worse letters were received. They were regularly beaten day after day, while going to work and during work, by the Gestapo and the German soldiers. Many of the boys who left hale and sound were brought back from work upon their comrades' shoulders. After a hard day's work, the Germans took them out "for exercise." Anyone not doing the exercises properly, with the necessary precision, was shot dead without warning.

The filth was intolerable. Lice simply devoured the boys' flesh. There was no provision for laundering and washing, and the hay they slept on was never changed. The stables and sheds where they slept were locked at night; all bodily needs had to be attended to right there. They lived amid a suffocating, deadly stench. Since there was so little food, they plucked all kinds of grass and ate it, and as a result dysentery spread. If this disease sapped the patient's strength too much, he was not cured but shot to death. For fear of death, no one wished to complain to the Germans of being sick. Because of the filth and insufficient food, blisters broke out on their skin. Very rarely did the Germans consent to free a sufferer from work for a number of days. They did so only when convinced that the person could not move his limbs for pain.

The boys were finally convinced that their days were numbered, that sooner or later they would die. They therefore decided to escape. Some money was sent them, sewn up in suits, so that they could buy railroad tickets; and little by little, in small bands, they began to make good their escape. Escape was a very serious business indeed. In winter, an ill-fitting garment could draw the attention of any passerby. They made their way through the woods and thickets in order to avoid people's eyes.

As a result, the fate of those remaining at the camp, who did not escape in time, grew even worse. When the Germans discovered that the number of boys was decreasing daily, they began pursuing the ones who had fled and cruelly tormenting those who had remained. Most never returned to Jędrzejów again; only those few who succeeded to escape did so.

The appearance of the returning boys was horrifying; they were skin and bones. Their bodies were covered with all sorts of blisters and sores; their clothes crawled with insects. When their beds were made on the floor, the space around them was at once covered with insects. Hands, feet, and bodies were inflamed, distended; altogether they made up a husk of wounds. And the faces of these youths were like those of the very old. For a long period after their return, they had to conceal themselves from the Germans.

Other groups of boys and girls were also sent to unknown destinations. No report was received from them. There was hardly a family that did not lose one of its members: a father, son, brother, sister, or mother. The rest of us were working for the German authorities, there in town.

In Flight

Another decree: the Jewish Council must transport from Jędrzejów to the nearby towns four hundred of the most prosperous Jewish families. No one knew why and for what purpose the demand was made. The wealthy hastened to pay their ransom of thousands of złotys to the council for permission to remain in town.

At dusk a man would receive notice, and by midnight he was compelled to gather his belongings, put them aboard a sleigh made ready for him, and travel into the unknown. It was intensely cold. The Jewish militia saw to it that every Jew receiving such notice evacuated his apartment by morning. Whole families had to leave Jędrzejów and travel to a nearby town designated by the Germans. Everyone received fifty złotys for travel expenses from the Jewish Council,[5] which used the ransom money from the wealthy for this purpose.

The sleigh would arrive at Wodzisław,[6] sixteen kilometers from Jędrzejów. Mothers and children were nearly frozen. The driver would unload the bundles in the street and continue on his way. The mother's heart was rent with anguish, seeing the flesh of her little children blue with cold. She stood helpless, awaiting succor from heaven.

Where, to whom, could she turn among strangers? But here, too, there were Jews. Seeing the mothers and the half-dead children, one of them, out of pity, would bring them into the shed in his yard. Here the wind blew in from every nook and cranny. There was no stove, and waves of shivering passed through one's body. But this, at any rate, was preferable to being on the highway, under the open sky. Funerals took place daily: one died of cold, another of hunger; both old and young alike. There were also some cases of suicide.

At length, we were all assembled and driven like a herd of cattle to the synagogue. It was a large, open room. The cold was fearful. In the center of the hall was only a small stove. The windowpanes were covered with layers of ice, and icicles hung from the walls. The people lay in a heap—men, women, and children. They got their food from the kitchen, set up for the refugees shortly before by the Jewish Council. The unfortunates, having no other alternative, made peace with their bitter fate. The thing that counted was life.

The afflictions that were brought about by the Germans, following one another in rapid succession, turned our hearts into stone. Everyone thought only of himself, was willing to rob his fellow of a crust of bread.

The members of the Jewish Council did not even know the meaning of kindness: "If wrong is being done to some of you, appeal to the Germans. We only follow their orders. Go ahead and complain to them. What do you want of us?"

The wealthy would find protection and immunity from being moved to another town. They could even obtain permits for travel by rail, as well as avoid work. They were respected everywhere: by the Jewish Council and the militia as well. The Germans alone did not differentiate between the rich and the poor.

Thus the Germans needlessly dragged the Jews about from town to town, with but one aim: to make them lick the dust, to deaden their will to live. But the very poor suffered most of all.

Our poverty grew worse from day to day. People sat idly, consuming every penny they possessed and all the goods they had. The food obtained daily on ration cards was insufficient even for breakfast; prices in the black market were sky-high. Out of sheer necessity one had to run deadly risks in the hope of gaining a livelihood. The women put on Gentile dress and wrapped themselves in all manner of clothing in order to smuggle goods by hook or by crook into the Aryan district, where they might sell them and earn bread for the children. Each mother knew what a risk she was taking. Were a German to recognize her, or a Pole to point her out to the Germans, they would kill her. If the militia seized the women leaving the ghetto, they did not refrain from beating them and even imprisoning them for many weeks.

Poles willingly bought the goods smuggled out of the ghetto, which they were forbidden to enter. They had much money on hand, but there was nothing to be bought; the trade with the Aryans had then just begun. The women received, in exchange for their goods, various foods, coal from the railroad laborers, or other products. With hearts anxiously beating, they went from town to town, from village to village.

There were some Poles who, upon recognizing the peddler as a Jewess, took all her goods away without payment, and told her that if she even dared to raise her voice or express displeasure, they would turn her over to the Gestapo. Silently she would return home, moneyless and without goods.

Trade was mostly carried on at night. In the darkness a Jewish woman would walk through a village, secretly knocking upon doors. Hastily completing her business, she would continue on her way. However, in almost every settlement or village, the Gestapo had its men who served for a monthly wage but also received special prizes for every Jew apprehended.

At times people warned the Jews to be on the alert. Nevertheless, scores of Jews were seized daily.

Yet every morning the mother would again go out with an anxiously beating heart. She could not help pitying the children who reached vainly for the slice of bread that was not there. Perhaps, once again, luck would smile upon her and indeed she would sell all her merchandise and make some profit besides. Ten times and more she succeeded—until someone informed. One evening while she would be returning from the village along a narrow path in the field, a German would leap upon her out of the grain fields. He would take everything she had, push her away, beating her over the head with his rifle butt, and then shoot her, thus putting an end to her misery.

The unfortunate children would remain alone, for their father had previously been sent to an unknown destination. Rather than die of hunger, they would stealthily leave the ghetto. They would go to some village in search of bread. Seeing the hungry children, a feeling of pity might stir in the peasants, and they would offer them some food. The children slept under the bushes or in fields. They lived until caught by a German or one of the Poles, who turned them over to the police or put an end to their lives himself, after tormenting them.

There were peasants willing to give shelter in their homes to these unfortunate, homeless Jewish children. They would give them food, and in exchange the children would help them with their farmwork. But there was widespread fear. The Germans issued a warning that if a Jew, or a Jewish child, was found in an Aryan's home, his entire family would be executed. A Jew caught and killed in the field was buried on the spot.

The police would bring men and order them to dig a grave for the victim—and that ended the matter.

Many, very many Jewish men, women, and children are buried somewhere in the fields. Birds, dogs, and worms now take their pleasure, do not lack for food. No one will weep at their graves—for who of their relatives knows their burial place?

Those fearing to endanger their lives by these devices expired together with their children. The people died one by one, bloated by hunger. Death from starvation is very terrifying.

Now the Germans invented a new method of murdering Jews. Almost nightly a busload of Gestapo men would arrive. They were drunk, lost to all sense. One of them bore a list of names. They would go to the president of the Jewish Council, give him a beating, then order him to lead them to the persons listed. The first time, about thirty persons, men, women, and youths, were taken out of their houses. The members of their families were warned not to dare show themselves. Then cries and shots were heard.

Toward morning the people were found killed, each flung in a different side street. Their bodies were black from the blows inflicted before they were shot. The weeping and wailing of the surviving members of the families was heaven-rending. The murdered were loaded by Jews on wagons and carted away to the cemetery. Jewish militiamen followed the wagons. Visiting the cemetery, which was situated out of town, was strictly forbidden. But this time people paid no attention to the prohibition. Many went to the cemetery stealthily, in indirect routes.

For some time after the first such occurrence, the people could not compose themselves. They were afraid to discuss it openly. No one knew of whom one ought to beware; unknown also was the man who furnished the secret police with the list of names. There was much confusion.

The case of the thirty murdered was not unique. Periodically the Gestapo would come in the night and take people away to be shot. A person going to bed could not know whether he might not be shot during the night.

One night, in 1942, many Gestapo buses arrived in the place. Almost half the population of the town were rousted out of their homes. The people were barefoot, dressed only in their nightshirts. The cold was intense and the snow very deep. They were ordered to run around the marketplace. Gestapo men followed closely, striking them with their rubber truncheons until the people bled. Anyone who stopped running was shot to death. They then were told to lie for half an hour in the snow. Several Jews were given whips and ordered to strike the others. Then some were again ordered to prostate themselves on the ground; and while they lay there, a heavy military vehicle passed over them. And still there was no end to the "sport." Now they ordered pails to be brought and all the remaining Jews were made to stand about the well. Several Jews then drew water from the well and poured water upon those standing in line.

All these doings had taken place at night. But soon the Germans started their excesses in daylight as well. Several Gestapo men took a number of men and women in their cars and drove them toward an unknown destination. Several days later, some peasants living near the forest related that the Germans had brought a number of persons there, stood them up under a tree, and killed them all with machineguns.

Such acts were daily occurrences. Anyone dying a natural death was envied, for he died as becomes a human being and the place of his burial could be identified. Nevertheless, no one wished to die.

One night, finally, the president of the Jewish Council and his family, as well as the members of the council and their families, were arrested. They were taken away somewhere and murdered.

At times the Gestapo men would take a group of men out and order them to dig their own graves. The Gestapo man fired a bullet into each; his victims would fall dead into the pits. Other Jews covered their graves with earth. Sometimes the Jews were not shot at all. When the graves had been dug, they were forced to jump in, lie down one beside the other, and so were buried alive. They would bring to the marketplace old Jews, wrapped in their prayer shawls, and order them to sing and dance. The Germans stood some distance away, watching, laughing, photographing the dances. They then pulled their earlocks and plucked out, one by one, the hairs of their beards. The old men cried out with pain, and the Germans thereupon slapped their faces so viciously that the beaten men spewed the last teeth out of their mouths.

Then came the young girls' turn. By the hundreds they were taken away to unknown destinations. No reports were received from them. A soldier, decent by comparison, let it be known that the majority of the young girls were sent to the front, as prostitutes. The girls soon contracted venereal diseases, and were then burned alive or shot.

The same soldier related that he was present on an occasion when hundreds of girls were brought in. The police told them that the next day they would start "working."

Upon being brought to the barracks and seeing what fate awaited them, some of the girls in desperation attacked the soldiers. They seized the bayonets from their hands, wounded them, and then plunged the bayonets into their own chests. Others fell upon the soldiers with their bare fists, shouting that as long as they lived they would not offer their bodies to shame. In the end, however, they were bound and raped. When this became known in the town, many girls put an end to their lives.

In the meantime reports came from other cities, from small to large ones.

Ghettos were erected, surrounded by high walls, in Warsaw, Lublin, Lwów, Radom, Częstochowa, Kielce, and elsewhere. People were dying of hunger en masse, daily dropping in the streets.

They asked us for potato peelings to be sent to them in tin packages, for hard bread crumbs and other inferior foods. In the large ghettos there were also some people who had money, but there was no one to buy anything from. The money lay unused while persons died of hunger in large numbers.

The hungry were compelled by the Germans to go to work every day. There was some chance of secretly buying bread-ration tickets from Poles on the way. However, it was impossible to bring bread into the ghetto. Upon entering there, everyone was searched. Possession of a slice of bread usually meant death.

In the cities suicides were common. Leading Jewish personalities, no longer able to witness such cruelties, committed suicide. Fathers and mothers killed their children in order to prevent their falling into the hands of the Germans.

Rumors were already abroad that people were being transported somewhere out of the cities. Large groups were selected, divided into categories, and supposedly taken to work. They left without knowing why or whereto. No word was received from the persons taken away. After several months reports came from only a few individuals. These the Germans temporarily allowed to live, in order to deceive the ones remaining behind and thus lull them into the belief that people had actually been sent to work.

Life in the large cities was much harder than in the small towns. In the towns near Warsaw and elsewhere, the ghettos had already been liquidated. All Jews were brought into the ghetto of the large city; it was easier to liquidate a population concentrated in a single place.

The massacre of Jews became a continuous activity and the removal of Jews from their dwelling places did not cease. From day to day, Jews decreased in number by the thousands, and still no one knew where they had been sent.

Everyone who could do so left the cities for the small towns, believing that the Germans were engaged in annihilating the Jews in the large cities only. It was no easy matter to disguise oneself as a Gentile. Many were seized in the street after they had slipped out of the ghetto, or on the train when their papers were examined. Wherever seized, a Jew was sure to be executed.

Announcements appeared in the ghettos of Warsaw, Radom, and other cities: Whoever possesses any valuables or a specified large sum of money may register, at appointed hours, for emigration to Palestine. There were many who came to register. Despite all the Germans' lies and deceptions, the Jews still continued to believe them. Jews who responded to the posters were seated in the body of a truck, separated from the driver. They considered themselves fortunate. Finally, they thought, we shall suffer no more hunger. It appears that the Germans aren't such bad people after all, if they agree to send us to Palestine in exchange for the Germans living in England. They assumed that they were traveling by bus to the railroad station.

After a few weeks the truth became known. The trucks drove some distance out of town; the driver pressed a button, and automatically the interior of the vehicle was filled with suffocating gas and all sitting within were poisoned. The driver unloaded their corpses in the woods and returned to take other people along with him. Thus more than ten busloads of people were taken to their death.

Mass Deportations

From the first the Germans carefully weighed the matter of liquidating the Jews. "Annihilation squads" were set up for the purpose. These consisted of Ukrainians turned savage, of Poles turned *Volksdeutsch*, and of young, healthy Germans to whom a human being meant no more than a fly. In their thirst for blood they found it easier to murder a man than to smoke a cigarette. This trait became second nature to them, a habit like inebriation, opium smoking, and the like. They wore black uniforms decorated with death's-heads, and black hats similarly decorated. The Jews called them the "Black Dogs."[7] Whenever they appeared, it was certain that half of the population was about to be murdered. Their very aspect was horrifying: hard faces, prominent, protruding eyes, big teeth, and furtive looks of beasts of prey. They were indeed ready at any moment to leap savagely upon their prey. Whenever they appeared in the ghetto, all hid like rats in holes and crevices. The men of the Jewish militia stood still as statues before them; nevertheless, they too were kicked and made sport of.

In the large cities, what the Germans called deportations were being ordered. At one swoop more than ten thousand persons were taken, among them entire families. The deportees took along food for a few days, and bundles of clothing. The Gestapo men and the "annihilation squads" led them from the ghetto to the railroad station. There was never a deportation without some killings on the way. The Jews entering a train took their dead along with them. To any questions as to their destination, the reply was given that they were being sent to live and work in the Polesie region.

The Jews willingly accepted the idea—it was better than death through starvation in the ghetto. If they could only get something to eat, they were ready to do the hardest work. They left one after another, and disappeared as into an abyss. No reports came from them. This was ominous and caused anxiety. No one wrote. Not a man returned.

Besides Warsaw, deportations were ordered in other cities too. But nowhere was the fate of the deportees known.

Jews were also being transported from France, Holland, Belgium, Denmark; also some remnants from Germany and other European countries. All were sent to an unknown destination. People arrived from other countries by passenger coach. They had food and drink. Women in makeup looked out of the coaches. They seemed fresh. They were all at peace. The boys and girls played mandolins, pipes, and violins. Even the sound of singing was heard from the distance. A guard of police and Gestapo men accompanied them.

At the station, men and women descended for a drink of water. Polish Jewish boys who worked at the station watched the people in the coaches. The boys saw that these were Jews, since they wore yellow stars upon their breasts. The foreign Jews approached the boy-laborers for a moment, seeing that they, too, wore white armbands with blue stars.

One of the boy-laborers went off into a corner and stealthily entered into a conversation in broken German with one of the passengers. To his question as to where they were going, the man replied: "We were told that we are going to Warsaw, and there we will settle in places abandoned by the Jews. Furniture, bedding, and house furnishings have been made ready for us. That is why the Germans told us not to take anything along. There we will get work and the abandoned Jewish possessions. The Germans treat us nicely." The boy then told him that he did not believe that they were being taken to Warsaw. There were still Jews in Warsaw, but they were being continually transported to unknown destinations. "It would be well," said the boy, "for you to flee now. The Germans aren't paying any attention to you now. Run for your life!" The man laughed aloud and said: "Why should I escape? I have been traveling for ten days already; we came from Belgium to Poland, and the Germans didn't molest us at all. They will take us to Warsaw, as they promised to do. I don't feel that I have to escape."

The train started moving. The man ran after it and hurriedly entered the coach. No wonder the Germans allowed them to leave the train at all the stations.

The fear of deportation came over the young people. Of their own accord, they volunteered for the hardest, most dangerous work, if only they could be saved from deportation. Many young men were sent by the Germans to munitions and armament plants. Such plants were located at Skorzysk[8] and other towns. The work was dangerous; an explosion might occur at any minute. The Poles were unwilling to work there for even the highest wage, but the Jews registered for such jobs together with their families.

Their life was horribly arduous. They worked from early dawn to late at night.

They slept in stalls, specially erected for the purpose, on the bare floor or on boards. The food they received was very meager, and even one not working would have found it difficult to subsist. For any cause they might expect whippings or death. No medical aid was tendered to the wounded. Anyone injured was taken by the Germans to a secret place and shot. Nevertheless, if only to save themselves from deportation, Jews were glad to get work under these terrible conditions. The hope that there might soon be a favorable turn in the war and that it might end quickly especially encouraged the Jews.

The deportations had not ceased. The officials of the community put on white caps and became militiamen. Single men among them were not apprehensive and dared to marry, for they supposed that the families of militiamen would remain in their place.

In mid-1942, rumors about the murder of the deportees became widespread. All now understood that deportation meant death. In the large cities people began seeking an opportunity to cross from the ghetto to the Aryan pale. An attempted crossing was not always successful; anyone caught was shot on the spot.

Those who succeeded to leave, with the aid of money and Aryan acquaintances, arranged matters as well as they could. For money they obtained forged documents. One who had acquaintances among Polish officials could get "original" documents if he paid for them generously. Most of the holders of such documents moved away to other towns. They did not dare to remain in their own town, fearing Polish acquaintances who might turn them over to the authorities. In his new place of residence, a man would register in accordance with his purchased document, find work, and live. Many such people still live in this manner to this very day, and it does not even occur to anyone that this or that person might be a Jew. Still there were many people whose secret was nevertheless discovered.

Jews with "Semitic" features, who together with their families succeeded to free themselves from the ghetto with the aid of their Polish friends, paid large sums of money for places to hide in. It was very difficult for them to earn a living. The Poles incessantly extorted money from them, or else turned them over to the police. Many Poles feared to hide Jews in their homes. In most cases it was easier for girls to pass, if they did not look like Jewesses. They somehow arranged their affairs. They worked in offices, as actresses, in stores, and also as domestic servants. Schoolgirls, who never in their life had known the meaning of menial labor, willingly came to work in a household. Such work offered more safety than could be found in an office. Girls entered convents, left for the front as nurses—anything to remain alive.

Most children were turned over to the orphanage. Anything at all could be accomplished by bribing the officials of an institution. There were Jewish children who sold newspapers, cigarettes, shoe polish, and other such petty wares in the Aryan streets. But woe to the boy who happened to meet Polish children who had known him before! They threw stones at him, lashed him with ropes, and then turned him over, barely alive, to the Gestapo. A Gestapo man would put an end to his torments with one blow of his rifle butt.

It was much more difficult for a man to find refuge. Any slight carelessness was apt to betray him. If the Germans suspected a man of being a Jew, they took him through any gate they happened to pass and ordered him to let his trousers down. There were cases of entire families being seized because of their baby boys. The Germans had no need to search and examine any further, for the babies were found to be circumcised. There were Polish doctors who learned to perform operations that eliminated all signs of circumcision, receiving ten thousand złotys for their labor. Often an operation did not have the desired results, and there were many cases of blood poisoning and death.

Whoever could do so established contact with the partisans and escaped to the woods. But those persons were few in number; the guerrillas did not welcome Jews. Most Jews accepted there were those who proclaimed themselves as Poles. Others set out to wander from place to place until they fell into German hands.

Life was hard for the Jews in the Aryan district. Bands of Polish extortionists derived a livelihood from the Jews. If anyone was suspected of being a Jew living in an Aryan neighborhood, he was pounced upon, and a sum of money was demanded of him. If he refused, they took from him, after torture, everything he possessed, and then turned him over to the Gestapo. The more "decent" scoundrels would take only money and valuables, then disappear without informing the Gestapo. It happened, too, that a Jew in concealment would receive anonymous letters demanding that he deposit, in an assigned spot, a certain sum of money. If not, he was to be turned over to the Gestapo the next day. If the Jew did not have the specified sum on hand, he was compelled, for fear of the Gestapo, to sell his last shirt and bring the sum of money at the appointed time.

In Warsaw, in the "Aryan" Żoliborz district, there lived a Jewish family of six. The people were once well-to-do. Their landlady was the wife of a Polish officer who was killed in the war. She knew that the family was Jewish, and they paid her very handsomely. They had lived there for a full month. One night, suddenly, the bell was sounded at the gate. The landlady leaped out of bed; what could be going on so late in the night? She asked: "Who is it?" The men at the gate spoke a broken German. The landlady did not get confused and kept the door closed. She hastened upstairs and warned the family to beware; she thought Germans were knocking. There was a drumming at the gate. The landlady came down; she was forced to open it. Men in civilian dress, masked, entered with pistols in hand, ready to shoot. They asked if a certain Jewish family lived there, and even stated its name. The landlady answered: "No, a family does live here, but it is not Jewish. It has a different, non-Jewish name. I had them registered in accordance with the passports they showed me. I think the passports are in order; the people are not Jews."

The men did not argue with her; they shoved her away from the door and went up the stairs. Two men remained at the gate, two in the kitchen, six went up to the apartment. The men they found were ordered to stand in a corner, with arms raised. The women were ordered to show their documents. The intruders said: "Your name is not Jdskulski, but Silberstein." The people in the house turned pale. All entreaties were in vain. The masked men, who spoke bad German all the while, searched the apartment.

They took all the valuables—watches, bracelets, furs, and good suits. They then demanded fifty thousand złotys, threatening that if they were not given what they asked for, they would shoot everyone. Pleas were of no avail. The Jews gave away everything they owned, down to the last penny, in order to be allowed to live. The blackmailers then left. Downstairs, the landlady asked them: "What then—are they really Jews?" The blackmailers replied: "Yes, Jews. If we find them here next time, you, madam, will be shot together with them."

The landlady answered: "Fine policemen you are! You say that if the people are Jews, you will certainly kill them, and now you leave without doing anything!" They threatened that if she did not remain quiet they would turn her over to the Gestapo. The Jewish family was compelled, in order to save itself, to leave the apartment.

Another case: A certain Mr. B., an old, grey-bearded man, unlike a Jew in appearance, met with blackmailing practices wherever he went to live. At one time he was living with some elderly people. Hoping to avoid recognition by the neighbors, he did not even go out of doors. Not a living soul knew him—except the family he lived with and the young Jewesses, disguised as Polish girls, who brought him money for rent and food. The girls, like himself, were members of a labor organization. No one but them knew the secret.

One morning there was suddenly a knock at the door. The man, apprehensive and pale, unlocked the door. Three young men, dressed in German police uniforms but speaking Polish, stood there. They demanded that he give them thirty thousand złotys at once or they would shoot him. He returned to his bed and took out his purse, which contained but three thousand złotys. He swore that he did not own a penny more. Mauling him about, they insisted that he bring them all the valuables he possessed and also turn over the rest of the money he had hidden somewhere. The old man produced more złotys. He begged the hoodlums at least to leave him something with which to buy bread and cigarettes. They laughed at him and announced that next week they would return again. He must have a sum of money ready for them by then—a definite sum. In case he did not have it, he could kiss his life goodbye. They took along all the booty, then searched again to see whether more money was not concealed somewhere; and showing him charity by letting him live, they put their pistols back in their holsters and left.

The old man remained without hope. That very day he must escape. Where to? He did not have a single penny left. It was still rather early, and he recalled his friend, a doctor, who had promised him aid in case of trouble, so he hastened to him. Leaving everything behind he went out into the street, covering his face as well as he could. Terror-stricken, he kept his eyes on the ground.

At last he approached his Polish friend's house. The friend offered profuse excuses: he was unable to help him in any way. He could not let him stay even for a single night; talk was superfluous. The doctor did not dare endanger his own life and the lives of his family. He only promised that in case he learned of any apartment suitable for hiding, he would inform his friend, the Jew. And so the old man left empty-handed. He walked brokenhearted, without any avenue of escape. Luckily he met a girl, one of the members of his organization, a Jewess too, and she found a temporary place for him to hide in.

During all this time, hosts of deportees kept leaving. Whither did the Germans transport such a multitude? Where did they find room enough for the housing of so many? The deportations had started with the largest cities and now the turn of the small towns had come. From the end of 1941 until the middle of 1942 more than two and a half million Jews had been deported.

CHAPTER TWO

Homeless

Last Days at Home

AUGUST–NOVEMBER 1942

What a dream, a nightmare of turmoil and struggle! I battled wildly with a nameless foe only to fall back, powerless. I felt all my strength draining, draining in my fight with the enemy in my dream. Suddenly I woke up. A bright, beautiful day. The sun was shining. One's heart broke through the breast, as it were, and soared toward life. It was the 15th of August, 1942. My face beamed. I was alive, the enemy had not conquered me. My fears and anguish were nothing but a dream.

But my good spirits disappeared instantaneously when I saw the faces of my dear parents. They seemed as if demented. They stood clasping their hands in woe.

Tonight again the neighboring city of Kielce had seen a mass deportation. As usual, this was accompanied by a massacre. Persons were killed like flies attempting to escape. The Germans buried others alive. They respected neither age nor sex. To be sure, the Germans did announce that the people deported previously were to be brought back, for England insisted that no wrong be done to the Jews. Furthermore, they announced, there would be no more deportations. Was this another attempt to mislead us?

My parents thought of nothing but how to find some den to hide the little children in and thus save them from death or deportation. I still recall my mother's words, as clearly as though she had only spoken them today: "Papa and I, even though we are still young, have already had some joy in our lives. But these poor children, now in their bloom, what have they had? Whom did they wrong? I would gladly die here on the spot, if only I could save them from death."

From hour to hour the situation grew worse. The nearby towns had been emptied of Jews. Poles came and told of horrible, abominable deeds. What was to be done? A few Jews who had escaped from the massacre into the fields around Kielce came to our house.

Those who succeeded to get away were not many. Young men captured by the Germans in the fields were killed on the spot. The Poles willingly cooperated in the pursuit of Jews, in order to win the favor of the Gestapo.

It was terrible to look at the faces of the runaways. Ragged, barefoot, small bags in their hands, they were barely able to stand on their feet. They had fearful stories to tell, such as the following: A woman of a family about to be deported, attempting at the last moment to save her little children from deportation, drew them aside from the group. Suddenly a German, crazed, frothing at the mouth, leaped at her wrathfully. He killed two of the children by kicking them with his hobnailed boots while the mother looked on.

He then forced her to dig graves for the children with her own hands. But he was still unappeased, and he smashed her skull with his rifle butt. For a time afterward, until she died, her body was convulsed with pain.

One day a band of half-mad women appeared. They were thin, pale, blue-lipped, like driven reeds in the wind. They were hungry and begged for a slice of bread. When this was given them, they burst into hysterical weeping and told, all at once, what happened to them: Without warning their homes had been surrounded by men in military uniform. Shots were heard on all sides. The children, playing in the street, grew scared and ran home. But some German caught them, and, striking deliberately, killed them one by one.

The women who had witnessed this stood before us half-mad, dressed only in their undergarments and nightgowns and barefoot. They had escaped with nothing but their lives; for life is the thing that counts. But where could they flee now? Into the fields, the woods, among the rocks. Polish peasant women from the village, seeing the half-clad and hungry women, brought them, at the risk of their lives, a slice of bread and some water. And so the women led an animal existence during the weeks of wandering. During the day they hid, at night they wandered aimlessly wherever fate might lead them.

One night more people came to town. They told us this tale: "We were one hundred and eighty persons wandering without a goal. Poles attacked us in the forest. They robbed us of everything we possessed, stripped us of our clothes and shoes. They threatened to turn over those of us who resisted to the Germans. Every one of us wants to live; we therefore gave away everything we possessed."

In mute evidence of this treatment, the men had nothing but their underwear; others were wrapped in shawls. The women wore torn undergarments; the children were stark naked. But with all this the people were pleased that they had escaped with their lives.

And they added: "For several days we have had neither bread nor water. The weak among us have fallen by the wayside; others, who could not bear their suffering, cut their veins and so put an end to their anguish. At least they are sure of never falling into the hands of the Germans. Many people left our company unseen and disappeared into the night. No one knows what became of them."

Only seventeen persons reached our town—and these too were barely alive. Young men turned grey from fear and concern for their families. With no dwellings available, they slept under the open sky or in some stable.

Each of us helped them as much as possible. They got clothing and food. We all lived like transients, awaiting the day when the catastrophe would strike here, too.

The arrival of a group of small children, all of a single family, plunged us into an even more depressed state of mind. They told us:

> When Mother saw that the Germans were concentrating on seizing all the Jews in the city, she did not become despondent. She hid us away in closets, under blankets and under beds. After some time the clatter of German boots was heard. We sat in absolute stillness. We knew that if the Germans discovered us we would die. A German entered, rifle slung over his shoulder, and started searching. Even though Mother hid us well, he found us all. Stealthily he gave each of us a small slice of bread and ordered us to hide again—for if another German were to come in, he would surely kill us. He told us to wait until night. He laughed and tears stood in his eyes. He told us that he, too, had children, and because of this he could not kill us. He patted us, closed the door, and went out. From the distance shots and cries were heard. We sat silently, awaiting Mother's return.

> Night fell; silence, as if everyone had died, settled over the town. We left our hiding place. But our youngest sister, only fourteen months old, who lay too long under a blanket, was suffocated; her tiny body was cold.
>
> "I," said the oldest girl, "am already eleven years old. I lifted up little Rosie in my arms right away. After death she was quite heavy. Crying I carried her into the cellar. I was afraid to dig a grave for her in the street, for the Germans might catch me.
>
> "Quickly I dressed the younger children; we waited for Mother. It was dark outside. I was afraid of what the coming day might bring. I said to myself: Mother probably ran away herself and she forgot to take us with her. The German said that Mother would return at night. How she will cry when she finds out that little Rosie is not alive! Still Mother did not come. I took the children by the hand and went out with them through the window, because the door was closed. The windows of our neighbor's house were smashed. I looked in. Everything was quiet there. Once more I looked around to see whether anyone had noticed us. All the time I felt as if Mother was following us. I didn't know the way. I walked a long time. I asked peasants for bread for the children; we slept in the field on the ground. The village boys would throw stones at us, but they did not hit any of us because we ran away very quickly. The peasants and their wives asked us many questions. We did not say a thing except that our mother was dead. But they kept telling us that we should not be afraid, they would do us no harm—they knew that we were Jewish children. We finally came here. A man told us that there were still Jews here."

The long walk had injured their bare feet, their faces and bodies had become bloated, their clothes were soiled and torn. They didn't want to speak to anyone for fear he might be a German in disguise. The eldest said that she would rest awhile and then set out again to seek their mother. "Mother certainly must be looking and crying for us. What will happen in case we don't find her?" In order to relieve their minds, temporarily, they were put up in the homes of well-to-do families. But where should they go? How soon now before we too, who had thus far escaped the hangman, would be subject to a life of wandering; before we too would go about naked and barefoot, half-crazed, begging for pennies and a slice of bread?

This question confronted us in all its enormity. To whom and where should we go, since almost all communities had already been emptied of Jews?

Every moment in our life seemed the last, every passing day came to us quite unawaited. We did not sleep at night. We feared the imminent arrival of the "annihilation squad." At any rate, at such a time it is well to be awake. During the day we slumbered, crushed and weary with the terror awaiting us, for the Germans did not usually start their activities until night fell.

Rumors were abroad that within a few days action would begin in our own as well as nearby towns. Only one subject claimed attention: What could be done so as not to fall into the hands of the Germans alive, since we were unarmed and had nothing but our bare ten fingers? Then again, another question arose: Where to hide and how to escape deportation?

In the street, everywhere, small groups of people were taking counsel—what could they do now? The wise—their wisdom had suddenly gone stale; the rabbis had lost their counsel. People shaved their beards and mustaches—and still they looked like Jews. Whither, whither escape, with their Semitic features?

During one of these days there came to us a young fellow who had fled from the train of deportees at Kielce. This was his story:

> Not far from his town, at a railway station—he did not recall its name—ten boys or more were taken out of the coaches and sent to a war plant in Skarzysko. There they were forced, under threat of beatings and death before the firing squad, to write to their relatives in other towns that they were well placed, had enough food, and lived together with their families: the people should therefore not be apprehensive about deportations; in reality it was hardly a deportation at all, but simply a trip to a place of work, and one was allowed to take along all the valuables one owned. There were boys who refused to write such lies and deceive their relatives. The Germans tortured them for a long time before the eyes of the others, and then shot them on the spot. The rest of the boys were compelled to witness this, so that they would know what to expect if they refused to write as ordered.

The boy did not know where the rest of the transport had been sent. He assumed they had all been murdered. The Germans' actions clearly indicated this: their crowding of people into cattle cars, for instance, without counting them, without supplying them with food stocks; the practice of throwing in the corpses of those shot on the way to the station together with the living; the beating of the heads and faces of mothers with rifle butts and lashes when they begged for mercy for their crying children. The cars had been barred and locked; armed guards stood on both sides, rifles ready to shoot.

In the meantime, in order to buy bread, people sold their last few pieces of furniture. No one thought of work, for the day of deportation was about to arrive. No one would be excluded; work certificates would be of no avail. They would leave no one except a few men picked to clear the neighborhood: to remove all unnecessary temporary structures, previously erected by the Jews for their brethren who came from other towns and neighboring villages, and to dispose of the dead who would fall, as usual, during the process of deportation.

The Poles felt elated; they looked forward to the chance to plunder to their hearts' content. When Jews went away or escaped from their residences, they had to leave everything behind, except some trifling valuables that they took along with them to exchange for bread.

It was difficult to stay in one's house. The emptiness was horrifying. Everything the house contained had already been sold for a few cents to the Poles or given away gratis. Whatever remained would also soon be theirs. There was confusion in the town.

Everyone tried to flee wherever possible. But where was a safe place? No one knew. Almost a fourth of the Jewish population fled at night to the woods and fields.

The well-to-do bribed the villagers to house and hide their children. The remaining children wandered about like sheep without a shepherd.

In our own family it was decided to divide equally among all the children the money obtained for the furniture we had sold. In this way, each one would have some money in hand in case we were scattered. The following night, we decided our parents, with our youngest brother, Jacob, would leave for the woods. Then, after they had left, my two sisters would travel to Warsaw disguised as Aryans, despite the great danger involved. There they would settle in the home of some friends and afterward try to bring over our parents too.

That very day, on Friday, August 22, 1942, I left for the Jewish camp at Sandziszów[1] to seek shelter with my brother Aaron. He and his friend made it possible for me to remain there. This was a Jewish camp under

German authority. Shortly before, more than five hundred boys and twenty girls ransomed from the Gestapo for many thousands of złotys had been sent to work there. We assumed that by hiding in the camp I might escape deportation. Parting from my parents was very hard. They were in deep despair, not knowing whether we would ever see each other again. And indeed, it turned out that those were our last embraces. The premonition that we were parting forever did not deceive us.

Some days after I began working in the camp, I spoke to the supervisor about letting my father and sisters into it. He agreed and wrote out transport orders for me, by means of which they would be allowed to come to work in the camp unhindered. But, alas, it was already too late. One bright morning when we got up as usual for our labor—we were building houses and railway bridges—a report reached us that struck us as a thunderclap. Early in the morning, at 4:30, deportation proceedings would begin at Wodzisław. There was no longer any way to get in touch with our parents and the other members of the family. Had they succeeded to flee in time, before the barbarians put an end to their lives?

The camp supervisor, a German, came running and showed us the order: the Gestapo demands that he add the girls working here to the transport about to be sent out, for women are not permitted to work.

He advised us to flee and save ourselves, wherever we could. In our great despair, we were unwilling to think of saving ourselves. But he did his best to persuade us: "You are still young, save yourselves, some of you might remain alive!" Had it not been for the fear under which he labored, he said, he would have hidden all of us; had it depended upon him, he would have kept us at work, without our having to beg him to do so.

In a very friendly manner he wished us luck and went away.

On the Road

My wandering began on the 27th day of August. That day I succeeded, with the aid of my brother Aaron and his friend, in slipping out of the camp. By untraveled roads I came, together with another girl named Joachimowicz, to the woods. From every direction horrible groans, shots, howling dogs were heard. Suddenly a shrill shout: "*Stehen bleiben, verfluchter Judel. Rexl, an ihn, beiss ihn!*"[2]

With beating hearts and complete abandonment to fate, we left the forest. A few moments later we saw two policemen pursuing us. They recognized that my friend was a Jewess. They brought us to a place where many Jews were already assembled—captured as were we. But fortune smiled upon us. After a long talk, full of arguments and counterarguments, we were freed. Since they assumed that I was an Aryan, my friend, at my intercession, was freed too. But now we were compelled to separate, each one going in a different direction.

From this moment on, I was alone.

September 12, 1942

The night was beautiful, I remember, and lit by the moon. I lay in a field, shivering with cold and trembling at my thoughts during these last passing minutes. Why, indeed, should one toil so arduously for a life as inane, foolish, and disgusting as this? Nevertheless, one does not wish to die.

It was quiet all about. Periodically the low barking of a dog from a nearby village was heard. I was utterly unable to think of anything. After a night that seemed as long as a year came a bright, sun-drenched day. But how dark and somber did the day appear to my eyes. . . .

At least I got warmed up a bit: I was alone in the field. There was not a single friend anywhere close by that I knew of. Very slowly the day passed. Again a night of cold and hunger. Crushed and oppressed in spirit as I was, I sank into slumber.

I awoke with dawn. What now? There was no reason to remain here any longer. One must go on further, wherever the path may lead. Perhaps I might reach a place where I would find my people, not yet deported. My feet moved on with difficulty. My sense of direction was gone. I regretted that I had separated from my friend; it is much easier for two to carry the burden of suffering. After wandering for hours I arrived in a small village. I ate some food, and after tidying up as much as I could, I turned toward the next railway station, Kozłów.

The tracks finally brought me to Charsznica. If my memory did not trick me, I thought, I had some acquaintances here among the railway workers.

I ran forward now. I was terribly tired. I would very much have liked to wash, to be like the people around me. Suddenly, something wonderful happened to me: on the ground before me was a woman's pocketbook, containing a small sum of money. But, besides this, I found something more important, a passport belonging to the owner of the pocketbook. Now, at any rate, it would be easier for me to continue on my way.

I came to my acquaintances. Their joy was indescribable. It was warm in their clean, pleasant dwelling. They did not know whether to be more surprised at my courage or at my terrible appearance. My face was very thin, but this meant nothing. After resting for a few days I would be able to travel on. I decided not to cause any unpleasantness to these kind people. Well did I know that if the police were to discover me in their house, the entire family would surely be lost.

My friends furnished me with a ticket and a few złotys. They tried to revive my spirits. If I could not find any other escape, they were willing to shelter me again. I knew how sincere they were.

And so—departure for another journey. I was offered work on an estate in a small village. But I was utterly weak and exhausted, unable to work in a household. Besides, I was afraid of registration. I feared that finally my identity would become known.

I was in surroundings completely unknown to me. After a long and arduous journey on foot, I arrived at a small railway station.

One dark night I bought a ticket for Kazimierz, where it was supposed that there still were Jews. I decided to stay there for a while and find out, if possible, whether my family was still alive. The train was moving. Suddenly someone peered searchingly into my eyes. A chill passed through me: they know my identity. It was a townsman of mine. He turned away from me. Now and then I overheard other people talk about me: "Yes, it is she. It was easy for her to escape, for she does not look Jewish."

I could no longer stay in the coach. I felt that if I were to remain there I would faint. I saw pursuers everywhere, at every step. I went to the rear of the train. It was chilly outside. Sparks from the locomotive rained pitilessly upon me. Suddenly the door of the coach opened; the conductor appeared. He started a conversation, probably trying to judge by my accent whether I was Jewish. He invited me to enter the coach. "It's chilly here," he said, "and the sparks are dangerous." I thanked him for his kindness and explained that I was standing there because of the congestion and stuffy air inside. He examined my ticket, noted where I was traveling to, and returned to the coach. I understood. Upon reaching the next station he would turn me over to the police. It was quite simple. It was well worth his while to do so, for he would receive a reward of several złotys.

Quickly, while my mind was still clear, I seized upon the moment when the train slowed down while moving up an incline, and throwing out my small suitcase, leaped after it. I lay unconscious for some minutes, but the cool breeze revived me. My feet were bruised and torn, but that was a small matter. The thing that counted was that I had saved myself again.

I kept running with all my might. It was dark all around; the places were strange to me wherever I turned. The grass, wet with dew, bathed my wounded, bare feet and soothed my pain.

Suddenly a gleam of light appeared in the distance. I was approaching a little house. A dog barked, aware of a stranger. The owner of the house appeared and asked me my business. I told him that I was on my way to my relatives, but that I had learned by chance that an ambush had been set up for the Jews in this vicinity. Since I had no certificate testifying to my Aryan descent, I must hide for a few hours until daybreak. Of course, if the Germans saw me in broad daylight they would never doubt that I was a pure Aryan. The man understood. I entered the house, drank something warm, and lay down to rest in the hay. At dawn the master of the house told me to go, since it was forbidden to admit a person to a house without first reporting the matter to the police.

Again I was afoot, but I was rested and invigorated. One thought spurred me on: if only I could find out something definite concerning my family, that they were still alive—I would then know that my life had an aim.

I finally reached Kazimierz. Jews still lived there, but there was great tension; the Jews knew quite well that their brethren from the neighboring places had already been sent off to be murdered. Only a few had plans for saving themselves; for the others there was no escape. First, they did not have the money required. Besides, they did not know a single Gentile, no matter how kind, who would give them shelter in his house.

As a Jewess I could not under any circumstances find any shelter there. The Jews were intimidated by the orders issued by the Germans that no shelter must be given to Jews fleeing from other towns. They were careful not to transgress this prohibition, thinking this might save them from deportation. But it was a meaningless, vain hope. The Germans had decreed our annihilation everywhere.

Life in Disguise

I was now completely destitute. I could get no material support from any source whatever. To continue my fight for life, I needed a roof over my head and sustenance, no matter how meager. I had to find work at any price. But how to go about it? I knew no one in the city. I wandered about in deep depression without anyone to lend me a hand. I was thoroughly revolted simply by the strange faces I encountered. Those wearing a Star of David on their arms were my only joy.

Sunday, at dusk, while passing a house, I noticed a Jewish militiaman nearby. Turning to him I asked whether he knew of any place where I might stay overnight. He took me into the hall of his house and there I stayed until morning. Thus I struck up an acquaintance with his family. From that day on, this was the only Jewish home in the place known to me; and only the members of that family knew that I was Jewish, and helped me afterward with my mail and in other ways.

After many unhappy adventures, I met a Polish girl who became friendly with me, not knowing I was Jewish. She introduced me to a partly German family who gave me shelter in exchange for household work. I was glad, for I would now be able to quiet my nerves somewhat and look for ways of establishing contact with my family.

A new way of life began. Work was the only remedy for the wounds and afflictions I had suffered. Evenings, I went to bed thoroughly tired. Yet something robbed me of rest and would not let me be for a moment. I was seized by spasmodic fits of weeping. But I must refrain; I must beware of my benefactors. I was compelled to pretend that I was only a simple girl, satisfied with my lot, content with life and my part in it.

My benefactress praised me highly. I knew myself that I accomplished a great deal of work. She behaved toward me as if I were a girl both experienced and intelligent. She declared, once and again, that it was the first time she had ever had a girl as good as I—clean, industrious, pious, even educated to some extent. I would explain there was no need to be surprised. I came from a well-to-do family; only because I had lost my parents was I compelled to look for housework. My mistress frequently gave me gifts. Generally speaking, the Germans and their children behaved toward me in the kindest manner possible; relations were unlike the usual situation between master and servant.

But there was one thing they could not comprehend. Why did I look so depressed, why was it impossible for me to brighten up a little? To allay any suspicions, I explained that this was because I lacked proper clothes. Because of this, I said, I dared not go to church.

After obtaining these necessities I had something else to be concerned about: How could I attend church, ignorant as I was of everything in the ritual? I knew no prayer, no religious chant, and I was terrified lest I arouse suspicion. As it was, my benefactress kept me in her home despite the fact that I was not registered with the police. She would certainly assume at the slightest slip that I was a Jewess. I must completely disguise myself so as to appear as a devout Catholic.

On Sunday I dressed hurriedly, and a strange horror took hold of me. Might not my conduct in church reveal that I was ignorant of the Catholic faith and its ritual? Would not the people there recognize that I was only playing a part in a comedy? A deep disgust filled me: wherever I turned I was compelled to play a new role, to pretend and assume disguises.

My heart beat madly. A crowd of people pushed into the church, myself among them. What would my father and mother have said had they seen me in this state? I watched the people about me. I was transformed into a parrot. Whatever they did—I followed suit. They crossed themselves and so did I; they knelt—and I did likewise. They prayed devoutly, lifted their hands and eyes to heaven, and I emulated them. I never knew that I was gifted with such a talent for mimicry.

The people finally rose from their seats and went to the door. I watched them. Going out they kissed the image of Jesus, and I did likewise. I was already outside—I could feel the pure air—I was on the way home from church. A heavy weight rolled off my chest. All had gone off well. The important thing was that the neighbors and the children of my benefactress had seen me in church, witnessed my ardent prayers. Now they would no longer suspect that I was Jewish.

Now that I had begun to live once more, I even experienced some happiness. I wrote to my sister Sarah who lived in Bendzin. A few days later I received a report that, whenever I thought of it, placed me in danger of committing some folly out of sheer joy. My dearly beloved parents, brothers, and sisters, I learned, were still alive. The brother who remained in the camp was still there. Surely there was none so happy as I. Suddenly the ties that bound me to my loved ones were renewed again.

They were still in the woods beyond Wodzisław, near Miechów. In that place, evidently, the few Jews still alive and in hiding had been cordoned off. I easily imagined how they lived in the forest, in the chill of late autumn, and pain stabbed at my heart.

How could I take pleasure in a warm, clean bed when my dearest ones must endure hunger and cold in the all-pervading mud?

I wrote to my parents and day by day, hour by hour, I awaited a reply to the letter. After prolonged anticipation I finally lived to see that moment. The letter that was to bring me so much joy came at last. But together with joy, it also brought inexpressible anguish.

Inconceivable want, exposure, filth, especially hunger were my parents' lot. Lord, what could I do? I was but a puny, helpless creature. I asked Sarah in Bendzin and Aaron who worked in the camp to send as much aid as they could and they did so indeed. Large sums of money were spent in supplying them with various goods, for the peasants in the neighborhood swindled them mercilessly. My little brother, Yankele, comforted our parents as well as he could, said the letters. He tried to awaken in them the will to live, he encouraged them. However, the letters did not tell me anything at all about my two sisters.

A letter from Sarah—I read it in frantic haste. My parents' joy at learning that I was still alive was indescribable. They had been certain that I was lost forever. There was another matter: they demanded, unconditionally, that I go to Bendzin to stay with my sister Sarah. They knew it was dangerous for me to remain where I was without proper documents (the passport I had found once in the Charsznica station was honored there only). They were right to a degree. If it were to occur to my mistress to register my documents, I would fall into the clutches of the police.

Everything was arranged. A smuggler would come and guide me across the boundaries between the part of Poland known as the General Government[3] and the part that had been annexed to the Reich. On my way from Kazimierz I was to stop over with my parents, who were now in Miechów. There the Jews had been temporarily concentrated; there a trap had been set for them.

Bitterly, sorrowfully I recall those moments. I was certain that I would see them, my dear ones, even if only once. But I was not so fortunate.

One fine November day I made the decision to leave Kazimierz and go to Bendzin,[4] where my sister Sarah lived with the other members of her kibbutz.[5]

On a Sunday, while I was on my way home from church with friends, the sister of the militiaman in whose hall I had spent the first night approached and told me that the smuggler had come from Bendzin to take me there. I served the evening meal in a rather excited state of mind. My benefactress noticed it, too. But after I had finished my work I hurriedly and without difficulty slipped out of the house and went to my friends. I returned after an hour with a detailed plan.

That day I was to leave. I invented a tale for my employers, telling them about an aged, sick aunt whom I must visit for two or three days. My benefactress, who understood, allowed me to go. Night, darkness, and silence were all about me; it was raining steadily.

Impatiently I waited for the train that was to take me away. If only it would hurry a little!

Finally I was on my way. The train ran at a good speed. Nevertheless, every minute was like an hour to me. In my imagination I pictured the meeting with my dearest ones. I saw the faces of my parents, grown thin, aging, yet shining with happiness. But at the same time I could not believe that I would really be fortunate enough to see my family again. I felt that there must be a stumbling block somewhere, which would prevent this meeting from taking place.

A small railroad station. Could this be Miechów? No, one still must travel on, but we would soon be there. It was not very far from the small station we had just passed. The woman who was to run me across the border had said that it was impossible to stop over at Miechów. It might cause me some difficulties during the remainder of the trip, and besides, she could not take the time to stop there now. But she promised me, upon her word of honor, that after bringing me to Bendzin she would return immediately and fetch my brother and parents. Under no circumstances did I intend to agree to this, and since she could by no means convince me, or compel me to continue the trip in the way she wished, she informed me that my sister in Bendzin had strictly forbidden her to stop in Miechów. I must cross the border of the General Government as soon as possible, enter Reich territory, and proceed to Bendzin. I thought: Sarah is older than I am, and she knows what should be done. The idea of bringing me across the border quickly is quite sensible. I therefore agreed to the demands of the smuggler and did not get off at Miechów. It did not occur to me that what the woman said was intended only to deceive me.

The meeting with my parents did not, therefore, come to pass. I cannot express how bitterly disappointed I was.

That very day, after midnight, we arrived at Częstochowa, the town where the woman lived. Tired and depressed, I hastened to her house. There I had a light meal and went to bed, sinking into a deep slumber.

After spending some days there, we started for the border, crossing it on the road to Bendzin. The trip went without any mishaps. I considered myself safer in those parts. I was a stranger here, and the terror that lay heavy upon me while on the way, the terror of being recognized, was now lifted. Now I must hasten and see my dear Sarah[6] first, and then all the people in her kibbutz.[7]

I walked unsteadily from excitement. What did Sarah look like? What would she say upon seeing me? What would my life be like from now on?

Arrival at Bendzin

December 4, 1942, was when I came to the kibbutz.

I ran up the stairs and at last opened the door. The hall was clean and brightly lit. The boys and girls, dressed in fine, clean clothes, sat around tables deeply immersed in their reading. I peered anxiously about, searching: Where is Sarah? Had something unforeseen happened again? The group knew well whom I was seeking. Baruch led me to the third floor, to the bedroom.

The room was in deep darkness. The hall was long, the silence absolute. Only a quiet, rather somber breathing disturbed it. Sarah was lying in bed. Yes, it was Sarah, none other than she. At last! Baruch guided me in the darkness toward the bed. He was a pleasant young man, lively, and very understanding.

"Sarah," he said, "would you like to have Renia come here?" She jumped up from bed, sensing that I was near. "Renia," she called loudly, "you are all I have left in the world! Worry for you made me ill."

Like a mother she kissed me and pressed me to her heart, weeping. She was very weak. Nevertheless, she led me to the kitchen where I could have some food. There in the light I saw how thin and emaciated her face had become. It was possible to read upon it the complete story of her sufferings and anxieties. Her face had grown quite aged, but she was still youthful in spirit.

And now—a new anxiety, and a new struggle with fate: What can be done to save our parents? It was difficult to bring them here: there were no housing facilities, no means of support.

A letter arrived from Sandomierz.[8] My parents had been there for some days.

They were living like cattle. The Jews had been concentrated in a narrow, filthy district, actually heaped one on top of the other in small, dirty rooms. They slept on the bare floor, or on a thinly covered straw bed. Lack of food caused great suffering. They were practically naked, the poor, miserable people. And there was no fuel for a fire. They lived in constant fear of deportation and mass murder. The ghetto might go up in flames at any moment. The inhabitants were in constant danger of death. Little Yankele begged to live as long as we were alive. "Save us," he wrote. "Our will to live, despite all these inhuman miseries, is great."

> I am the only solace and support of our dear parents. They are happy that Renia has gone to a safer place. I would have liked

> to join you, together with our parents, even though no one can know for how long a time the Germans will let you be. You are the only persons we can depend on, you alone can help us and take us away from here. Our parents are likely to commit some horrible act; they may kill themselves. But I am with them, and this alone preserves their mental balance.
>
> Every day I leave the Jewish district, despite the strict watchfulness of the police. One must earn something, even if only enough to pay for overnight shelter in the narrow, crowded, cold, and filthy room. It is December weather. We are sparing of our food, because it is the only way we can save 120 złotys, the price for a night's lodging on bare boards. The people lie crowded, literally like fish packed in a barrel. Each warms the other. Insects fatten on our flesh. It is not surprising. For months we have not changed our outer garments or underwear. There is no place for washing clothes, and nothing to wash with.

What could we do to help our dearest? There was no possible way to send them money or food parcels. We ran about distracted, fearful of the thought that one day all connection between us would be broken. Such a break would be clear proof, indeed, that they had been done to death.

What was to be done? Our nights were sleepless, haunted by a weird feeling that the end of the world had come for all of us.

A letter, the last letter that forever engraved itself in my memory. A letter of parting, written in the hand of Papa, Mama, and little Yankele. It read:

> If we are not found worthy of remaining alive, you, at any rate, keep on fighting for your lives with everything you possess, so that you may be witnesses to the world; so that you may testify by what cruel means your own dearest ones, and your whole people, have been robbed of their lives. May God protect you always.
>
> We are about to die, believing that you, at least, will remain alive. Especially intense is our anguish because of our youngest son, Yankele, beloved of all of us. But we have nothing in our hearts against you. We are certain that if you could but act, you would have done everything. Assuredly, it has been thus decreed. If such is the will of the Holy One, blessed be He, we must accept His judgment.

From this letter we also learned of my sisters' end in Wodzisław.

They were hiding in the lavatory. At the last moment, as the deportation of the Jews was about to be completed, the landlady's son, a boy of about seventeen, entered the lavatory. Seeing them there, he called in some Gestapo men. And they made both of my sisters join the throng being taken away to Treblinka. . . .

Everything was now lost. There were no tears. Our hearts had turned into stone.

All contact with the family had been broken. I was an orphan. I felt that from day to day my memory and my very senses grew steadily weaker. Had it not been for my sister, for whose sake I now lived, and had it not been for her "group"—I do not know myself to what a pass I would have come.

Suddenly contact with my brother Aaron was also interrupted. However, indirect reports reached us that he had been transferred to the Skorzysk[9] munitions plant. Work there began with the break of day and went on until late at night. A slice of dry bread and cold water were the staple foods, and these were carefully measured and weighed. Many fell dead every day. Their clothes were filthy, torn, and ragged; they walked about in bare feet. There was a typhus epidemic and Aaron and his comrades had fallen sick. Because of the goodwill of their attendants in the sickroom, they were not taken out to be shot as were the others who were stricken with the typhus. Aaron had already partially recovered, but he was still very weak. After such a severe illness, cold water, with a tiny bit of bread, was again his ration. He got nothing else, for he was not engaged in productive work. Beyond this, we had no definite news about him.

Despite everything, we were still alive, even if we walked about like shadows, with our dear ones taken from us. Nothing was left for us but to continue to struggle against fate. Who could know what it held for us in the future?

But this I did say to myself: If it were destined that I, too, should fall—I would not fall like a hunted animal.

CHAPTER THREE

The Bendzin Kibbutz

How the Deported Jews Were Destroyed

From November 1, 1942, to Deportation

Several days had passed since I came to the kibbutz. The group consisted of thirty-seven people. Everyone worked at his particular job, for every Jew was obliged to have a special work certificate, what we called a *sonder*.[1] Without such a certificate no one could leave their house, for they might at any time be transported to forced labor or transported out of this world altogether. The Jewish Council, serving the oppressors as it did, took good care that none of the Jews meandered about idly.

The comrades were, therefore, all at their places of work. The household of the kibbutz itself was shorthanded, and many of the group, upon returning from work, had to help with the laundry[2] or lend a hand in the barn.

Soon after my arrival, I, too, entered into the routine of the kibbutz. Eventually I was assigned to work in the laundry, which previously belonged to the kibbutz but now was owned by the Jewish Council.

The new life that began was quite a paradise to me, though a temporary respite. Here one was not continually aware of the horrible massacre that had taken place before my very eyes only a short time before. At times I would contemplate the group and the other Jews living there, and I could not believe my own eyes. Were there such Jews, Jews who lived like human beings, people of vision who looked toward the future? These people lived for the sake of the distant motherland and all their thoughts always revolved around Eretz Israel, the Land of Israel, which was the hub of all their talk, studies, and songs. Was it not a dream? Had not these people heard of the barbaric murders and abominable deeds that took place in the General Government? That was impossible. By now all had been deported or were still being deported from their homes—to be murdered.

The following was reported by a Polish engineer on a train heading for the extermination site. So that no one might know where the train was going, the Polish engineer was replaced by a German several stations before its destination was reached. It was known, however, that the place was Treblinka. Here trains arrived not only from Poland but also from other European countries.

At the Treblinka station, Germans and Ukrainians stood in rows along the tracks, prodding the people on with blows and curses. So that they would have no opportunity to look about them and observe the place, the hastening people were not allowed to halt for even a single second. The Jews were gathered into a wide enclosure.

First, a hundred boys were selected from the group. Later, those selected had to sort the clothing of the persons put to death. It was then asked who was sick, and the sick were gathered separately in a specially erected tent and shot to death. Those left, not knowing that the others had been taken to be shot, thought that if the sick had thus been separated, it was clear enough proof that they had been brought there to work and not for slaughter.

The corpses of those who were shot were put in big electric ovens for cremation.

Now the men and women were separated. The children were given bread and milk. All were told to take off their garments; all bags and valises were put aside. Their clothes were then thrown upon one steadily growing heap.

Everyone was now undressed. The Germans hastily apportioned clean towels and bars of soap. They told the people to hurry, for the water might turn cold. They were led in a row, naked, towels and soap in their hands.

In large groups they were brought to the "*Automat*" building. The Jews were herded forward by police wearing heavy masks for protection against gas fumes. The building was full to overflowing with naked men or naked women, in turn. Only a few realized at first that this was but a cunning design of the murderers, and that in a few minutes their end was sure to come.

Then at last sobs, prayers, and confessions were heard. At a set moment, the guards opened the gas valve. The bodies became tense all at once, like taut strings.

Thousands of people closed their eyes, suffocated, and were practically fused together in one lump, turned into a kind of solid, consistent mass. The lump was then broken up, it was reported, and divided into parts. Its components were lifted up by derricks onto wagons; and by machine they were deposited into pits. The pits were wide; the earth swallows all. But the secret of this frightful deed was not swallowed up by the earth. The fact must be proclaimed. Some Jew who escaped those bloodstained hands will surely make the abomination known in full detail.[3]

A burning urge for revenge flared up in the hearts of the comrades of the kibbutz who listened to this story. They solemnly pledged not to go to their death as the Jews of the General Government had done—like sheep led to the slaughter. "If it be our fate to fall and die—let us at least defend ourselves. No, we will not be taken away to be murdered in such a shameful, degrading manner."

Daily, large companies of Jews over forty years of age were dispatched from Bendzin, Sosnowiec, and Dombrowka. These, the Germans stated, were selected only because they were no longer fit for work.

All these operations were carried out by the police, aided by the Jewish Councils and the Jewish militia. They were the servants of the Germans, their tools, and these Jews blindly obeyed each order given. The slightest "transgression" was enough to send a man to his death. Capital crimes included crossing the street diagonally, walking on the right or the left side of the street when prohibited by law, or leaving a house during curfew hours. Jews were strictly forbidden to smoke cigarettes. To engage in petty peddling, sufficient to earn the price of a crust of dry bread, was also prohibited. Jews in whose houses were found eggs, onions, garlic, meat, milk products, bread made of white flour, or a little fat were ordered deported, and no appeal was permitted. Periodically the police raided Jewish homes and conducted minute investigations, even into pots.

Even in the kibbutz, deep dejection was already prevalent. Several weeks after my arrival, Frumka Plotnicka,[4] of the Warsaw Central Committee of the Polish Hechalutz,[5] came to stay with us for a while. There seemed to be some prospect of sending her over to Slovakia and from there to Palestine as our representative. Evening after evening she told us of new abominations perpetrated in various cities such as Vilna, Białystok, and Warsaw. Everywhere murderous "operations" were being carried out by the "annihilation squads," companies of Ukrainians and Gestapo men specially trained and experienced in murder, as well as some of the regular police. The men of the Jewish militia acted as auxiliaries, of course. Upon completion of their job they, too, were put to death. At times they were granted "special consideration": at their request they could be killed by firing squads, somewhere behind a small ruin or under a dilapidated fence, out of the way; or in the Jewish cemetery.

Until this very day I can visualize the horrible events that took place in Vilna, as Frumka related them. The Jewish district was turned into a pool of blood, while the cruel men of blood walked in it taking their pleasure. The streets, alleys, and residences were covered with a carpet of corpses. Groans, sobbing, wails like those of wild animals were heard. Now and then Frumka's story would be interrupted by a quiet sob. No help was in view. The world permitted everything to pass in silence, turning its eyes away from us.

I recall the bewilderment of our group. Why live? What value and what justification does such an abominable life hold? Why read, why study, of what value are culture and enlightenment?

Our first misfortune befell us. Pinek Elbaum, the youngest member of the kibbutz, was taken away from us and deported. For what reason? Because of an insignificant incident. In the morning there was talk among us about a small iron bar that we needed for repairing the stove. Little Pinek, who was only seventeen, decided without further ado to get us the necessary piece of metal from the shop where he worked. He did not even have time to conceal the metal bar. He had merely picked it up and examined it when the German who was his foreman became aware of it. That was sufficient cause for deportation. He had no time to appeal to a higher authority. At dusk, when we inquired why he had not yet returned from work, we were told that he had been deported. The news plunged us into extreme depression.

Meanwhile the manhunt continued. The chase was aimed at those who had succeeded to escape from the General Government or from other places where deportations had occurred and had found refuge among us, after hiding and disguising themselves near the borders of the expanded Reich for long periods. The hunt usually took place at night. The Jewish militiamen were employed in it as well as the "Aryan" police. Persons who gave shelter to refugees from the General Government were subject to immediate deportation.

There were many other "illegal" people among us in the kibbutz, in addition to myself. Most nights, we "illegals"—Mordecai Bachazh, Zvi Brandes,[6] the two sisters Hancia[7] and Frumka Plotnicka, and myself—would stay in hiding. After a night of sleepless torment we had to get up and work the next day at the laundry trough in place of the "legal" members of the group, so that they could do other work. But we accepted everything gladly. The instinctive will to live was stronger than our suffering.

From day to day conditions grew worse. Rumors were current that within a short time all the Jews of the town, for whom segregated districts had only recently been set up, would be deported. For the time being, however, we suffered from the process of the concentrating of all Jews in the ghetto, the Jewish quarter. People who have lived for a time in such a ghetto know well the meaning of this.

Frumka Plotnicka and Hershel Springer, our secretary, went about distracted. What was to be done? Should we move to the ghetto, or should we rise up and fight? After much deliberation we came to the conclusion that we would not benefit from even the fiercest resistance at this point; that it could only lead to disastrous results. We decided that the time was not yet ripe for a stand.

Hence we were compelled to accept the latest decree. In the kibbutz, preparations were underway to bring all the most essential household chattels to Kamionka. This was a part of the town that had been emptied of its Aryan inhabitants and made ready to absorb twenty-five thousand Jews. The housing problem there was severe. Only ten thousand people could find any kind of dwelling for themselves, even the most rudimentary; the others were sentenced to rove aimlessly under the open sky.[8]

Hershel and Frumka spent almost all their days in the office of the Jewish Council. They tried to obtain some sort of dwelling in Kamionka both for us and another kibbutz of younger boys called Atid ("future" in Hebrew).This was the group of nineteen boys, ranging in age from ten to sixteen, who had been removed from the Bendzin orphanage during its liquidation. They had been housed until now in a number of rooms and lived the way our kibbutz did. We were trying to bring them up in accordance with our ideals. Eliza Sittenfeld, a member of our kibbutz, and Marek Folman, one of our people from Warsaw, were engaged in this work. After Marek left, his job was taken over by Baruch Gaftek,[9] another member of the kibbutz.

We saw in these children the embodiment of our future.

Removal to the Kamionka Ghetto

Horrible days came—the transfer to the ghetto. Every day it was necessary to clear the Jews from one of the streets they inhabited. The number of dwellings was limited. It was easier for the well-to-do to find some space in the newly created ghetto, for they could bribe the Jewish Council. But what could the poor people do who could offer no bribes?

There was continuous commotion in the office of the council. Shouting, sobbing, weeping, and wailing—all in vain. Without money you were like an unarmed soldier. The wealthy were the strong, even in those unhappy days. The well-to-do received preference because they could afford to pay the sum demanded for dwellings. Before each house were heaped furniture, tableware, packs, and parcels. Nearby, on the ground or on bare boards, were the little children. Little innocents, what are they guilty of? A fearful, indescribable scene that can scarcely be imagined by any human being.

Persons having no money and no roof over their heads hastened to build shacks similar to poultry roosts for shelter against the elements. Four walls made of clapboard were now considered excellent living quarters. Sheds, stables, garrets, and the large lavatories were turned into apartments. Ten persons lived in a small shed, and they were considered fortunate. It was no small matter for a person to have a place of his own, a refuge that could be called a home. Those who had no place as yet slept on the ground under the open sky. Furniture, except for beds and tables, was not brought into the new dwellings at all. In many places the beds had to be taken outside during the day to leave a passage wide enough for people to pass without stumbling over one another.

In the daytime the ghetto looked rather like a Gypsy camp. Small stoves were set up everywhere, each a few steps from the other. Smoke rose out of their stacks, poisoning the air. People sat on the ground, plates in hand, eating porridge. They were like wandering shadows; they moved about miserable, emaciated, and ragged. To be more exact, they were living corpses.

But the Poles, the Aryans, were happy. Shamelessly they plundered Jewish possessions left behind in town. "Too bad," they said, "that Hitler did not come sooner."

There were Jews who did not want to cause the Poles such gratification, and they burned everything, or chopped their furniture up into firewood.

The day arrived when we, too, left for the ghetto. We packed those things without which it would have been impossible to get along, and had them transported by car. Thanks to the efforts of Frumka and Hershel, we got rooms that seemed magnificent compared to those obtained by others. We occupied an entire two-story house.[10] Part of the house was ours, the rest belonged to Kibbutz Atid. It was a narrow, uncomfortable place, and it was difficult to walk through the passageways. The closets and tables were in the courtyard; for the time being, at least, we would have fuel to burn in the stoves.

We found our situation quite satisfactory; compared with private dwellings thereabouts, our house was practically palatial. It was clean, well-ordered, and pleasant. We began once more to order our lives in accordance with our aims, even though we were certain that we would be able to do so only for a very brief time.

The ghetto was shut and barred, guarded well by the Jewish militia. The penalty for leaving the ghetto area was deportation, and many were those who suffered that penalty.

Our people went to work in groups, accompanied by a militia guard. The militia also escorted them upon their return. The Jews worked in government-owned tailor shops, shoemaking shops, and plumbing shops, set up by the Germans. Labor was obligatory and the German management made immense profits. But even that did not spell security for the workers, as the following days proved.

A rebellious spirit seized hold of the people in the ghetto. Some who still were without a roof over their heads did not go to work. They would claim that they could not leave their children without proper care. The Jewish Council, therefore, set up nurseries.

Early in the morning the children were turned over to the nurseries, and there they remained until their parents returned from work. They had adequate supervision and received nourishment regularly. The parents could, therefore, be at peace as to the fate of their children. But at night they had to sleep, and where could they rest their heads? It was decided to erect huts that would shelter as many as possible.

The huts were erected near the smithies. Each smithy had its particular hut encampment. In some cases the people came to live in their shack before it was completed. Quite a long time passed before people gradually found shelter for their families under conditions of abominable overcrowding.

Preparing for the Defense of the Ghetto

February 1, 1943

Gradually we became accustomed to the disgusting sight that was the Jewish ghetto. The huts, tents, and sheds that served as living quarters for human beings were a far from pleasant sight.

There were filthy alleys, unpaved and without sidewalks. At times there were so many people that it was difficult to pass through. They were all Jews, marked by the Star of David patch worn on the left side of the breast. The yellow patch could easily be seen at a distance. The penalty for leaving the house without the Jewish patch was immediate expulsion; the slightest pretext was enough to lead to death.

At night the ghetto was shrouded in deep darkness. The ordinances called for a complete blackout. Occasionally there was the gleam of a flashlight; it was probably a policeman visiting the district, or a militiaman hurrying to his watch. Dead silence. Eight o'clock struck, and after that hour no one dared show his face outside. In every alley a militiaman watched over the deathly silence. Suddenly a shot would ring out. We were forbidden to go out to investigate, but what everyone assumed proved always to be true: there was a funeral in the morning. The unfortunate person had died while attempting to pass from his neighbor's house to his own. Such incidents were quite frequent.

Week after week, masses of people were being transported to Oswiecim[11] to be exterminated. The transports were made up of old persons; fathers and mothers who hid their children to prevent their being sent away to forced-labor camps; young children and babies torn from their mothers' breasts; young men caught evading forced labor or suspected of political activity; men and women who slipped away from work for a few days. All these regularly made up a parade of many thousands under police guard, marching to the station to be transported to Oswiecim. On the way they were beaten and tormented.

The crowd was at the station. The cattle cars were expected to arrive soon. Suddenly there was shouting and wailing. A policeman pulled a baby out of its young mother's embrace. He seized it by its feet and beat its head against a brick wall. The skull, in two parts, fell to the ground; blood sprinkled the wall and sidewalk. Nearby lay the tiny body, already beginning to grow cold.

Nearby, a person was found with something of no importance "concealed," and now he got his due reward. They whipped him, they trampled upon him with their boots, and afterward they fired a bullet into his head. But this was no longer necessary; the man had breathed his last. The others witnessed these cruelties in utter terror. The children screamed with heaven-rending voices. There was no one daring enough to complain or protest.

There was more space in the ghetto now, as the Germans cleared the place of its inhabitants. Someone was gone from every house. Here a father or mother, there a son or daughter. All our hearts were broken. It was surprising indeed that the entire district did not become a madhouse.

We gave up all our projects of training and education in the kibbutz, for the day of decision had come.

Certificates started coming in that made departure for some internment camp possible.[12] There was excitement among the people of the Palestinian movement. Who would be the first to receive the certificates and thereby be saved from the forthcoming deportation?

Some of us already had such papers. It must now be decided: Should we remain and resist, or be rescued and live to work in Palestine? The group unanimously voted to make immediate preparations for resistance. Hershel demanded, however, and in Warsaw it was likewise demanded, that Frumka go with someone else as a delegation to The Hague. Frumka definitely declined: "No," she said, "if it is decreed that we must die, let us all die together; but insofar as possible, let it be an honorable death."

A bold resolution had thus been agreed upon: defense! At once, we energetically set to work. The leaders in this activity were Baruch Gaftek and Zvi Brandes; they had some experience in resistance tactics. All groups were divided into units of five: four persons and an officer, whose orders they were to obey.

The officers would receive directives and assignments from Baruch and Zvi. Unit meetings were held daily. Everyone had to learn how to use various firearms that were soon to be brought from Warsaw. We learned not only the use of firearms but of axes, hammers, scythes, hand grenades, and incendiary fluids as well. The comrades were aflame with exaltation, ready for anything. They all set aside various kinds of sharp tools that could be used in a fight. After a time we had accumulated such weapons in quantity.

From early morning to eight o'clock in the evening—when curfew began—the rooms and courtyard of the kibbutz were astir with a changing throng of young people. Baruch was busy all day long, working on secret plans with our group. All matters pertaining to resistance were his special responsibility.

The people of the district started whispering among themselves; they craved to know what the young people of the kibbutz, and the youth who were continually getting together with them, were planning. The brick house where we lived became the focus of universal interest in the ghetto. Everyone wanted to have the honor of belonging to the circle of people who were allowed entrance to the kibbutz, even if for a while. We became well-known as "practical" people who were the masters of their own future; who knew what to do and how to behave at a given moment. The people became respectful toward the kibbutz members and we were greeted with a show of friendliness everywhere.

Most important, we began to construct bunkers wherein to resist, even if for a short time, deportation. After a full day's work the comrades of the kibbutz, together with the members of the Zionist youth groups, devoted their nights to the secret task of building the bunkers. They worked with extraordinary intensity, without either the Jewish Council or any outsiders knowing anything about the matter. Our comrades invested their entire energy in this project. One was shocked at the sight of their thin, emaciated faces.

The plans had been formulated by Alter Goldbrom and David Kozlovsky. For entire days they were preoccupied with questions such as: What place is best adapted for building bunkers? How to build the bunker so that the approach and entrance would be unnoticeable to strangers? Directives and blueprints were received from Warsaw. Ingenious stratagems were thought of, such as making the entrance to a bunker pass through a stove, or through walls, closets, or under sofas, or by way of chimneys and garrets. Also, a brick wall might be erected in such a way as completely to hide a room. Other hiding places were found in stables or woodsheds. All the innovations of our group cannot be detailed here. They included methods of installing electric lighting, small stoves, water, sleeping berths in the bunkers. In short, everything was well and properly done. When the hour of our final reckoning came, we hoped we would have nothing to do but stock the bunkers with a supply of food for a time. We had already begun to prepare toasted bread for the comrades who suffered from stomach ailments.[13]

The bunkers were completed but not yet entirely supplied. Our group decided to build bunkers in a number of private homes as well. The youngest of our boys, eighteen-year-old Gutek Goslavsky and his friend Tuvia Kalmanowich, showed marvelous talents, and their inventiveness amazed us all. They planned and designed things as if they were actually reliable, experienced engineers. From day to day the number of bunkers grew.

People did not know how to thank us sufficiently for our generosity and hard work. We did not wish to accept any money.

Clash with the Militia

February 1943

Work in the laundry had temporarily ceased. There was a great demand for recruits for the militia. To us this indicated that the deportation was about to begin. The Jewish Council sent "invitations" to our young men, requesting them to appear on a certain day at the office of the Jewish militia. There they would get uniform caps and documents. If they did not appear, their "special passes," that is, the work certificates, would be taken from them and the very next day they would be transported deep into Germany. These invitations were received by: Baruch Gaftek, who taught Hebrew in the Jewish school; the laundry workers Abraham Hershlikowitz, Yitzhak Kruvka, Aaron Schoenthal, and Tuvia Kalmanowich; and Tuvia Dvorsky, who was the supervisor of farmwork in the ghetto.

Our young men said that they preferred to return the work certificates rather than wear the militia caps. They did not want to be executioners of Jews and aid the Germans in leading Jews to the scaffold. Nor would they ever agree to leave for Germany. The Jewish Council had already sent some young fellows to Germany—and not one of them had returned.

On the appointed evening, after the young men failed to appear at the office of the militia, a militiaman with a written order from the head of the council, Molchadsky, came to take away our work certificates. The young men returned the certificates without ado.

The council did not expect such a response. To be without a certificate meant assignment to forced labor—it meant being deported. The next day a squad of ten or more men, armed with clubs, surrounded the kibbutz. The assistant commander of the Bendzin militia, Kaufman, was at their head. They came with an order to seize the specified young men and ship them off to Germany. Two militiamen stood at the door to prevent anyone's escaping; others examined the papers of all the young men. Aaron Schoenthal and Tuvia Kalmanowich leaped out of the window. Several militiamen went after them and were so badly beaten by the young men that they ran away as fast as their feet could carry them. The boys and girls shouted defiantly that they would not allow even one of ours to be taken, whatever the militiamen did. Kaufman ordered the militia to beat us all. The young men were to be seized forcibly and taken as hostages to replace those who had escaped. The militiamen, upon receiving the order, attacked us with their fists. The boys and girls seized anything at hand, and a fierce fight ensued. The heads of several among us were cracked by militiamen's clubs.

Frumka was apprehensive that someone might be killed and the police would be called in; then everyone would surely be killed. She therefore ordered all the young men whose names were listed to go to the police—but we would not give hostages. The militiamen went out, taking the young men along with them, while the members of the kibbutz followed in their wake. All the residents of the ghetto stopped to observe us; the street was black with people. On the road a bus stood ready to take the prisoners away. Suddenly Yitzhak Kruvka, a strong, sturdy young man, slipped away from the militiamen and started to run at top speed. The militiamen could not, of course, pass over the matter in silence. A battle started anew in the street, all the people of the kibbutz actively participating. Zippora Bocian and Alter Goldbrom fell upon the vice-commander Kaufman from behind, raining blows upon him especially. The fight lasted only ten seconds; the militiamen and our group were all beaten and bruised.

Kaufman, rather confused, ordered the militiamen to get into the bus: "Drive directly to the police office. Let them come and deal with them."

The spectators, noting that there still were Jews unafraid to oppose the misdeeds of the militia, started to applaud loudly. The militiamen were consumed with wrath, as if they were Germans themselves.

Frumka was certain that if the affair became known to the police not one of our group would remain alive. She therefore began pacifying Kaufman and the militia. They respected her highly and agreed to keep silence, but only on condition that hostages replace the escaped persons. The remaining boys and the hostages were taken to the bus. The hostages were Hershel Springer, Joel Springer, and Frumka herself. The bus set out for police headquarters.

When the story was reported to the commander of the militia, Heniek Bornblatt, he ordered the quarters of the kibbutz padlocked and the group moved out into the courtyard. In the evening the militia padlocked our rooms; we remained in the yard. That evening Frumka and Hershel returned with a report that the head of the Jewish Council and the commander could not be dissuaded from their decision; all argument was in vain. For the offense of disgracing the militia and its vice-commander, all were to be taken away to Germany.

The whole night through we sat outside, under the open sky. Many neighbors came and invited us to sleep in their houses but Frumka forbade us to do so, even though after eight o'clock we were risking our lives as curfew breakers. Let the militia find out that we are quite capable of squatting outside throughout the night, if necessary.

Frequently during the night militiamen came to inspect the leaden seals upon the doors. Luckily the night passed without incident and the German guards, who wandered about in the ghetto on spot patrol, did not come across us.

Throughout the following day we suffered hunger and cold, since we did not wish to enter anyone's home. Most of the neighbors sympathized with our action. That day Frumka set out again to intercede with the authorities for those arrested.

Toward evening we had a light repast with Kibbutz Atid, which still lived in the house. Late at night the militia opened the doors for us: a sign that the penalties had been remitted. But what will be the fate of those arrested? Frumka and Hershel have not yet returned. Who knows whether they have not all been deported by now? Late at night all the arrested comrades returned, together with Frumka and Hershel. Had it not been for these two, all the young men would have been in Germany by now.

Thus, not one of us was drafted into the militia or sent to forced labor in Germany. For a long time afterward the bold defiance shown by the kibbutz was a favorite topic in the ghetto. As a result of this incident, Baruch Gaftek, who had been deprived of his certificate, was no longer able to teach the children. Several children, aged nine to eleven, came to the kibbutz to inquire about Baruch. At that time he was ill and bedridden; the children surrounded his bed, begging him to come and give them instruction, for he was well loved by all of them. Baruch, who also liked the children, explained that his work certificate, the *sonder*, had been taken from him. Apparently, in the Jewish Council's opinion, further instruction was unnecessary.

The children did not long remain inactive. Leaving Baruch, they went to see the head of the council. They started with entreaties, speaking softly; then turned on him, shouting their protests at his revoking their teacher's certificate and demanding that the council return it.

The children's mission was successful. Two days later, a militiaman brought Baruch's work certificate. But Baruch was unwilling to take it as long as his comrades had not had their work certificates returned, too. In the evening a militiaman came and brought with him all the other certificates that had been revoked.

We were obliged to struggle continuously against the council and the Jewish militia. There were cases where the militia behaved as viciously as the Germans. It was commonly called the "Jewish Gestapo." At times, it knowingly conveyed Jews to prison and into the jaws of death. Not a day passed without a clash between the residents of the ghetto and the militia.

The militiamen behaved arrogantly. They prided themselves upon the white hats they wore, and some of them had to be feared like Germans. They were pleased with their lot. If one of the militiamen obtained information that someone had concealed goods, they forthwith came to demand a bribe. They would impose fines for trivial reasons and keep the money for themselves.

However, there were a few militiamen who acted compassionately, endangering their lives by their acts during deportations, smuggling Jews out of concentration camps. Such a "crime" was punishable by death. If they happened to know that the Germans were about to arrest someone or take him away for forced labor, they would warn the person while there was still time—in deep secrecy so that the other militiamen would know nothing of the matter. The militiamen also had permits to leave the ghetto, and some of them used this privilege to bring medicines and other necessities from the Gentile quarter that could not be obtained within the ghetto.

Many were punished for their good deeds. For the most insignificant cause, they were mercilessly beaten by the Germans.

Hancia's Journey and the Battle in Warsaw

We had been in continual contact with Warsaw throughout that period. Zivia Lubetkin[14] and Isaac Zuckerman would inform us of their defense preparations. They wrote that in Warsaw, deportation proceedings had ceased temporarily. But this silence only foretold a heavy storm; wholesale deportations might start at any time. True, there was no longer a large number of Jews in the ghetto; out of six hundred thousand, only fifty thousand remained. But the few who did remain would not let themselves be annihilated as easily as were the others.

Preparations for defense and drills went ahead, day and night. Everything was done secretly. Those engaged in this work were mostly members of the socialist-Zionist parties, but no one now paid any attention to party and ideological differences. The thing that counted was whether a person was known, from his work in any party, to be reliable and capable of being entrusted with some activity, without fear of betrayal on his part.

Our contacts wrote that it was possible for them to save themselves by leaving the ghetto and either finding living quarters in the Aryan section or escaping to other countries by way of a route they knew. But all plans for the salvage of individuals were rejected. No one was interested merely in saving his own skin. The last handful of Jews were determined to stand against the enemy, face-to-face, and fight him to the very last drop of blood.

In the next letter, dated February 1943, Zivia demanded categorically that Hancia Plotnicka go abroad. It was imperative that someone who had witnessed the barbaric massacres of the Jews remain alive. If the world was in deep slumber now, at least let it know at the proper time how millions of Jews had been wiped off the face of the earth in Europe. Let someone remain, a living witness to the horror that no language could adequately describe. She must leave at once, without delay—perhaps she would succeed to get through alive. Zivia wrote that she would listen to no excuses or arguments. This was a definite decision and we must carry it out.

Hancia rebelled against this. It was difficult for her to part from Frumka without knowing what tomorrow might bring. The two sisters had vowed to stand by each other through thick and thin. Frumka, too, could not imagine parting from Hancia, her last surviving sister. Nevertheless, the day after receiving the letter from Warsaw, we communicated with the smuggler from Częstochowa, urging him to come as soon as possible.

Hancia's preparations for the journey began. She went about depressed and despondent. Who knew whether she would ever again meet the friends she was to leave? Especially painful was the prospect of parting from Frumka. She tried to persuade her sister to go with her, but Frumka flatly refused.

It was queer to see Hancia, with her strongly Semitic features, dressed as a Gentile country woman. We became deeply worried. Would she arrive safely in Warsaw?

Hancia parted from us, tears choking her. We, too, wept; parting was very hard for all of us. Aided by the smuggler, she left the ghetto safely. She tore the Star of David off her breast to complete her transformation into a Gentile girl. Her heart certainly must have been pounding. The road to Warsaw was still rather long.

Two days later we received a telegram from Częstochowa. She had crossed the border safely. Everything had gone well. She would not stop there for long, but continue on her way.

Now a telegram and a letter came from Warsaw. The journey thus far had been successfully completed. The Germans had not identified her. The group at Warsaw was overjoyed. She would set out for abroad in a few days; all formalities were already arranged.

Another letter. For the time being, Hancia was not leaving; various rumors were afloat that prevented her from doing so. Until things were definitely clarified, neither she nor the others in the same position would leave.

The last letter was received at the beginning of March 1943. The situation was grave indeed; in the very near future wholesale deportation was to begin. "If you do not receive any more letters, let this be a sign that action has started. But this time the Germans will have a rather difficult affair on their hands, by far more difficult than before. They are not prepared for this at all."

Smuggling of Arms and Reports from Warsaw

During those days, A. used to come to us secretly from Warsaw. She was accompanied by the runner with whom Hancia had set out on foot from Częstochowa. He was very well compensated and it was worth his while to take these risks. On each such trip, A. would smuggle through some arms—especially pistols. She transported these by various means: they were concealed in large dolls, in toys, in a bread loaf, in dough, or in a jam container with a false bottom. It was no easy matter to transport arms from Warsaw to Bendzin. A. was liable to be caught at any moment. She would also bring with her, sewn into her garments, papers in which the plans for self-defense were outlined in detail.

The papers included maps showing the sites of the bunkers and describing how they were constructed. They were long corridors, built underground and beneath buildings. The corridors were several kilometers in length, in most cases stretching from one end of the ghetto to the other. The doors usually led into the Aryan section. The entrances and exits were properly camouflaged and would hardly be noticed. Subsidiary lines, such as dwellings and cellars, branched out of the main corridors. Light, water, and radio facilities were installed. There was also a stock of food sufficient to keep the people from dying of hunger while in action.

If the Germans failed to discover those bunkers, a few individuals might remain alive. Also stored underground were caches of arms and incendiaries. These bunkers really made up an underground world. They were constructed at night so that no one might learn what was going on.

Everyone belonging to a defense group knew his bunker password. The units comprised five persons each, one of whom was the leader. All of them were thoroughly trained in the use of various sorts of weapons. They also learned how to fight with their bare fists. They were under orders to fight to the very last, and never to be taken alive. It was of the utmost importance that all the preparations be kept secret, that the Germans know nothing.

We were sent specific directives from Warsaw as to our preparations, as well as a list of materials for making fire bombs. When these devices are thrown, the bottle bursts and pours forth lethal incendiary fluids.

The letters also notified us of relations established with the PPR,[15] who helped us obtain arms and transport them to the ghetto. They were also of assistance in housing people in the Aryan section of the town. They promised that when the operation began, they too would join the battle from the other side of the ghetto and beyond it.

Each letter we received from Warsaw mentioned a certain Polish woman named Irena who was particularly devoted to the cause and had performed a great many good deeds. She helped in various ways and had already, many a time, risked her life. She had forged a true, firm friendship with Tuvia, Zivia, Frumka, and others. She furnished various addresses in Warsaw and other cities; established necessary contacts and kept them active; made all the necessary arrangements, wherever she could, for the young men and women who had to engage in various activities in the Aryan sections of the town. With all this, she was very careful, too; no one in her home knew anything. She worked for our movement wholeheartedly and devotedly. We all admired her greatly even though we had never seen her.

At the same time we learned of the failures of some men and women comrades on assignments in the Aryan districts of Warsaw and other cities. Many of the young women, such as Chavah Folman, Lonka Koziebrodzka, and others, were caught and sent away to the camp for political prisoners at Oswiecim, to the Pawiak prison in Warsaw, and to other camps. Many others disappeared without a trace.

Other reports told of negotiations with a group of partisans and also that Jews were not being received in the partisan units. Addresses were sent to us from Warsaw so that we might know where and with whom to establish contact that would enable us to send people to the partisan units. We were asked to do everything possible to evacuate our whole group to the woods. This was indeed the only way out. We were exhorted to prepare for resistance as early as practicable, for it was not well to tarry too long. They were anxious to give us all the aid they could: to transmit money, smuggle through arms, give instructions. In short, they would do everything to make things easier for us.

Early in March, A. came. She reported that the people in the Warsaw Ghetto were living in great apprehension. The Germans were likely to besiege the ghetto at any time, thus launching the final action. Our people there were ready. This time A. returned to Warsaw hurriedly, for she still desired to contact the ghetto. By that time she was already living in the Aryan section.

After a few weeks the report of the horrifying massacre in Warsaw reached us. We suddenly received a telegram from someone in the Aryan part of Warsaw telling us that Zivia, Tosia Altman,[16] and many others were no longer alive and that the battle was still at its height. Meanwhile we heard nothing of Hancia. This affected us all deeply; Frumka was quite distracted with sorrow. Hancia, her sister, and Zivia, her best friend! The group, knowing Zivia as it did, spoke about her incessantly; "A girl like Zivia," they said, "cannot be found anywhere in the whole wide world."

Afterward things grew quiet. All reports ceased. Had everyone been murdered by then?

Frumka, Hershel, Zvi, and Baruch decided to send a courier to Warsaw with some money to obtain information. Since my appearance was not markedly Jewish and they thought that I might successfully carry out this mission, I was assigned to it. The runner from Częstochowa was informed and that very day he came to take me. He cleverly managed to cross the wall of the Bendzin Ghetto and came to us at the kibbutz.

I had sewn several hundred dollars in my garters.[17] We thought that this money would be useful to the Warsaw people. Up to the boundary at Trzebinia I traveled by train, equipped with the fingerprint certificate I had once found in the street. I got off at a station this side of the border, accompanied by the runner. A highway twelve kilometers long confronted us, traversing fields and woods. The border had to be crossed stealthily, on foot. The runner knew the way well, and he also knew the soldiers on guard. The border strip was but a small forest, which we had to cross as quickly as possible so as not to fall into the hands of the guard. If we met with a soldier of the runner's acquaintance, he was to get from us a bottle of whiskey. In exchange for this favor, the soldier, without saying a word, would permit us to continue on our way. He would even show us the way.

Quietly, cautiously, we slipped through among trees and bushes. We took care not to let our footsteps be heard. The mere rustle of the leaves and the slightest movement of the trees called forth fear. Someone seemed to be following us. Suddenly we noticed a shadow. We fell prone to the ground and crawled under the bushes. Very slowly and carefully the steps drew closer. We peered out of our hiding place: a man, trembling with fear, was approaching from the other side of the border. He was certain the police were lying in wait behind the bushes. Seeing us, he breathed freely. He told us that things beyond were quiet.

After a few moments we left the forest and came at once into a "foreign country." At the nearby station we boarded a train and rode up to Częstochowa. Here the ghetto still existed. A handful of Jews, engaged in hard labor day and night, lived within its walls. Only the young and skilled remained. The police conducted daily raids by to see that everyone was at work. The aged and the children had long since been put to death. Periodically a review took place, and the people were divided into categories. The weak were killed, and those still able to work were temporarily allowed to live. They carried out street cleaning and garbage removal in the ghetto and at military establishments.

The runner gave me his sister's identification card, minus photographs and fingerprints. I had learned the essential details by heart, and the following morning I was on my way to Warsaw.

In Warsaw it was difficult to pass through the streets; at every step documents were examined. Luckily, I succeeded somehow in boarding a streetcar. Drunken, riotous Germans rode toward the ghetto and back. The whole city was full of smoke and foul with the stench of buildings put to the torch and of burnt human bodies. A drumfire of shots was heard, bomb blasts were felt. Voices like those of jackals and other savage beasts rose up in the air; it was an uncanny kind of noise. Policemen were halting all passersby and searching each bag and package. All streets and alleys were filled with gendarmes and secret agents dressed in civilian clothes, searching for survivors escaping from the ghetto. Anyone arousing the slightest suspicion was shot in the street without ado. I grew dizzy at the sight of all this.

Clouds of smoke rolled above the ghetto. I kept going and arrived finally at an address that had been given me. The landlady was unwilling to admit me, saying that Miss Zosia (that was A.'s assumed name) was not at home.

It was dangerous to go out in the street: documents, as I have said, were examined at one's every step. Ten times things might turn out well, but on the eleventh I might stumble and be caught in the net. I did not know anyone here.

After lengthy explanations, the landlady agreed that I should wait—perhaps Zosia would come soon. She half apologized for her caution, saying there were announcements in the streets forbidding the admission of a stranger to one's home, even for a minute, on pain of death. She also told me of her suspicion that Zosia might be Jewish. She had already asked her to move away from her quarters, for she, the landlady, was afraid of endangering herself. The neighbors were already beginning to suspect her. I listened and pretended to be greatly amazed. Then I remarked: "I don't know, I made Zosia's acquaintance accidentally. I met her on a train. She asked me to stop in to see her when in Warsaw, and gave me this address. But I do think that Zosia is a Catholic, for she does not in the least resemble a Jewess. If she were Jewish, one could tell it immediately."

Then Zosia came. We went into the city. She told me that for some days now she had had no contact whatsoever with the ghetto. But she knew that the report of Zivia's death was incorrect. Zivia was alive, still in the ghetto, and fighting together with the others. But the report about Hancia's death was correct.

She told me how Hancia fell. After the Germans put the ghetto under siege, Hancia decided to return to Bendzin. She wished to die together with the comrades with whom she had spent the last years. Two comrades, with pistols in their pockets, accompanied her to the open space leading from the ghetto to the Aryan district. They went through byways and alleys so as to avoid the Germans. They were already approaching the exit when suddenly, a call: "*Stehen bleiben*!" (Halt!) Someone had recognized them. There was nothing for them to do but shoot. The men fired and started running. One German fell, a second was wounded, the third pursued the men, shouting. One of the comrades was hit by a bullet and fell, but the German also fell, struck by a bullet from the other man's gun. Then suddenly, several policemen emerged from behind. The surviving comrade slipped through one of the gates and disappeared; the Germans were unable to seize him.

Hancia ran breathlessly. Suddenly they overtook her. The Germans heaped their furious vengeance upon her. They beat her mercilessly, kicked her, and pulled her by her hair. She was dragged for some distance and killed "gradually." They finished their work with bullets. The story of Hancia's death, A. concluded, came from a comrade who succeeded to slip out of the ghetto after this happened.

A. took me to an inn, where I stayed that night. The next day I went to the ghetto, accompanied by a woman I made friends with, to observe more closely what was happening there.

All streets leading to the ghetto were crowded with soldiers in tanks, buses, and on motorcycles. They wore helmets and were equipped for assault. The heavens were red with the flames of buildings afire. The cries were deafening. The nearer I came to the place, the more horrifying and distinct the shrieks and groans became. Shots rang out. The ghetto was surrounded on every side by the Germans of the "annihilation squad." Behind ramparts hastily erected by the Germans lay soldiers and police, manning machine-guns.

Tanks appeared from every direction, firing. Planes flew over the ghetto, dropping bombs and incendiaries. The streets adjoining the ghetto were also in flames. It looked as if a major battle was underway.

Poles and Germans stood about, contemplating the sight from some distance—a sight that human imagination could scarcely conceive.

Young mothers were dropping their babies from fifth- or sixth-story windows; husbands were pushing their wives off the roofs; sons—their aged parents, then leaping to death themselves. Elsewhere lay men with gouged-out eyes, screaming, begging the Germans to shoot them. The Germans laughed derisively. After some moments, the men disappeared in the flames.

Others, situated on an upper story, were in no position to commit suicide. The floors below were already enveloped in flames and the fire broke through, extending higher and higher. Suddenly the brick walls tottered and fell. A roar arose from among the mounds of ruins. Mothers saved from the flames, babies in their arms, wailed with inhuman voices, entreating the Germans to spare the little ones. But the Germans were doing what they had set themselves to do. They tore the children out of their mothers' arms, dropped them to the ground, trampled upon them with heavy boots, split them with their bayonets. The little bodies squirmed with pain, as if they were worms split apart, crawling on the ground. Afterward the Germans threw the corpses into the fire; they then stabbed the mothers with their bayonets. A tank finally crushed the mothers to death.

The Jews defended themselves valiantly. On the roofs of houses not as yet enveloped by flames, boys manning machine-guns could be seen through the smoke as through a heavy fog. Girls fought heroically, armed with pistols and fire bombs. Small boys and girls attacked the Germans with stones, sticks, and iron bars. People in the street, seeing the developing battle, seized whatever weapon they could find and joined the fighters, for, to them at any rate, nothing was left but death. The ghetto was full of corpses. Many Jews died, but Germans, too, were falling.

Every onlooker reacted in his own way. There were Germans who spat at the sight and turned away; they could no longer endure the horror. A Polish woman stood at the window, stripping the garments off her body and shouting that there was no God in heaven if he could see all this and remain silent. She had become crazed at the awful spectacle. I felt that my legs would no longer support me and was therefore compelled to move away. I was crushed with sorrow at what I had seen; yet I was somehow glad that there still were Jews alive who could fight back.

Broken in spirit, I returned to the inn. The sights I had witnessed pursued me and distressed me. At times I could not believe that my eyes had actually seen all this. Hadn't I somehow been deceived by my senses? How could Jews, crushed as they were and weak with hunger, battle so heroically? Was it true indeed that millions had fallen quietly without resisting, without revolting, yet now others had arisen who wished to die like self-respecting human beings?

It was rumored that proclamations from the ghetto were circulated daily in the city. Listed in detail were the number of Germans killed, the weapons taken from them, and the number of tanks disabled. It was also stated that the Jews would fight on to their last breath. The din of planes was heard throughout the night and the ground trembled with the bombs they dropped.

Early the next morning I went to the station. I went from car to car, and all the people were marveling at the heroism and bravery of the Jews. There were others who said that many Poles were probably fighting with them; it was inconceivable that mere Jews were capable of such a valiant struggle.

The battle of Warsaw lasted approximately six weeks. Zivia Lubetkin and Isaac Zuckerman miraculously arrived safe in the Aryan section. They reported that scores of fighters still lived in the tunnel beneath the houses. Comrades living in the Aryan pale, Kazik[18] among them, decided to save these people. One day, disguised in police uniforms, they drove a bus to the site of the tunnel serving as an exit to the Aryan side. The uniforms had been removed from the bodies of Germans killed during the battle in the ghetto. With great effort they succeeded in removing to safety approximately eighty persons.

This is how it was done: German guards still continued to rove about the ghetto; it was necessary to be very careful. The young men dressed as policemen sat armed on top of the bus, surrounding their counterfeit prisoners. When halted in the street, the "policemen" showed their false papers. The Gestapo examiners saluted and went on their way. The bus drove out of town, toward the forest.

Our people got off the bus, entered the forest, and the bus driver returned to town to fetch other "prisoners." Some of those rescued continued moving ahead in any direction they could. Some lived in the woods, heedless of the Germans into whose grasp they might fall at any time. As luck would have it, a decent watchman was living in the forest, and he brought them some food daily.

The Germans were still kept occupied in the ghetto. They dynamited houses to make certain that there were no more Jews left in the bunkers; they sprayed gas into every sewer. Occasionally at night, one of the watches failed to return from its beat. The guards were found dead, killed by Jews wearing police uniforms.

Not many persons succeeded in making good their escape. Once one of the young men, dressed as a policeman, was standing at the gate of the ghetto with a group of bona fide policemen. No one recognized him, for the gendarmes did not know one another; they had been brought from the environs of the city. The young man started calling upon the Jews to come out. He then approached, dragging a couple of "prisoners" by their hands along with him. Other Jews, noticing that this gendarme did not shoot, quickly followed. The Germans paid no attention. They probably assumed that a new system was being tried—the gendarme was merely taking the Jews away before killing them.

Scores of Jews were thus saved. The persons rescued fled without knowing where they would be safe. Many fell into the Germans' grasp while wandering about the streets, not knowing where to go. However, many did save themselves. To this day no one knows who this kindhearted gendarme really was.

Comrades Are Being Deported

We were still busy in Bendzin bringing in arms from Warsaw. Gisya Pesachson, one of the girls, fell into the Germans' hands while carrying arms. The place where she was murdered is unknown; she went away and never returned. There were various rumors about it. It was said she was seized while on a train; others maintained it happened at the Częstochowa station. Nothing is definitely known.

Thereafter we went on our journeys in pairs. For instance, Ina Gelbart[19] and I went on a trip together. Ina Gelbart was an alert, tall, brave girl, typically Silesian. She traveled everywhere, fearless of death. We both had forged passports and transit permits for the border. There were persons in Warsaw who provided such passports at a high price, but in time of need no one haggled over price. When crossing the border the transit permit issued by the government, with its attached photograph, had to be shown, and also the identification card and its accompanying photograph.

The trip to Warsaw was not especially dangerous. If the examination of documents passed without incident and no one recognized me on the train, the trip was practically accomplished.

A Jew formerly named T., now K., lived in the Aryan district. He was the one who contacted the passport forgers and arms sellers. He supplied us with both commodities, passports and arms, and was well compensated by us for it.

The way back from Warsaw was more dangerous. There were endless searches on the train, with every tiny bundle examined. Weapons were sought in food packages, which were taken away from the passengers.

Throughout the trip you had to be ready for anything, not only ready to be shot, but to leap out of the train in case of emergency. You had to know beforehand what to do during a grilling. Above all, it was imperative, in case of failure, to bear the most extreme suffering without divulging information. A strong will was the greatest requirement.

Every weapon was treasured. It cost us a great deal of money, infinite energy, and nervous tension. Both the couriers and those who awaited their return suffered unbearable anxiety all the way. If the messenger did not return at the appointed time, his comrades simply lost their senses with worry; who knew what could have caused the delay?

Sometimes weapons were successfully smuggled in, and then we discovered that it was impossible to use them. Some part, for instance, was rusty, or else there was no ammunition. There was neither time nor any place to test the weapons in Warsaw. They were then immediately repacked in some out-of-the-way secret place, and some of us hurriedly got on a train to return the weapon to Warsaw or exchange it for a serviceable one. Again people had to risk their lives. Most of the pistols and hand grenades originally came from German arms stores. One of the soldiers would steal a weapon and sell it to someone, this someone in turn sold it to someone else. We would receive things probably at fifth hand.

In the beginning of May 1943, policemen, Gestapo men, and soldiers surrounded the Bendzin Ghetto in the dead of night.

The sound of shots was heard from afar. We looked through the window: dawn was breaking. There was panic, many people running about in confusion with nothing but their shirts on. They look like bees chased out of a beehive.

We leaped out of our beds: deportation!

Frumka and Hershel ordered all of us into the prepared bunkers, all except a number of persons who had *sonder* certificates from Rossner's[20] workshop. This workshop was owned by a Gestapo man, and persons possessing such a *sonder* were certain not to be deported. They were to remain in their quarters, for if the Germans were to come and find empty rooms, they might start searching and discover the bunkers. Then we would all be lost.

There was no time for lingering. Nine persons remained upstairs, the others went down into the bunker. The entrance to this bunker was through the kitchen stove; we lifted its top and went in. Those remaining upstairs put the iron cover back in place.

After a time, the sound of heavy hobnailed military boots reached us.

Immediately afterward we heard a running of feet in the room above, curses in German, a clatter of opening closets and furniture tipped over. They were searching for people they supposed to be hiding there. Then a stamping of boots on the stairs, noisy talk and shouts: "Get out—damned Jews!"

Silence settled over the place; everyone had left. Thus we sat for several hours. We were thirty persons in a small bunker. The air drifted through to us by means of a narrow crevice. There was tense silence all around; the air captured even the quiet buzzing of a fly.

The air grew steadily more suffocating; the heat was unbearable. One girl fanned another's face to prevent her from falling into a faint. Zippora Marder fainted suddenly. Fortunately we had some water with us, and some spirits of ammonia. Still, we were in a desperate state. There was not enough air to draw a breath, and it proved difficult to revive her. There was commotion in the bunker, and it was fortunate that no soldiers seemed to be out there. What were we to do? We were at our wit's end. Zippora was now thoroughly drenched by the water poured over her. We finally started pinching her until we managed to revive her. She had been greatly weakened; the rest of us, too, were seized with faintness for lack of air, our mouths parched.

The German operation had begun at four in the morning. It was now eleven, and none of our comrades had returned yet. We sat silently for another half hour. From the distance a sound of weeping, arising as though from a tomb, reached us. The people of the ghetto were coming back crying and wailing.

We waited for someone to come and lift up the cover of the stove. Frumka said: "Who knows whether they haven't been deported, since no one seems to have returned." We then heard the sound of steps, a spasmodic weeping, and the quivering of bodies on the floor. Only two persons out of nine had returned—Max Fishel and Ilsa Hansdorf. For some reason they were not deported and were allowed to remain here. A shuddering cry escaped Ilsa. Seven of our best people had been deported!

We could hardly believe what was told us. They were all gathered in an empty lot, ordered to stand in one long row. Work certificates were of no avail. To make sure no one would escape, the lot was roped off by the Jewish militiamen. They did not distinguish between old and young. A Gestapo man strolled about, holding a small cane. He was separating the people; some were sent to the right, others to the left. People did not yet know who among them was destined for deportation and who was to be left alone. Those on the right were being led away to the railroad station, while the others scattered and went home. The simple wave of a cane, either toward the right or the left, decided whether one remained alive or died. Many were shot to death trying to escape.

We went out and stood before the house. There was nothing at all we could do to save them from being sent away. These are the names of those deported on that day: Hershel Springer,[21] Joel Springer, Max Perlstadt, Sarah Rubinstein, Gutek Goslavsky, Abraham Hershlikowitz, and Fishel Wnuk.

Outside we saw weeping people returning from police headquarters. One came without his mother; another without his father, son, daughter, brother, or sister. Everyone remaining alive had lost someone close and dear. People fainted in the streets. A mother, quite demented, ran to join the deportees because her three grown sons had been taken from her. Five children returned in tears: their father and mother had been taken from them. They had no one to come back to; the eldest was only fifteen. And then came another unfortunate girl, the daughter of the vice president of the Jewish Council. Her father, mother, and brothers had been deported, and she remained alone. She fell to the ground, tearing off her garments. What could life mean to her now?

Everywhere there was weeping and despairing. But it was all in vain—those taken to the train would never return.

Hershel Springer was beloved by all the residents of Bendzin. He devoted his days and nights to helping others in every way possible. He was respected by the heads of the council. Now Jews from the ghetto came to us and said: "If Hershel Springer could not be saved, it is certain that not a Jew will remain alive in the end." Both we and the rest of the Jews wept as at a father's death, remembering him as we did.

The street was covered with people in states of collapse. The passersby stepped over them; there was no one to revive them. Everyone had his own among the missing; everyone thought his anguish was the deepest of all.

After the police departed, the dead were gathered in one place. Several wagons were filled with the corpses, soon to be carted to the cemetery. The grain in the field had been trampled by people hiding amid the corn. There, too, lay those felled by bullets; the groans of the dying were heard. In front of the houses lay people shuddering with agony, their bodies shattered with poisoned dumdum bullets. Their relatives deposited them there helplessly.

These sights become unbearable. We returned home. The beds were overturned; in every corner lay a person wailing in despair. The children of Kibbutz Atid were crying bitterly, and it was impossible to quiet them.

Frumka was tearing her hair and knocking her head against the wall. We were afraid that she would attempt suicide. She cried aloud: "I am guilty of their death! Why did I tell them to remain in their rooms? I am their murderess, it is I who sent them to their death!" It was utterly impossible to explain to her that she was not at fault.

The shots did not cease. Those to be deported had been turned over to a military guard. Some attempted to flee, trying to leap over the iron gate dividing the enclosure from the highway. On the other side of the gate, in the street, stood Poles and Germans watching the spectacle. They were well content. Snatches of conversation were to be heard: "Too bad that some have still been left. But the end of these, too, won't be long delayed. It's quite impossible, of course, to take them all out at once." Indeed, the Poles generally said: "Whomever Hitler will be unable to kill off now, we will murder after the war."

The train arrived. With blows and shouting, the deportees were pushed into the cattle cars. There was no space for all; the cars were filled to overflowing. Those who could not be taken by train were packed into a large building, which had once served as an orphanage and home for the aged. Here the Germans would concentrate Jews whom they were about to kill.

The train left for Oswiecim. That very day they would be put to death.

Those remaining stared out of the windows of the fourth floor of this large death house, as if grasping at a straw to save themselves. The house was surrounded by a strong contingent of police and Gestapo. The militiamen still roamed about the place, hoping they might still save some family members or friends. In the end, several men did return from the orphanage. Rossner had them brought out from there as craftsmen without whom it would be impossible for him to continue working. Rossner, though a German and a Gestapo man, wished to save his laborers from the claws of death. As long as he was alive, he said, he would not permit any of his men to be taken away from his workshop.

But the Gestapo men did not consider his request important. They did as they pleased, without paying any attention to Rossner. The Gestapo men knew that, one way or another, sooner or later, all the Jews would assuredly be killed.

Hershel's Return

One day we were given a note by a militiaman returning from the workshop. We scarcely believed our eyes. The note was in Hershel's handwriting. He asked that one of us come to see him, and we would learn what had happened.

Eliza Sittenfeld, Max Fishel, and I accompanied the militiaman to the workshop. As soon as we left the ghetto, a Gestapo man halted us and examined our papers. He blustered and threatened, but finally permitted us to proceed. Near the workshop we saw a wounded militiaman running for shelter and first aid. His face was shattered almost beyond recognition; his white coat and cap were smeared with blood. He briefly told us what had happened: one of the Gestapo men had shot at him "for the fun of it."

Our guide brought us to the upper story and led us to a small room filled with merchandise. We looked about, but saw no sign of Hershel. Could the note have been only a ruse? We were not inclined to believe anything until we saw Hershel. The militiaman shoved aside some heaped-up crates of merchandise, and behind them, as in a nest, was Hershel.

He was in indescribable agony. His face was smashed, his feet were badly wounded, his clothes torn to shreds. Nevertheless he smiled courageously and embraced us in a surge of emotion. Tears of joy at the reunion with us flowed down his cheeks. But his condition belied his words. He was so badly mangled that he could not stand up. "What counts," he said, "is that I am still alive and seeing you." He showed us the contents of his pockets; everything was in order. "Nothing was lost," he reassured us.

> We were jammed into a [train] car that could not accommodate all of us, and we were severely beaten. I at once studied the car for possibilities of escaping. Joel Springer, Abraham Hershlikowitz, and Gutek Goslavsky were in the same car. The others had been shoved into other cars.
>
> I had with me a penknife and a chisel and after much effort I succeeded to pry the window open. The car was unbearably jammed and no one noticed that I had opened the window. But when I tried to leap out, two men seized me and shouted: "What are you trying to do? You will only make it worse for all of us. They will shoot us like dogs because of you."
>
> The train rolled on. Joel and Gutek had razors and wanted to commit suicide. I dissuaded them. "Wait until the others are busy with their own affairs," I said, "and we will leap out." Finally there came a moment when the attention of the people in the car was diverted from us. I sprang out of the window. I heard someone else jump behind me, but I did not know whether it was Joel or Gutek. Shots were fired at us by the German highway guards, but I preferred death on the spot to being taken to Oswiecim. I made it into a ditch without being struck by the bullets. The train didn't stop and was soon out of sight. At some distance I saw bodies lying along the track. Evidently others had also attempted escape and been shot down.

> After a while I climbed out of the ditch and started across the fields. A woman was working in a field and she motioned me to follow her farther away from the tracks. She showed me great kindness, bringing me food and fixing up some bandages for my feet from my shirt. She said that Oswiecim was not far away and that all the Jews on the train were being taken there for extermination.
>
> Night fell. The woman showed me the direction I was to follow and warned me to beware of the peasants in the villages, who would certainly turn me over to the Germans if they saw me. Slowly I started walking in the direction she had pointed out. During the following days I hid in the fields and subsisted on beets, carrots, and other vegetables. At night I continued my journey. After seven nights I arrived here. Only a few militiamen know of my return. This is my second day here. They bring me food.
>
> I very much want you to take me home with you. I want to be together with the bunch.

The following night, with the assistance of the militiaman, we brought Hershel to the kibbutz. Our joy was unbounded—Father had returned. Life would now have meaning again. At first we could scarcely believe that Hershel was indeed back. He had to hide in the bunker because the Gestapo was searching for him.

Chavka Lenchner, our nurse, attended to his wound. We knew that the joy of our reunion was to be short-lived. And indeed, after a few days we had to leave our dwelling. We had aroused suspicion and drawn the attention of certain officials of the Jewish Council.

Many houses had remained vacant after the Jews had been deported. We therefore divided our thirty members into three groups and quartered them at three different ends of the ghetto. Each group was organized as a separate entity, but we continued the life of a kibbutz as before; we were still one family.

We Try to Join the Partisans

At the end of May 1943, Marek Folman,[22] our comrade in Warsaw, came to our kibbutz in Bendzin. After the children had been ejected from the orphanage, he, together with Eliza Sittenfeld, had undertaken to look after them. In December 1942 he had joined a partisan unit in the region of Radom. It was a very active unit and had considerable accomplishments to its credit. They attacked German barracks, blocked military trains, set fire to buildings and installations housing German offices, and caused great additional damage. Among the partisans, he concealed his identity and passed as a Pole.

Marek had a plan. The partisan unit with which he had been associated refused to admit Jews. But he had established contact with a Polish officer of the partisan army living at 23 Modrzejewska Street, and this officer consented to bring Jews into contact with other partisan units.

This was a welcome development. We had sought ways of contacting the partisans for some time but had been unsuccessful. Now that such an opportunity presented itself, we were anxious not to miss it. We had some doubts at first about the integrity of this officer and wondered why he should go out of his way to help Jews join the partisan army. Marek and Zvi Brandes visited him at his home, and they were favorably impressed by what they saw. The household seemed to have been carefully camouflaged and at first glance looked like the home of a simple proletarian family.

Arrangements were made with this officer and the day and hour for our departure were set. He was to wait for us at an appointed spot outside the ghetto. Our comrades were to meet him there and follow his lead. The arrangements inevitably entailed grave risks but we had no choice.

Marek and Zvi returned and reported the plans to us. We were confronted by the problem of who was to go. After weighing the matter, several members of the various groups were agreed upon.[23] They were all armed with pistols. Before leaving they promised to keep us informed of what would happen to them.

The young men set out. When they reached the end of the ghetto, they removed the Stars of David from their clothes. They met the officer and followed him. A week later the officer returned. He could not contact us because we had been careful not to give him our address, still being somewhat uncertain of his integrity. Marek Folman and Marcus Pohorilla therefore visited him at his home in the Aryan part of the city. The officer informed them that our comrades had reached their destination safely, that they had been received by the partisans very amiably and been assigned to units. They were probably in action against the Germans already. But, he said, in their excitement they had forgotten to write us a note.

We therefore organized a second group. Those chosen considered themselves lucky and were overjoyed. Again about fifteen comrades were selected. Everyone was eager for a chance to leave; it was known that a general deportation from the ghetto would soon take place.

I felt very depressed that I had not been selected for the second group. I, too, wanted to be among the fortunate ones. Frumka's and Hershel's arguments that there was much work still to be done in the ghetto did not relieve my depression. I was the one charged with maintaining contact with Warsaw, they asserted. After some more groups left, I, too, would be free to go.

Again we asked the departing comrades to inform us by a note of their safe arrival in the partisan camp, and to give us information about the plans for the subsequent groups. Meanwhile, with people continually leaving, our supply of arms dwindled steadily. Yet we kept on deceiving ourselves that we might succeed to transfer everyone to the partisans before the general deportation.

The following comrades, members of Dror and Hashomer Hatzair, represented the kibbutz among those who left to join the partisans: Alter Goldbrom, Shmuel Finkelstein, Zippora Marder, Yitzhak Kruvka, Mordecai Bachazh, and Ubek Goldstein. The young Kibbutz Atid was represented by Yitzhak.

Several days passed after the departure of the second group and we received no word from them. Then one of the group, Yitzhak Kruvka of Hashomer Hatzair, returned. His face had changed almost beyond recognition. His clothes were torn to shreds and he was suffering from a bad case of nerves. He told us what had happened:

> We left the ghetto after removing the Stars of David from our clothes. We all felt cheerful. The man who was to guide us met us at the appointed spot and we went ahead. He said we would meet our friends who'd gone before us after passing through the forest. We walked all day and reached the forest by evening. We were no longer in danger, our guide assured us. We sat down in a clearing in the forest to rest and eat. Our guide went away to bring water. We suspected nothing and were all quite happy at our successful escape from the ghetto. Our guide returned with the water, then he left again, telling us to get some rest before we resumed the trip.
>
> Suddenly mounted soldiers appeared on all sides and before we had a chance to disperse they opened fire on us. All the other comrades were killed instantly. I was sitting under a bush and

> I escaped miraculously. The soldiers searched the bodies and, while they did so, I crawled some distance away and hid in the undergrowth. When they left, I slipped away and escaped.

We could hardly believe this story. Marek Folman, who initiated the plan to join the partisans, considered himself responsible and wanted to commit suicide. The best of our comrades were now dead, some as a result of the deportations and others in this attempt to join the partisans. We had hardly enough people left for self-defense.

In addition to the members of our Dror group, the following members from Hashomer Hatzair lost their lives while being deported: the brave sisters Irka and Leah Pesachson; David Kozlovsky, who dreamed of but one thing during his last days—to meet with an honorable death (his wish was fulfilled and he did kill quite a number of Germans before he lost his life); Halla Katzengold; and members from Gordonia: Kalman Blochatz, Moshe, and several others.

Yitzhak's report overwhelmed us. Bad luck seemed to pursue us no matter what we tried. Marek Folman went about like one deranged. Altogether about twenty-five comrades had been lost in the two attempts to join the partisans. If Yitzhak had not returned, still others would have walked into the trap.

That very night Marek left for Warsaw in despair. He slipped out of the ghetto and disappeared. Since then no trace of him was found. It is presumed that he was caught by the Gestapo at the border of the Reich and the General Government.

My Last Trip to Warsaw

One night our instructor, Moszek Merin,[24] was arrested and taken away. To us, this was the signal of the approaching general deportation. Eliza Sittenfeld, who was in charge of the children of Kibbutz Atid and others, therefore decided to send the children to Germany as Aryans. In Germany they would be able to work for farmers and thus probably survive the war.

They immediately began working on this plan. Eliza prepared the children for the trip. Their documents were fixed up with new names and ages. Early each morning a few of them would stealthily leave the ghetto accompanied by Ilsa Hansdorf, one of the girls of our kibbutz. Once they were safely outside the ghetto, they would depart for Germany. In Germany they reported to the community offices of villages, declared themselves to be orphans and asked to be assigned to work on farms. The German farmers were glad to hire them; even if they were of a tender age, they could easily earn their keep tending the livestock and doing household chores. Ilsa chose eight children whose appearance belied their Jewishness. We received cheerful letters from them, sent to the address of a Polish woman living outside the ghetto.

From two of the girls we received letters once only. Evidently they had been identified; we did not know what became of them. The other children wrote that they continued working until their German employer began to suspect that they were Jewish; then they fled to another village to begin all over again. The work was hard, but there was no alternative. With us remained only a few of the children, those of a clearly Jewish appearance.

We received frequent letters from Zivia. She urged us to move to Warsaw if we wished to save our lives. Those of us who looked Aryan could easily be taken care of with forged identification papers, she wrote; for the others bunkers could be set up in the Aryan part of the city. There were Poles who would permit us to live in these bunkers, for a price of course. Passports and travel certificates could be forged in Warsaw. Those with Aryan features could travel by train; for the others Yitzhak would try to get a bus and smuggle them over the border between Bendzin and Warsaw.

Frumka, Hershel, Zvi, and Baruch decided that the children and the weaker comrades who were incapable of fighting should be sent first. The others would follow, if time permitted. It was idle to dream now of a well-organized defense; the majority of those fit for defense were dead. Those who were able to depart in time would do so. The remainder of our strong and fit comrades would leave last.

Passports and travel certificates began coming from Warsaw. At first only a few documents arrived and we were informed that the others would be ready when Ina Gelbart or I would arrive in Warsaw. Ina set out on her journey in the evening and took with her all the addresses and money. I followed the next morning; with me came Rivka Moskowitz. She looked like a Polish girl and had been provided with a passport and travel certificate. She carried a valise containing the bare necessities. I had arranged to meet Ina at an appointed place.

We traveled by train. Rivka now passed as "Zosia" on her forged passport. At the border documents were checked; I trembled lest Rivka fail to pass this ordeal, but the inspection of documents went off without a hitch.

The train was terribly overcrowded and Rivka, being rather sickly, had to have a seat. With difficulty I found one for her. A German soldier in the car was telling of the deportation of Jews from Silesia to an extermination camp, which he had witnessed. The other passengers refused to believe him. They were fresh from the front and did not know about what was going on in Poland. But the eyewitness continued his tale. "It's a delightful sight, really a pleasure. They go to their death like docile sheep."

We traveled an entire day and finally arrived in Warsaw, weary and exhausted. Hastily we rushed through the streets. On the opposite sidewalk documents were being checked, so we slipped away into the crowd. Our papers were useful for the trip only; a Warsaw policeman would easily recognize the forged seal. Without looking backward we rushed to the place appointed for the meeting with Ina. But she was not there. Could she have been caught on the way? I did not know what to do; I had no address to report to, and the money in my possession would not last more than a day. I was becoming frantic. Where should I take Rivka? And what should I do if I did not meet with any of our people? Should we then return to Bendzin?

I left Rivka at an inn and hurried to the address of a sister of one of my acquaintances in Bendzin, who had been living in the Aryan section of Warsaw. Perhaps she would know Marek's address. Indeed, after a long search, she found the address of Marek's mother. The following day I went to see her together with Rivka. I found Marek's mother and sister-in-law, whose husband had been killed while fighting with the partisans. But Marek's mother did not know anything about his whereabouts; she only knew that he had been with us in Bendzin. She put up Rivka for the night at the home of a Polish friend. She could not take her into her own home; blackmailers had been badgering her and she was afraid of the risk.

The following day, aided by Marek's mother, I found Kozik. He, in turn, arranged for me to meet Isaac Zuckerman, who went by the name of Antek. He was a tall, blond, young man who looked unmistakably Polish; I would never have believed that he was a Jew. Only a slight accent marred the perfection of his "disguise."

I found him to be keen and cautious, and, though he never showed any furtiveness, he was always aware of what was going on about him in the street and who was apt to be following him. He was the commander of all the organized Jews in the Aryan section of Warsaw and one of the busiest men I have ever seen. He attended to housing and financial matters, maintained contact with the Polish underground, arranged the transfer of persons from the city to the partisans, and obtained arms for hundreds of Jews.

I discussed Ina's disappearance with him. "She must have made some slip while the documents were being checked," I guessed. He consoled me: "Perhaps she had to return home for some reason." He promised to have passports ready for the others in our group in Bendzin as soon as possible and undertook to arrange for a bus to bring across the border those of our comrades who, because of their distinctly Jewish appearance, could not risk traveling by train.

Rivka was temporarily put up in the apartment of a house superintendent. We paid him two hundred złotys per day, and her meals had to be paid for separately. I slept in the cellar. A Jewish boy disguised as a Pole was already there, and I was supposed to be his sister. To mislead the neighbors I said that I had illegally returned from Germany and therefore could not register my passport.

With great impatience I waited for the passports and definite information about the bus. I saw Isaac Zuckerman daily and urged him to hurry, since the general deportation from Bendzin might start at any time. I thought it was best to go at once with whatever was ready rather than wait until all arrangements were completed. A strange premonition that each day might be decisive obsessed me.

But matters dragged and there were postponements from day to day. I finally told Zuckerman that I could wait no longer. Several passports were already on hand. A bus had also been arranged for; we were to be informed by telegram when the bus would arrive. But we could obtain no weapons.

I began the return trip. I carried with me twenty-two forged passports with photographs and travel certificates attached. My heart beat with apprehension and I could not help thinking of Ina. Would I learn what had happened to her when I returned?

The examination of documents and searching of the baggage dragged on interminably. I tried to pretend calmness. The gendarmes were drawing closer. Bravely I untied my bundles; they dug into their contents. I engaged them in conversation hoping to divert their attention and prevent them from searching my person, as many others had been searched. I summoned all my courage and faced them confidently. They finally went on to the next passenger, suspecting nothing of the forged passports in my possession.

On the way I stopped at Częstochowa. I wanted to see Rivka Glanz,[25] who headed the Jewish Council. But I found the ghetto already burned and no trace of its inhabitants. Local Poles told me that the ghetto had fought a tough battle against the Germans and that many Jews had fled and were now in the woods, whence they continued the fight against the Germans and raided the villages for food. But Rivka Glanz was known to have died in the battle. During the last days of the ghetto, Rivka was like a mother to the Jews of Częstochowa. She had wanted to leave the city, but the remnant in the ghetto pleaded with her to stay with them; they felt more secure as long as she was around.

Oppressing premonitions continued to haunt me the rest of the trip. Who knew what was happening in Bendzin?

I spent the night on the train. I felt worn out, but sleep was not to be thought of. I had to remain alert in case of a search or another passport examination.

General Deportation

AUGUST 1, 1943

Dirty, depressed, and tired from my journey I arrived in Bendzin. We were immediately driven out of the station. Ear-splitting shouts could be heard from all sides and the turmoil was indescribable. "What's going on?" I asked some Poles. They told me that the Jews were being deported, and that since Friday, group after group was being taken away. It was Monday now and the deportation had not yet been completed.

A general deportation from Sosnowiec, Bendzin, and Dombrowka was on. I asked whether all the Jews were being taken. I tried to sound gay because I had to pretend that not only was the affair of no concern to me, but I was actually glad of it.

My heart was torn with anguish. My comrades were being taken away, and I had no way of knowing what had become of them. The deportation was in its fourth day. Bunkers were being broken open and everyone found within was shot on the spot. Jews rounded up in the ghetto were being loaded into cattle cars. The SS "annihilation squad" and German military surrounded the ghetto on all sides, and it was impossible to enter it.

Jewish militiamen carried out the dead and the wounded on stretchers. Gestapo men led Jewish boys and girls in chains along the street to the cattle cars. Other Gestapo men, dressed as civilians, dashed about town, examining documents, peering into people's faces in search of Jews who might have escaped from the ghetto.

On the square before the railway station, behind a barbed-wire enclosure, I recognized some friends. Poles and Germans outside the enclosure were staring at them as if they were beasts in a zoo.

My strength ebbed away. I felt that I would collapse if I were to remain there any longer. If my documents were checked now, I would be lost. Life had lost all meaning. Why go on living when everyone had been taken away from me—my family, relatives, and now my comrades too? When I risked my life, it was for their sake. They alone gave me reason for living after my family was gone.

Put an end to it all, my weakness counseled. But I was immediately overcome with shame at the thought. What, that I should help the designs of the Germans? Perhaps I would still have a chance to share in the revenge against them.

One way only remained open to me—to return to Warsaw. There was a train leaving at five o'clock the following morning.

I felt weak and exhausted. I had traveled all night. It was three in the afternoon and I had had no food all day. If only I could get some bread! But all food was rationed. Lacking a ration card, I could not enter a store without arousing suspicion. I suddenly recalled an acquaintance in Sosnowiec, the dentist Dr. Weiss. I boarded a trolley. At the other end of the car documents were being examined. I transferred to another trolley.

Thus transferring from one car to another I finally reached Sosnowiec. Here, too, the deportation was still going on and the ghetto was besieged.

Dr. Weiss, a Russian woman, stared at me in disbelief when I knocked at her door.

She could not understand how I had got there. But she noticed the expression on my face and asked me to come in. She offered me a seat and began preparing some tea for me. In the momentary security of her home, my remaining strength vanished. I tried to tell what I had seen, but could not and gave way to hysterical weeping. She gently caressed my head, soothing and encouraging me. But the measure of my suffering had brimmed over and overflowed in convulsive sobs.

I had hoped to stay in Dr. Weiss's house till the following morning, when the train for Warsaw was departing, but she apologized and pointed out that it was impossible. It would mean risking her own life, since private homes were frequently raided by the Germans in search of Jews in hiding. Being a Russian, she was suspected of maintaining contact with Jews. Where could I turn, I wondered in despair, where could I go for the night? At the railway station documents were constantly checked. To walk about the streets was also extremely risky. And I had no other acquaintances in the city.

Dr. Weiss prepared some sandwiches for me and bid me a tearful farewell, again begging my forgiveness for not sheltering me through the night. I went out of her house and aimlessly walked. I left the town behind me and approached a sparse forest. Night fell, a bright August night. I sat down on a bench among the trees. In my imagination I saw my parents, brothers and sisters, and comrades. They stood before me, their faces distorted with suffering. I tried to see them more clearly, and their images vanished. Great grief seized me. What had I done, whom had I wronged that so much suffering was my lot?

Suddenly I noticed the figure of a man approaching between the trees. A chill passed through me. Who could it be at this hour of the evening? He came nearer and I noticed that he was drunk. He sat down beside me on the bench. I moved away. He stared at me and began asking me questions. I was alert again and gave him inane answers. The time passed; I realized I must flee. Slowly I rose and began walking away. The man followed. I began to run back toward the town; I hid in a dark corridor cowering under the stairs.

In the morning I left for Warsaw.

The Battle of the Ghetto: My Comrades' End

A casual glance at my face, after I returned to Warsaw, was enough to tell the story of what had happened in Bendzin and the nature of the reports I was bringing. My comrades in Warsaw did not know how to calm me, and I felt that I was losing my sanity. Impatiently and without reason I awaited a letter from some survivor in Bendzin. And, as if by a miracle, a postcard from Ilsa Hansdorf did arrive. She requested that I come immediately and I would learn what had happened.

After consulting with Isaac Zuckerman it was decided that I should leave the same day. At great expense I obtained three forged travel certificates, one for myself and two to be used in case there were any survivors. I also took along several thousand marks that might be needed while I was within the borders of the Reich.

I reached Bendzin and reported to a certain address as directed. There I found only Meyer Shulman and his wife.[26] The landlord, a Pole, had formerly been a machinist in the laundry of the kibbutz and had promised all possible aid in case of deportations. His address was known to all our comrades.

Meyer was not a member of the movement. He was a very capable man; he lived in a house near the kibbutz and had helped us build the bunkers. Being mechanically inclined, he had installed a secret radio set for us. He would also repair damaged weapons. On instructions received from Warsaw, he had made explosives and forged seals that we required for documents. Toward the end he even tried to counterfeit dollar bills. He was very friendly with the people of the kibbutz and helped us in every way possible.

Mrs. N., the landlady, cautiously opened the door to admit me. Meyer and his wife sat at the table in silence. Their faces were thin and emaciated, their eyes expressed fear. They met me cordially and I began asking them what had happened. They told me the following story:

> The moment the deportation proceedings started, we hid in the bunker. There were more than twenty people in our bunker. We lost contact with the other bunkers and for a time did not even know whether the others had succeeded to hide. Thus we lived for several days. We soon ran short of water and although there was constant firing outside, several young men went out each midnight in search of water.
>
> After four days the ghetto was still surrounded by the Germans. The firing continued. At night the entire ghetto was illuminated by the glare of searchlights that the Germans directed at it.
>
> One night the men returned with empty pails—the Germans had shut off the water supply. Our situation steadily worsened. The lack of water and the stale air began to tell on us. To remain in the bunkers would have meant certain death. We therefore decided that each night three or four of us should leave the bunker and try to reach the Aryan section of the town. It was worth taking this risk since we faced certain death at the hands of the Germans, who were bound to locate our bunker eventually—if we did not die of thirst before then. So each night a small group crept out. We had no reports from any of them. Perhaps some of them did succeed to escape from the ghetto.
>
> Finally there remained in our shelter only a handful of people whose features were distinctly Semitic and who could

> therefore not hope to pass unnoticed in the Aryan section of the city. Despite the grave risk we sent one of the young fellows, Moshe Marcus, to find out what was going on in the city and whether any Jews were left there. After several hours of tense waiting, Moshe returned. He reported that the Germans had left about two hundred Jews who were assigned to gather Jewish possessions and bring them to a collection center. The leader of the camp where these Jews stayed was a certain Boehm, who had been acquainted with the members of the kibbutz, especially with Hershel Springer. It was then decided to contact Boehm and beg him to arrange that the inmates of the bunker be taken to the camp.
>
> Boehm bribed some policemen and sent them to us. On the way they encountered a little boy and took him along. The policemen had no difficulty in locating our bunker by following the instructions Boehm had given them. First they lowered the little boy they had brought along and ordered him to tell the people within to come out. No one within knew who the policemen were and we felt certain that we had been discovered by a German search party.

"My wife and I," Meyer continued, "hid under some boards that had served us as beds. We were resolved not to go out. The others considered for a few moments whether the ones going up should take arms along. It was decided to put two pistols into the handbag of one of the girls, to be used in case of an emergency. The other weapons were hidden under some coal in a bin."

> The policemen ordered those who went up to hand over all the money and valuables in their possession. Then they set out to make a search. The two pistols in the handbag were discovered. The other weapons hidden under the coal were also found.
>
> The policemen started jeering and scolding: "We came to free you and you meet us with arms."
>
> Everyone was ordered to stand against a wall, as if about to be shot. The policemen then called Gestapo men and the torture commenced. Everyone was mercilessly beaten. All day long they were kept standing against the wall, without food or water and in expectation of instant death.

One of the young men, Zvi Brandes, who could no longer stand the torture, ran out of the line and tried to escape. He was pursued by a number of Germans who opened fire on him. After a few minutes the Germans returned. "*Er ist erledigt*" (He is done with), they announced, and they ordered three of the young men to carry Zvi's body back. The dead body was lying in the young grain some distance away. They carried it under police guard to the wall where the others were lined up.

Night fell and they were still kept standing along the wall. All had been beaten so cruelly as to be unrecognizable. The police tried to find out where the arms had been obtained but were not successful.

Late at night they were all taken to the camp. They were sentenced to be shot the following day after an additional questioning. During the night the girls managed to change their appearance—their haircomb and dresses—and to mix in with the other women in the camp. The young men hid in the camp as best they could. When the police came the following day they found only Hershel Springer, who happened to be in the open, in search of water, and they included him in a transport of Jews leaving for the extermination camp in Oswiecim. Hershel thus did not succeed to escape the fate that dogged his steps. Not many days of life were vouchsafed to him, after his earlier escape from the deportation train.

"One night some days later," Meyer concluded his story, "we slipped out of the ghetto and came here. As long as we have some money we can manage to exist. We do not know what we will do when the money gives out."

I learned that two girls were also living in the Aryan quarter disguised as Poles.

Finally Ilsa Hansdorf arrived. She was badly shaken by the past days and was overjoyed to see me. She told me how Frumka Plotnicka and the other comrades had died.

"It happened on the fourth day of the deportation," she said. "Groups of Germans were scouring the ghetto for Jews still in hiding. The comrades were in a well-camouflaged bunker under a basement laundry room. Seven comrades hid there: Baruch Gaftek, Frumka Plotnicka, Frumka Dolnorowa, Zippora Bocian, Hedva Bernard, Tuvia Dvorsky, and Penina Yakubowitz."

They were constantly on the alert for any sound. On the fourth day, as Baruch was standing guard, he heard voluble German conversation in the courtyard. He felt certain that the bunker had been discovered and opened fire on the Germans through a small opening in the wall. He did not miss; two Germans were killed by his bullets. A large number of Germans then besieged the house. They were amazed that there were Jews left ready to give battle. Afraid to approach the house, they threw a large number of grenades through its windows. The house burst into flames. It burned for several hours and all this time the Germans kept it under fire. Finally there were no more sounds from within. The Gestapo brought the Jewish militia, which they had organized to handle the remaining Jews in the ghetto, and ordered them to extinguish the flames.

Within the ruins were found the severely burned bodies of the seven comrades. One by one the militiamen brought them outside. They were almost beyond recognition—bare skulls, bodies completely nude. Yet some of them were still alive.

Frumka Plotnicka was still alive, although badly burned. She muttered something, frantically looking about her. One of the Gestapo men bent down to hear what she was saying, hoping to hear something of value. But another Gestapo man stomped upon her body with his booted feet. Then they killed those who were still breathing and viciously kicked the lifeless bodies.

A Narrow Escape

Only a few members of the kibbutz still remained in the camp: my sister Sarah, Marek Folman, Eliza Sittenfeld, Chavka Lenchner, and the two children from Kibbutz Atid, Moshele and Estherke.

Somehow a way must now be found to get them out of there. Every day the Germans transport small convoys of people out of the camp; the kibbutz members, too, are likely to be taken. I myself cannot go into the ghetto; I do not know the guards or where to get in.

And then I hear that one of the members of the Hanoar Hatzioni movement, B.,[27] knows some of the guards; he goes in and out of the camp a few times a day. He is living in the Aryan part of the city, disguised as a Catholic. B. is a good friend of the kibbutzniks. I hope he will help me or give me instructions on how I can save my friends in the camp. Now for the second day I stand in the street like a watchdog in order to meet B. Ilsa Hansdorf is also with me.

At long last I can see him in the distance. I run toward him; I feel that he is the only person who can help me now. But my hope is soon shattered. I sit down with him on a bench in the market. We try to be as quiet as possible since there are two Polish women sitting next to us on the bench.

I beg B. to help me as much as he can. He tells me that first and foremost he has to save the people in his "Noar" youth movement. After a great deal of negotiation, I tell him that I can give him a few thousand marks if only he will rescue one of our people. We agree to meet in a certain place in two days' time at six in the morning. We part company. Ilsa and I go one way and he—the other.

Ilsa and I hurried along to take the trolley to Katowice. Turning back I saw two women running breathlessly after us, followed by a mob of children and shouting: "Jewesses! Jewesses!" Ilsa suggested that we flee. I dissuaded her, since by doing so we would only confirm the suspicion. But we hurried our pace and turned into an empty house. The crowd continued to pursue us. The two women at last caught up with us and pointing at us kept screaming: "Jewesses! Jewesses! You only pretend you're Polish." We were surrounded by the mob, which kept growing in number. One of the women started to drag me toward the police station. "We'll murder all of you! If Hitler doesn't take care of you, we will!" she screamed. Realizing our peril, I slapped the woman's face in pretended anger. "If I'm a Jewess, you may as well know what a Jewess can do! Say once more that I'm Jewish and I'll slap you down altogether!" I shouted.

Two Gestapo agents appeared. They inquired what was the cause of the commotion. In pretended indignation I told them, in Polish, that I was being humiliated by the woman who accused me of being Jewish. I asked the Gestapo agents to examine our documents, with a show of great self-confidence. One of them casually questioned me about my age and birthplace. Ilsa, too, answered the random questions courageously and correctly. Another German approached and remarked: "If they don't speak German, it's evident they're Polish. All Jews know German." This bit of wisdom had its effect. Several in the crowd, seeing our self-confidence, began to whisper that we really didn't resemble Jewesses. The woman who had tried to drag me to the police station stood somewhat abashed. I again slapped her twice to strengthen the impression of self-confidence I had made on the Germans and demanded that they question her. They laughed loudly: "You are a Polish swine, and so is she." They went away and the crowd dispersed.

We continued on our way. A couple of boys followed us approvingly. "You should have knocked her teeth out," one of them said, "for even daring to call you a Jewess." I told him I would have were it not for her age.

We would be spending tonight with a German woman in Holohita, a Bendzin suburb, whom my sister knew. Tomorrow morning we would be meeting with B. I would at least tell him about the incident that occurred because of his Semitic-looking features.[28]

P. K., in whose house we stayed, was very welcoming toward us and completely sympathized with us. If she could have, she would have helped me rescue comrades from the camp. She tried her best to calm me down as much as possible.

Five in the morning. The town was still fast asleep. I went by tram to the place where I had arranged to meet with B. I waited for one, two hours but he didn't show up. No trace of him. I had never thought that this would happen.

Pain gnawed at my heart and I start resenting B.—particularly since he knew how dangerous it was to loiter in one place, waiting for someone. After waiting impatiently for two hours, I took off.

I was now at a complete loss; I needed the help of people who knew all the different ways of stealing into the camp.[29]

Suddenly, like an apparition from another world, my sister Sarah appeared at the house of the German woman. Our joy was unbounded. She told me how she had escaped from the camp. She had dressed as a Polish woman, and a militiaman with whom she was acquainted, Heniek Bornblatt, had bribed the guards and arranged an opportunity for her escape to the Aryan section. There she was arranging accommodations for our people. Sarah promised to do everything in her power to help our remaining comrades from the ghetto escape. That very day she returned to the camp. I had to escort Ilsa to Warsaw so as to bring her to the Aryan side of the city.

That evening Ilsa and I began our return trip to Warsaw.

CHAPTER FOUR

In the Toils of the Gestapo

An Unsuccessful Journey

Our tickets from Katowice to Warsaw had been bought. Both Ilsa and I had passports and travel permits. Our only worry now was the crossing of the border. After two hours of traveling we arrived at Trzebinia, a station on the border. I sat in one car, Ilsa in another. Since both our passports were forged and bore the Warsaw imprint, it was best that we stay apart at this point. I recalled the way Rivka Moscowitz had gone to Warsaw. Everything had worked out well that time. Perhaps we would succeed now too.

It was fifteen minutes past midnight. The examination began. Ilsa was in the third car ahead of me. Heavy steps were heard: Why is there such a delay in the front cars?

The examination of documents usually proceeded much faster. Perhaps it just seemed to me to take so long. Finally they reached me. With an air of unconcern I took out my passport and travel permit, and handed them to the examiners with a casual gesture. They looked at the papers for some moments, then carefully scrutinized my face. "Yes, just like the one in the front car," they said. I knew at once what they meant but feigned calmness, as though I didn't understand German.

My heart skipped a beat, then began racing wildly. They did not return the papers; instead they sharply ordered me to take my belongings and follow them. I pretended I did not understand. A polite man in the car translated their command into Polish. I still tried to look unconcerned, but through my mind the thought flashed: we are lost.

My mind remained clear. Although I was surrounded by policemen, I managed to open my bag stealthily and to take out the Warsaw addresses and swallow them.

Unnoticed I threw away the money. But some addresses were sewn in my garters and these I could not destroy. We approached the customhouse. Ilsa stood in the hall surrounded by police.

They asked me whether I knew Ilsa. I said I didn't. Ilsa turned red. Her face bore an expression of profound dejection and her eyes plainly betrayed her feelings of despair.

In a tiny room specially set aside for this purpose a fat German policewoman searched me. Carefully she examined every piece of my clothing, ripping every seam. She discovered the Warsaw addresses. I began to plead with her, trying to appeal to her conscience. Then I took off my wristwatch and offered it to her if she would destroy the addresses. But she refused the bribe. After the search we returned to the large room.

There she reported that I had tried to bribe her and handed over the addresses. Many policemen were standing about, jeering at us and speculating on who we might be and what should be done to us.

I stood barefoot, my shoes having been torn in the course of the search. My coat was also torn, the handbag cut into shreds. The tube of toothpaste had been pierced to see if anything had been concealed in it, the small mirror smashed, the watch taken apart. Each insignificant item underwent repeated examinations.

Ilsa was questioned first. Then they began questioning me. Where did I get the documents? How much did I pay for them? How did I manage to get my real photograph on the passport? Was I Jewish? From what ghetto had I escaped? Where was I going?

I clung to my story that I was Catholic, that the passport was genuine, and that I had obtained it from the firm where I worked as an office clerk.

Concerning my destination I told them that I had gone to visit relatives working in Germany, but I chanced to meet a woman who had worked with them, and she informed me that they were no longer at their previous place of employment and that she did not know their present location. I was therefore returning to Warsaw. While in Silesia I had stayed overnight in the home of people whose identity was unknown to me. My examiners asked whether I could find the place again. I told them it was the first time I had ever visited Silesia and I was unfamiliar with the district; I therefore couldn't possibly identify the place or the people. I said I regretted not having made a note of these, but that I certainly would have if I had known anything like this would ever happen to me, so that they might check the truthfulness of my story.

My replies aroused their anger. One of the policemen began beating me and pulling my hair, meanwhile screaming at me that I dare not talk to them in such a tone. But my determination to stick to the story as the only possible path to safety increased with their beating.

One policeman reported that they had shot more than ten Jews that week alone who had been caught with passports like mine. I tried to laugh it off: Could it be, then, that every passport issued in Warsaw was forged and was issued to a Jew? They urged me to tell the truth, promising me an easier lot if I did. At the same time they made thinly veiled threats: "We always discover the truth once we make up our minds to do so." I repeated my previous statements.

Then they prepared an official report. They scrutinized me again and compared my face with the photograph. I was made to sign my name many times for comparison with the signature on the passport. Actually, everything in the passport was correct except the seal, which differed slightly from the genuine one.

My head ached badly. The floor was strewn with the hair they had pulled out of my head by the roots. The grilling lasted until four o'clock. Then they set me to work scrubbing floors and putting the rooms in order. I looked for a chance to escape but all doors and windows were locked and barred, and an armed guard stood over me constantly.

At seven in the morning the other officials began to arrive for work. I was locked up in a small cell. What would happen now? Would I be shot immediately? It was my first time behind bars. I began envying those who were already dead. I would have preferred to be shot at once and thus end my tortures. Who could tell what inhuman suffering was in store for me?

Utterly exhausted, I was overcome by sleep. The turning of a key in the lock woke me. Two policemen entered and led me to the hall. They scrutinized me carefully. One was an elderly man, the other quite young. The young one smiled at me in a friendly manner. I recognized him; he had always examined my papers in the past when I was crossing the border. Whenever I had with me something dangerous on the way from Warsaw to Bendzin, I would turn it over to him to keep during the examination. I would tell him it was food that I didn't want confiscated at the border.

Now he stood beside me and patted my head. "Don't be afraid, my girl," he said. "I will help you. Nothing will happen to you. Cheer up." And he led me back to the cell.

Had he known that I was a Jewess I am certain he would not have spoken that way. Through the door I overheard the discussion in the main hall. I recognized the voice of the young policeman. "No, it can't be," he said. "She isn't Jewish. She has crossed the border with me many times. Only last week I examined her documents on the way from Warsaw to Bendzin. I will vouch for her. She should be freed right away."

Another voice, curt and sharp, answered him. It was evidently the policeman who had beaten me the night before. "Until now you couldn't know that her papers were forged," he said. "But now we have information that Warsaw passports bearing a seal like the one on hers are forged."

Wild laughter followed this remark and the conversation continued. "You should be as clever as I am. This is her last journey. In a few hours she'll sing for us and tell everything. We have a way to make people like her talk."

The conversation ceased. At intervals of a few minutes, the door of my cell would open and someone would look in to see what I was doing and how I looked.

At ten o'clock police came into my cell to lead me into the main hall. Ilsa was there already. Chains were clamped on our wrists and we were ordered to take our valises. The watch and other valuables were kept by the Gestapo man. We left the customhouse and turned toward the station. The young policeman cast a compassionate look in my direction, as if to say: "I wish I could help you, but your crime is very great." A train pulled up to the station. Passengers getting on and off turned to stare at us. The Gestapo official shoved us into a car with barred windows; then he too entered and barred the door from within. Through the barred windows the sunlight streaked the floor, offering us a little consolation.

The Gestapo official continually talked of the terrible treatment awaiting us, trying to break down our morale. He rolled his protruding eyes, slapped us, and did not permit us to sit down. Thus we rode from Trzebinia to Katowice.

We got off the train and a large crowd followed us. The chains cut our wrists as we walked. Ilsa was pale and trembling. A great pity for her filled me; she was so young—she had just turned seventeen. I whispered to her not to admit that she was Jewish. Every few steps we were kicked by the Gestapo guard to make us walk faster or slow down.

After half an hour we came to a large building on a side street decorated with German flags and swastikas. Several cars were parked outside the door. Kicking and shoving us, the guard took us to the fourth floor.

I shuddered. From other rooms were heard weeping and shouts. We were taken into one of the rooms. Behind the desk sat a fleshy, tall man of about thirty-five. His hard face and bulging eyes were enough to inspire fear.

We were ordered to face the wall, and did so. The Gestapo man who had brought us up now told our story to his chief, accompanying each sentence with blows. He produced our passports as well as the brief against us that had been prepared at the border station. A young Gestapo man came in to take off our chains and again we were beaten. Our guard laughed viciously: "This is the Katowice Gestapo. Here you will be flayed alive if you refuse to tell the truth."

Our belongings were left upstairs and we were taken to the cellar. Each was shut up in a separate cell. Though it was a warm day, I shivered in the cold, damp cellar. It was difficult to see anything clearly in the gloom. In the middle of the cell there were two long benches. I wanted to sit down, but the benches were covered with dried blood. I approached the window; two iron screens prevented escape. Frantically I began shaking the screens and, to my surprise, succeeded to pry the first one open. But my labors were in vain; the second screen would not budge. I carefully replaced the first screen and covered up the traces of my effort.

I was at a loss as to what to do. The thought of the tortures that seemed to be in store for me tormented me. I felt colder every minute. Drops of water were trickling down the walls. I began to cry. I sat down on the edge of the blood-stained bench and tried not to think of the future.

Through the window the sound of church music reached me. I had forgotten; it was Sunday and there was probably a church nearby. Again fear of the future assailed me. I could not keep the thought of it out. Was it worthwhile to go on living? If only I could have helped the people who were awaiting my return from Warsaw. But I had accomplished something; I had left the Warsaw address of our good friend "Zosia" with Meyer and Sarah. They might be able to contact her.

Last Days with Ilsa

Toward evening we were brought out of the cellar. Our feet were chained and so were our hands. We were ordered to take our valises along, a sure sign that we were not to be shot yet. A Gestapo official led us as one leads dogs, holding in his hand the ends of the chains that were about our wrists. I suddenly recalled how once, years before, I had seen a criminal led this way. He had murdered an entire family of seven and everyone turned out to watch him being led by. German children now followed us, throwing stones. The Gestapo man smiled with satisfaction.

We approached a building several stories high, surrounded by a thick, high wall. Its windows were small and heavily barred. We came to an iron gate. An inscription in German announced that it was a prison. The heavy gates opened with a screech. The guards saluted our Gestapo guide and the gates closed behind us. Our chains were removed and we were handed over to the prison supervisor. The Gestapo guard left; I felt relieved again.

The prison clerk took down the necessary information about us. He wrote down all the details concerning our appearance and measured our height. Then we were led to a cell. At eight o'clock the door opened and two emaciated girls brought us small slices of black bread and black coffee. We took the food and the door was locked again.

Although we had not eaten all day, we could not even take a bite of the black crust. For a few minutes we deliberated on how best to put an end to our lives. Escape was impossible. Ilsa said that when they started beating her again she would tell the truth and admit to being a Jewess. "Then they will shoot me and there will be an end to it all," she said.

I tried to dissuade her. If she were to tell the truth, many others would suffer, I pointed out to her. But I was not sure she could continue to undergo torture without breaking.

Crushed in spirit, we lay down on the filthy benches. But we could not sleep because of the insects that immediately swarmed all over us. The stench was suffocating. We decided to try to get some sleep on the bare ground.

At midnight twelve more women were led into our cell. They were seasoned prisoners. They were going by transport to Germany and had only stopped in this prison overnight. There were old as well as young women among them, and each had a different story to tell. One had been engaged to a Frenchman, although she was German. For this she was sentenced to five years' imprisonment. She had already served three years and was now being taken to the Cieszyn prison for forced labor. Two young girls wept continually. They had worked in Germany on farms, but because of poor food and overwork had finally fled to their homes near Warsaw. They had been at home for nine months; then some neighbors had denounced them and now they were being returned to Germany.

Two elderly women related that this was the sixth prison they had been detained in. Their original crime had consisted of transporting by train a quart of liquor and a pound of lard. They had been sentenced in absentia and did not know what fate awaited them ultimately. They had already spent a year and a half in prison. Others told of petty offenses that led to their wandering from one prison to another for years. Most pathetic of all was a woman about seventy years old. She sat hunched up and could only speak with difficulty. Her son had fled his home to avoid being conscripted into the German army; for this reason she had been arrested and had already spent many months in prison.

Ilsa and I nevertheless envied these women. We wished that we, too, were being transported to compulsory labor and thus could be free of the nightmare that awaited us. The women inquired why we were being held, and we told them we had been caught trying to cross the border illegally. They comforted us saying that this offense only carried a sentence of six months' imprisonment, and then we would be sent to Germany for compulsory labor.

We lay on the floor tightly packed against one another. Here, too, the bugs pestered us unbearably. We covered ourselves with dirty blankets, permeated with the smell of sweat and drugs. Several of the women were very dirty. For months they had been transported from one prison to another and from train to train without a chance to wash. They were infested with lice, which very soon spread to all of us. We kept the light burning all through the night as a deterrent to the insects, but we could not sleep anyway.

By morning the transport of women was taken away and Ilsa and I were again alone in the cell. At eight o'clock breakfast was brought to us, again a slice of black bread and some black coffee. We were also allowed to go to the lavatory. There I met the wife of a Polish officer, a young woman suspected of anti-German activities. She was extremely thin and could barely move about. Some weeks before she had been sentenced to hang, and she comforted herself with the hope that the war would end before the sentence was carried out. Her husband had been killed in the war and she had left three little children at home. Since her imprisonment she had heard nothing from them.

Another prisoner told me that some days earlier her sister had been decapitated in this prison. She was a relatively young woman and the mother of seven children. At the time of her execution she had been pregnant. She had been sentenced to death for slaughtering a pig for her own use in contravention of the law.

We would have continued talking but for the steps of the women guards that were suddenly heard outside. The guards were known for their cruelty in beating the prisoners with the heavy keys they carried about. We therefore fell silent.

Through the heavily screened windows we could see the emaciated faces of the male prisoners, who were confined to another section of the building. Executions were carried out right near the prison. In most cases a headsman was used. The condemned were not informed when their sentence would be carried out, and final parting with friends and family was not permitted. Confession to a priest was also forbidden.

After the midday meal we were taken to a bath and furnished with prison clothing. Ilsa and I were glad; it seemed that we had been forgotten by the Gestapo and might thus remain in prison for a few months. Who could tell? Perhaps the war would end by that time? We sat in the cell until evening. We looked at each other attired in prison garb and could scarcely believe our eyes. We were dressed in long shirts made out of crude flax linen, long patched drawers, ill-fitting dresses, and blouses made of multicolored patches. Each part of the uniform bore the stamp of the Katowice prison.

Night fell. Our condition was somehow more easily borne at night. We did not listen so intently to the sound of footsteps. In most cases the Gestapo people did not bother us at night. Our nerves, tense with the horrors of the day, relaxed. Only the bugs prevented us from resting.

I must have dozed off and awoken with a start. Could it have been a nightmare?

Ilsa was trying to hang herself with the belt of her dress, unsuccessfully. The belt snapped, unable to bear her weight. I burst into hysterical laughter. I seemed to have lost my sanity for a moment. Some moments passed before I composed myself again. I went over to her but she angrily pushed me aside, overcome with humiliation at her failure.

At dawn the supervisors came shouting obscenities at us and drove us out of the cell. We were each transferred to a different cell.

In my new cell, which was cleaner and had bunks covered with mats, I was met by eight women. One of them, distinguished by a delicate face, at once approached me and struck up a conversation. She asked why I had been imprisoned, and I told her. She, in turn, informed me that she had been imprisoned for fortune-telling. She had been a midwife by profession. She had two grown sons, one an engineer and the other an office worker. One of her neighbors had denounced her to the Gestapo as a fortune-teller and she was arrested. That was several months ago; no sentence had been passed. She cautioned me to be careful in conversation with the others because there were spies among them.

Everyone soon began addressing me in the familiar second person. Formalities were not indulged in the prison. The veteran prisoners constantly repeated their prison histories to each newcomer. One woman related that she had been in jail since the beginning of the war. She had long since become reconciled to her fate and felt destined to spend the rest of her life in prison.

After breakfast we were chased from our cell into the corridor. For no cause whatever I received a rather heavy blow from the guard, who shouted at me: "Looks as if you want to go about idle! We Germans don't stand for this sort of thing. Get to work!"

In the corridor there were long tables at which women sat plucking feathers. I sat down among them and got busy. Carefully I looked about, searching for Ilsa. She was there, sitting not far away. But I could not get closer to her, for a number of supervisors, armed with whips, were about and saw to it that the women did not talk to one another.

A pleasant feminine face looked at me from the opposite bench. Soft eyes, dimmed but still unextinguished, smiled at me. I read in these eyes a great pity for me. The woman did not say anything but her face spoke of the tortures she had endured. Tears rolled down her face, and my heart contracted within me.

Time passed quickly at work. My thoughts turned on one subject: What will happen next? It would be well if they either left us alone or shot us without delay. But this waiting, punctuated by beatings and abuse, intended to draw out our secret knowledge—this was intolerable.

We returned to our cells. For the midday meal we were given some soup containing grits and vegetable leaves. Despite my hunger I could not touch the revolting mess; I pushed my plate away. The other women avidly grabbed it and greedily ate the soup to the last drop. They comforted me: "After you're here a while, you'll beg them on your knees for some soup like this." Two peasant women whispered among themselves: "She is a lady. The soup doesn't suit her. She'll learn to like it."

Torture

We returned to work after lunch. Time now dragged more slowly. Hours and hours would pass before we were returned to our cells. A great unease seized me and strange premonitions troubled my heart. Every few minutes one of the prisoners was called by name and taken away for cross-examination. Suddenly a voice called out: Wanda Wyduchowska! I was petrified. The blow of a whip brought me to. What awaited me now?

I cast a fleeting glance at Ilsa. A pitiful expression was her only response. I was taken upstairs to the supervisor's room. In the hall I was met by a Gestapo man. I recognized him, the same hard face and bulging eyes that I had previously noted so well. It was he who had sat at the table when Ilsa and I were first brought before the Gestapo. A mist seemed to rise before my eyes and faintness overcame me.

He ordered me to go back and put on the clothes I had worn when arrested. The woman supervisor asked him the cause of my arrest. In reply he whispered something to her. Then he said loudly: "At the moment her name is Wyduchowska. After the hearings we'll know her real name." The woman asked him whether I would be returned to the prison after the hearing, but he said he did not know.

Chained, I was again led through the street, a Gestapo guard at my side. He spoke German to me all the way; I pretended not to understand. But his words became engraved on my mind. "Look well at the dress you are wearing," he said, "for after the beating you will now get you won't be able to recognize it. It will be torn to shreds right on your body."

I was amazed at myself. Somehow his words did not inspire within me the fear they were intended to arouse; it was as if he were talking about someone else.

Again we came to the Gestapo building. One of the men asked me whether I understood German. I said I did not. Two heavy blows that set my ears ringing were the acknowledgment of my reply. I stood quietly as if nothing had occurred. Four Gestapo men and a girl entered; the girl was to serve as interpreter. The Gestapo man who had brought me to the building acted as the chief interrogator. The others addressed him as "Chief Gehringer." The cross-examination began.

A multitude of questions were shot at me, each examiner trying to outdo the other in an effort to confuse me. But their hard faces, instead of frightening me, aroused me to greater determination. I resolutely maintained my original assertions: that my passport was genuine, that I was the daughter of a Polish officer missing as a prisoner in Russia, that my mother was dead, that I supported myself by working in an office and from time to time by selling family heirlooms, which by this time were all gone. One of the Gestapo men went over to the table and took out a package of forged documents from the drawer. The owners of these documents had also been seized at the border. All of them bore the seal of the same office where I had obtained my travel certificate. The documents were all alike, apart from the surnames.

I knew very well that the forger of the documents was selling them for large sums to all comers. My courage, which had held up well so far, suddenly ebbed at the sight of the forged certificates. I felt that I was losing color, and were it not that my cheeks were still burning from the blows I had received, my face would undoubtedly have betrayed me.

The Gestapo agents stood awaiting my reply, and I was momentarily at a loss. Then I said: "It's possible that those other documents are forged, but that doesn't prove that mine are forged, too. The firm I speak of does exist. I have been working for it for three years. My travel certificate is in the handwriting of an officer of this firm. The seal is that of the mayor of Warsaw. My papers aren't forged."

My statement only exasperated them still further. "All those caught with these papers also maintained they were genuine!" they shouted. "But they all turned out to be Jews and were shot the next day. Confess your guilt and you will live."

I only smiled. "I can't lie," I insisted. "My papers are genuine, how can I say they are forged? Since I am a Catholic, how can I say I am Jewish?"

Heavy blows were the answer to my statement. The girl who acted as interpreter was willing to vouch that I was not a Jewess. "She has definitely Aryan features, and besides, she speaks Polish perfectly," she declared.

"Then she must be a spy," one of the Gestapo men concluded. The others agreed with him at once.

Now their questions proceeded on this assumption. For which organization did I act as courier—the PPR, or that of Sikorski?[1] What was my salary? What kind of materials did I transport? Where were the main positions of the partisans?

One of my tormentors tried to break my resistance with kindness. "Don't be a fool," he said. "Why should you protect your superiors? They wouldn't do anything for you even if they found out you were caught. Tell us the truth and we'll set you free."

I obstinately pretended ignorance. "A courier? Is that a person who distributes leaflets? I have heard talk about the PPR and about Sikorski, but I don't know anything about them. I don't know anything about the partisans except what I hear in the street now and then. I'd gladly tell you where they are, if I knew. I am telling the truth. If I wanted to lie I could easily invent some names for you."

They were furious. The cross-examination had been going on for more than three hours and they still had obtained no information. They asked me about my education. I told them I had completed seven grades. They grinned at each other. No wonder I so stupidly endangered my life by refusing to give information. What else could be expected of one who had only gone through seven grades?

But the same Gestapo man who had previously concluded that I was a spy now advanced another theory. "She's lying," he declared. "Here we've been trying to gain information from her for three hours unsuccessfully. No one with only a grammar-school education could possibly deceive us so well."

The others again agreed with him. They decided further cross-examination would be useless and their chief ordered me to be taken to another hall. It was large and bare of furniture. Several Gestapo men armed with whips came in. "After we're through with you, you'll sing like a bird," they muttered. One savage kick threw me to the floor. Then one of the men seized my feet and another grabbed my head. Two others began to whip me mercilessly. I clenched my teeth. The pain blinded me. "Mother!" I screamed as the whips continued beating down. One of my tormentors twined my hair about his hand and began dragging me along the floor. An uncontrollable trembling seized me. The whips continued to rain blows upon me. I felt myself growing weaker. I could not scream anymore. Then darkness enveloped me.

I came to, lying in a puddle. The upper part of my body was nude. Pails of water had been poured on me to bring me out of my faint. Two Gestapo men helped me rise. I put on a sweater.

They renewed the cross-examination. They tried to find discrepancies between my answers and what I had said before. They urged and threatened. One of then pointed a pistol at me and ordered me to follow him. "If you refuse to talk," he said, "I'll shoot you like a dog." I went downstairs, happy at the thought that my tortures would be coming to an end. "This is the last sunset I will ever see," I kept repeating to myself without any sense of grief or loss. My guide stopped: "Aren't you sorry to die so young? What makes you so stubborn? Why won't you tell the truth?"

I told him: "As long as there are people like you in the world, I don't want to live among them. I tell the truth and you try to force lies out of me by torture. I'd rather be dead." He kicked me a number of times and took me upstairs once more.

Again they tried kindness for a while and one of the men pulled up a chair for me. He promised on his word of honor that I would be sent to Warsaw if I told the truth, that I would be employed by the Gestapo there. I agreed to everything he said, but insisted I was telling the truth all along.

Their chief thereupon ordered them to stop "playing" with me and to give me twenty-five more lashes, or as many as would force me to confess the truth. Two Gestapo men began lashing me. Blood began to flow freely from my nose and head. The woman who had acted as interpreter could not stand the sight and left the room.

The chief, seeing the effects of the beating, urged them to redouble their efforts, and, apparently not satisfied with what they were doing, began kicking me himself. But the pain seemed to recede: I no longer felt the blows. I dropped in a dead faint.

A long time seemed to have elapsed. Then I felt water trickling down my face and running into my mouth. I regained consciousness but kept my eyes closed. "She's already cold," I heard one of the men saying. Another pail of water was dumped on me. Two Gestapo men bent over me and felt my pulse and the beat of my heart. "She's all right again, her pulse is beating again." "She's lost her reason," one of them said pointing at my eyes that were bulging out of their sockets. They lifted me and placed me on a bench. A chill racked my body. A great regret that I had regained consciousness overcame me. Now I would be beaten again. But I had grown dreadfully weak and could not possibly endure much more. That was a consolation. Still another idea comforted me—since they had obtained no information from me so far, they would probably shoot me.

I could not get up without assistance. A Gestapo man bandaged my head with a soiled rag, put my sweater over me and led me to the table. He handed me the written records and said: "Here, sign these lies." As he spoke, his wife came in. She looked at me and grimaced; evidently I didn't present a pleasant appearance. She noticed my watch lying on the table among the other articles and asked her husband to give it to her, since I would be shot anyway. He promised she would get it after a while. She got angry and left the room in a huff.

The Gestapo man helped hold the pen as I signed the document. Then they phoned for a closed taxi and a few minutes later, accompanied by a Gestapo guard, I was taken away. The guard sat near me and locked the door. The driver asked him to come and sit up front, but he refused: "She may be almost a corpse, but she is the sort that might still try to escape."

Outside the sun had set and there was a grey twilight. From casual remarks I gathered that I was being taken to Myslowice,[2] evidently a place of terrors, for the driver grinned as he said: "That's the only place that will cure her of her obstinacy."

Four Months in Myslowice

Evening fell; we entered a large courtyard. Big dogs sprang out from all sides and surrounded us. My guide left me at the office, together with all the papers pertaining to my case. In the yard, guards walked their posts armed with rifles. In the office, a young man of about twenty-two looked at me with a grin and said: "They thrashed you properly, eh?" I did not answer. He beckoned to me with his fist and I followed.

He showed me into a cellar. There was a bunk along the wall. I tried to lie down but could not. Making another effort I finally succeeded to stretch out facedown. The pain increased in intensity. Every bone felt as if it were crushed. I tried to sit up, again without success. After some hours my entire body swelled and I could not move a limb. I never would have believed a human being could withstand such a beating. Yet there I was, still alive and even capable of thinking. Only my memory seemed to be confused.

For a week I remained imprisoned in that cellar. My condition seemed to grow worse each day. Once a day, at noon, a little watery soup and a cup of cold water would be brought to me. All week I did not wash. All bodily needs were attended to within the cell itself. The stench was suffocating. I did not see the light of day. I prayed for death, longed for the moment of its coming, but to no avail.

At the end of a week, a young woman came and conducted me to the office.

Again I was questioned in detail. I was amazed. Will they let me live? Will they take me to still another prison? After the questioning, the woman led me to a bathhouse. Out of pity she helped me undress. Now I saw the effects of the beating I had received; my entire body was discolored. Tears streamed down the young woman's face. She began speaking Polish to me, caressing and kissing me. Her tenderness found a response within me, and tears began rolling from my eyes. Who could she be, I wondered. Is there a German woman left capable of pity and compassion? After a while she told me her history:

> I have been under arrest for two and a half years. The last year I have spent in this prison. This is an investigation center, and

> people are held here for some time until thoroughly investigated. There are two thousand people in this prison now.
>
> Before the war I was a teacher. Shortly after the war broke out, everyone suspected of political activity in Cieszyn was arrested. My friends were all imprisoned; I hid for a time before I fell into the hands of the Germans. I, too, suffered not a little.

Here she showed me traces of being beaten with chains and the marks of pins having been stuck under her fingernails.

> My two brothers are also held in this prison. They were caught six months ago and have been kept chained to their beds ever since. They are under constant guard, and their slightest moves are punished with severe beatings. Terrible acts that human imagination can scarcely conceive of take place here. Not a day passes but that ten or more prisoners die from torture. Nor do the jailors distinguish between men and women. This is primarily a prison for political offenders and all will be killed in the end, anyway.

After the bath the woman continued talking to me. She promised to be my friend and to help me in any way she could. She explained her position in the prison. "Until recently I, too, was kept in a cell. Now I manage the bathhouse. I get the same treatment as the other prisoners, except that I can go about the grounds freely."

I was then taken into a long dormitory. A row of double-tiered bunks lined the wall. Two heavily screened windows admitted light. At the door there was a table for the use of the attendant. She turned out to be one of the best-liked prisoners and was responsible for the cleanliness of the place. A heap of platters was stacked in the corner. There were many women in the room. Their faces, pleasant and evil, old and young, examined me as I came in. One of the women, evidently demented, began to dance as I entered.

They crowded about me, jostled me, showered me with questions: Where did I come from? Why had I been arrested? What other prisons had I been in? When I told them that I had been arrested a fortnight before, their curiosity mounted. They wanted to know everything about the outside world.

What a conglomeration of human beings! One woman took me aside and eagerly asked what were the prospects for an early end to the war. She was a converted Jewess who had been married to a German. For months the Gestapo in her town had sought a pretext for her arrest; finally they had arrested her for playing cards. Among the women there were others who had been seized for similar "lapses."

I was especially drawn to a small, fifteen-year-old girl. She had a very pleasant face and I developed an immediate liking for her. She watched me with curiosity for a while, and finally, gathering up her courage, she approached me. She was Jewish and she inquired whether any Jews were left in Bendzin and Sosnowiec. She and her sister had been deported from Sosnowiec. They had both leaped out of the train that was taking them to an extermination camp. Her sister was severely injured during the leap and the girl did not know what to do. In desperation she had reported to the nearest police station and they had turned her over to the Gestapo. Her injured sister was supposed to be taken to a hospital, but there was no news of her and she was probably shot. The girl had been brought to Myslowice, where she had been held for three weeks. She had no idea what fate awaited her, but she did not wish to die. "Maybe the war will end soon," she said. "I want to live so much. Every night I dream of leaving this prison."

I kept up my pretense of being a Catholic but drew continually closer to this girl. I tried to comfort her: "The war is bound to end soon. You will yet be free."

We became good friends in a short time. She explained to me the routine in this prison and saw to it that I had a bowl to eat from and a straw pillow at night.

There were about sixty-five women in the ward. After the daily examinations and beatings several would be taken away, somc to other prisons, others to be shot. And daily fresh transports of women arrived.

The daily routine was as follows: We were awakened at six in the morning. We were taken to the lavatory, ten at a time, and waited our turn to wash with cold water. Only a few seconds were allotted for these ablutions. By seven o'clock the supervisor came in and then no one dared be caught in the corridor. She was a cruel woman. At the slightest pretext she used her whip and her bunch of keys, falling upon one or another of the prisoners and beating her mercilessly. We would clench our fists and indulge in daydreams of what we would do to her as soon as the war ended. I learned that the supervisor, who was a Pole, had declared herself to be a Volksdeutsche. Before the war she had had a small notions store and traveled about the fairs. When the war broke out, she had left her husband and joined the Germans. Thus she had risen to her present position of authority as overseer of about five hundred women. "You Polish swine, you cattle," she screamed as she beat her charges. The Gestapo appreciated her methods, which fitted their needs and temperament so well.

Shortly after seven we were mustered in three long rows. Two Gestapo men called the roll. Then we were given our breakfast—a small slice of bread, weighing about fifty grams, and a quarter of a liter of black coffee. The doors were locked and we would then sit idle and hungry, waiting for eleven o'clock. At eleven we were taken for a half-hour walk. Often many of us would have preferred not to go for this walk, which was a form of torture in itself. As we walked about the yard, the screams of the tortured in other wards assailed us. Sometimes we saw them being taken to or from the interrogation chambers; then they looked altogether inhuman—living corpses, their eyes blackened or gouged out, their heads bandaged, hands broken and arms twisted out of their sockets.

Their garments were bloodstained and torn by the blows. At times we saw dead bodies carried out of the interrogation chambers. These we envied. The dead bodies would be put in coffins and loaded on the same bus taking prisoners to Oswiecim.

At the end of the walk, we would return to our room. The guards and supervisor would be walking about in the corridors, and no one dared utter a sound. We were all bitterly hungry. Each stood with a bowl in her hand, waiting. We had no spoons and whenever we found anything solid in our food, we would simply use our fingers. Then we would hear the din of kettles being hauled from one ward to another. It was now twelve o'clock. We waited our turn, standing in line, trembling in hunger for the sound of the door opening. Two prisoners, held for only light offenses, doled out the lunch. An armed guard accompanied them. But no matter how great our hunger, none dared show any impatience. The supervisor stood at the door to see that order was enforced.

We received a little water in our bowl, a few cooked leaves resembling cabbage, and some other scarcely identifiable greens. Worms floated in the soup, others were among the leaves. The ones floating on the surface we skimmed off; the less obvious ones we ate together with the leaves. Anyone getting a few extra leaves in her soup considered herself fortunate; the less lucky ones got only some water in their bowls. For some time after eating, many would be nauseated by the unspeakable mixture, and our hunger remained as intense as before. I felt as if my stomach was daily contracting from hunger. At first I did not think I could possibly down the vile mixture, but after a few days I prayed that I would get an extra spoonful. Each of us dreamed of the day of liberation, which we visualized as one glorious opportunity to eat one's fill—a whole loaf of bread, sausage. No one dreamed of fancy foods, just of quantities of wholesome, wormless food. But who would live to see that happy day?

At seven in the evening there was another roll call and dinner. The slice of bread doled out was somewhat bigger than the one in the morning and sometimes a dab of margarine was added. There was also black coffee. We swallowed the bread at one gulp. At nine we had to turn in for the night, but for many hours afterward we could not sleep for the hunger pangs.

This prison was much cleaner than the one in Katowice. I learned that early in 1942 there had been a typhus epidemic here because of undernourishment and dirt. Many prisoners had died at that time, and since then more attention had been paid to cleanliness. We slept on boards covered with a thin mattress of straw, with clean but torn blankets over us. We generally slept dressed on the chance that a partisan attack at night would require us to flee at a moment's notice, without any opportunity to dress.

Throughout the night the corridors were patrolled by armed guards. The slightest rustle in any of the wards brought down their wrath. No one could leave the ward during the night, nor could the door be unlocked for any emergency. Occasionally shouting would be heard; apparently someone from the men's section had attempted to flee. But escape was impossible. I spent numerous nights thinking of escape. The windows were heavily screened, the doors locked and barred, the entire building surrounded by guards. Watchtowers were erected all around the building; the guards were changed every two hours.

In the morning we would be aroused by the sharp pangs of hunger and gnawing fear—what will this day bring? We would learn invariably of a number of suicides that had occurred during the night. One morning one of the women attempted to flee while in a group being led to the lavatory. She did not get very far before she was caught. She was mercilessly beaten and confined to a dark cell.

One day five Jewesses were brought to the prison from Sosnowiec. They had dyed their hair and tried to pass as Poles, but they had been apprehended at the Katowice railroad station. A Polish boy had become suspicious and called the Gestapo. I talked to them at night, while the others were asleep, but I did not reveal my identity to them.

Every few days more Jewesses who had been hiding were caught and brought to our prison. One of them fell into the hands of the police quite accidentally, when documents were examined in the street. Another woman lived for months in the home of a policeman who suspected nothing, and she had no idea who had denounced her. Her German hosts, who had harbored her unwittingly, were arrested together with her. One old woman was arrested on a train together with her two daughters during a check of documents. But the majority of them had been denounced by Poles.

When a group of twenty Jewish women was assembled in our prison, they would be sent to Oswiecim. Until the very last moment they all clung to the vain hope that the war would come to an end before they were shipped to the extermination camp. They would depart tearfully, knowing that they were being taken to their death. All of us wept in unison, the ones remaining behind tormented by their own fears for tomorrow.

Names of persons to be cross-examined would be announced without previous notice. Later they would be brought back on stretchers. On the following day they would be beaten again and again, frequently until death.

There were entire families in our prison, mothers and daughters in the women's section, fathers and sons in the men's wards. It frequently happened that one of the women prisoners would learn of her husband's death in the course of his cross-examination, or of his being sentenced to be sent to Oswiecim. Despair would then seize the entire ward.

Many men and women in our prison were sentenced to death because they had either hidden a Jew or helped one escape from a ghetto. One day one of the women was hanged for having sheltered a Jew, her former employer. She was only twenty-five years old and had two small children.

Some women were imprisoned as hostages for their sons, brothers, husbands, or even cousins. Others did not know why they had been arrested, and had been transported from one prison to another for as long as three years without being told what their offense was. One day several hundred people were brought from a village; a partisan had been caught in the village and shot. All the men in the village were executed, and the women and children were brought to our prison. Other villagers were brought in when Germans from bombed-out German cities had taken over their homes.

One day, during our half-hour walk, four trucks arrived. Gestapo men leaped out, followed by tens of boys and girls. They had been gathered in the vicinity of Zywiec. Partisans had been active in that region and in retaliation the Germans had imprisoned the boys and girls.

The children received the same food as we did. They were kept in a separate ward supervised by an older prisoner. They, too, were interrogated. At the sight of the whips and other instruments of torture they readily told anything they were asked to tell, the truth as well as imaginary stories that they concocted to please their tormentors and avoid punishment. The Germans were satisfied and eventually they would send the children to Germany to work and to be raised as Germans.

A month had gone by and my fate was still a mystery to me. Many women from our ward had perished during this month, and new ones had come to take their place. One of these new arrivals showed me her hands: there were no nails on her fingers. They had dropped off after red-hot pins had been stuck under them. There were chain marks on her arms; she had been hung by her hands for half an hour while the Germans beat her. Then they had left her, hanging down for several minutes. During the first months of the war her son had vanished without a trace. Later rumors spread that he was at the head of a partisan detachment. The entire family became suspect, and, indeed, she was the only one who had remained alive.

Among the inmates of the prison there were also petty offenders, speculators, peddlers, persons who had disobeyed the blackout regulations. These led a somewhat easier life and were permitted to receive packages from the outside. The Germans naturally opened all the packages and appropriated whatever took their fancy. Even so, the position of these prisoners was considered highly privileged.

One day the supervisor entered our ward and asked me the reason for my arrest. I gave the usual answer, that I was caught trying to cross the border. I was taken outside and told that I would be sent to work in the police kitchen. A great relief swept over me. A lightning thought flashed across my mind that I might yet be able to get away.

For the first time in a month, the gates of the prison opened before me. Again I was in the street on the way to the police barracks. My eyes wandered in vain searching for a familiar face, but I saw only strangers.

My work was to begin at four o'clock in the morning and to continue till four in the afternoon. I received sufficient food. One of the guards regarded me with much pity. Whenever he took me to or from work he offered me bread, apples, cigarettes. He told me he was from Berlin but had lived in Poland for many years. When the Germans came, he registered as a Volksdeutsche. They forced him to divorce his Polish wife, and she went back to her parents together with their child.

Something within me prompted me to believe his words. I trusted his sincerity and felt that he might be able to help me. At night, when the others were asleep, I wrote a letter to Warsaw. I knew that I was taking a great risk, but I had no other choice. The next day, when I went to work, I asked the guard to mail the letter for me. I told him it was to my parents, that they did not know what had happened to me since I was arrested. He agreed to mail it. As we turned in at the gate I gave him the letter. He again promised to mail it and shook a warning finger at me to mention the matter to no one.

The following nights I could not sleep a wink, wondering, hoping, despairing about the letter. Did he really mail it? Could he have turned it over to the Gestapo? That would be horrible, for in the letter I had mentioned some of the contacts in Warsaw.

Various incriminating articles were to be removed from those places, but most important of all was that they should know my whereabouts.

Late one night four women and a baby were brought to the prison. We learned that the baby and three of the women were Jewish; the fourth was a Russian woman born in Poland. I sought the acquaintance of the fourth one and we soon became close friends. Her name was Tatiana Kuprienko. In broken Polish mixed with Russian she told me the circumstances of her arrest. The three Jewesses were her friends and she had wished to help them. She had succeeded in smuggling them out of the ghetto and hiding them in the attic of her house. For some time she had kept them hidden and it looked as if no one was aware of their presence. Altogether there were six adults and the baby in the attic.

"I wanted them all to go to work in Germany," she related.

> I had a friend, an official, and at great expense I prepared documents for them, stating that they were Poles. One of the women left for Germany, and a few weeks ago I heard from her that she was working and all was well with her. The other women could not go because their husbands looked distinctly Jewish and they refused to leave them behind.
>
> One day a policeman appeared, accompanied by a Polish boy of about seventeen. Before I could say anything the boy accused me of harboring Jews. All of us in the house, as well as my two brothers and the official who had prepared the documents, were arrested at once. To this day I do not know

> how they found out about the hideout, for they seemed to be informed even about the woman who was already in Germany. Before I was questioned, they read the charges to me, and their information was complete and correct. At the police station I was terribly beaten. Now I am threatened with the death sentence. My brothers and the official face similar punishment.

Two days later the Jewish women and their husbands were taken to Oswiecim. The Jewess who was already in Germany was brought back. She was utterly dejected; in Germany she had hoped to survive the war. Now they had brought her from her relative safety and her fate seemed sealed. She was interrogated at once, and when she returned from this ordeal she was unrecognizable. Yet, despite indescribable torture, the Jewish woman did not reveal the name of the man who had prepared the forged papers for her, and consistently maintained that she did not know the Russian woman.

Once, when Tatiana was in a hopeful mood, she said to me: "No matter what they do to me, I feel sure I will eventually be freed. I have a premonition that I will survive. I left an old mother at home and I must go on living for her sake. I have a rich brother-in-law in Warsaw—he will get me out." I could not refrain from smiling when she said this, and then I wondered: Could her sufferings have affected her mind?

Some days passed and Tatiana was suddenly called. She turned pale; evidently she would be questioned again. Thoroughly crushed and apathetic she followed the Gestapo guard to the interrogation room. A few minutes later she came running into our ward, hysterically crying and laughing. We were certain she had lost her reason. She dashed from one to another kissing and embracing us. "I am free!" she shouted. "I am being sent home!" In parting from me she hastily whispered: "It was my brother-in-law, he ransomed me out, he gave them half a kilogram of gold." I scarcely believed her, yet the thought flashed through my mind: if it is possible to bribe the Gestapo, perhaps I too would yet get out alive.

Another incident that occurred shortly afterward also raised my hopes. One afternoon a taxi drew up to the gates of the prison. Two men in civilian dress emerged and presented Gestapo identification papers to the guards. They were admitted without question and at once went to the ward where important political offenders were kept chained to their beds. Removing the chains, they carried two of the prisoners to the car outside and drove away without delay. The guards became suspicious at the manner in which they handled the two prisoners; they had never before seen Gestapo men carry political offenders in their arms. The guards therefore reported the matter and inquiries were made. It turned out that the men were partisans who had obtained Gestapo identification documents. They were never caught.

This incident aroused great consternation among the prison authorities. The guards were at once arrested. The supervisors were brought in and the watch was redoubled. As a result of the changes that were made and the general tightening of discipline, my fate, too, took a turn for the worse. My case was investigated again and I was transferred to the political section of the prison as a possible spy. I no longer went to work in the police kitchen; in the political section, prisoners did not work. Occasionally we were questioned by Gestapo commissions. Otherwise we were kept in our cells awaiting our ultimate doom.

The hope of emerging alive from the prison, which had glimmered in my mind for a while, now faded. I sat in my cell brooding about what had happened to all the people I had known. It seemed to me that my memory was failing me. Past events were becoming confused. I could no longer concentrate; I couldn't recall what statements I had made to the Gestapo before. Had they interrogated me then, I would undoubtedly have made some incriminating statements. My head ached constantly. We were not permitted to lie down during the day. I often disregarded this order, but whenever the sound of the key turning in the lock was heard I would jump up quickly.

At this time I also learned, from a woman who was transferred to our prison, what had happened to Ilsa. Unable to withstand the tortures, she had confessed to being a Jewess and was hanged a few days later. Her face began to haunt me.

I Meet Sarah Again

One morning, while I was being marched to the lavatory, one of the women stuck a note into my hand and whispered that it was given to her by a woman while she was working outside, and that the woman would call for an answer the following day and would also bring a package of food. My hand trembled violently as I grasped the piece of paper. I carried it about with me all day without reading it, afraid of attracting the attention of my cellmates. Only after they had all fallen asleep did I open it. The note was in Sarah's handwriting. She wrote that our comrades were alive. She had learned about me in a letter she had received from Zivia in Warsaw.

She urged me to keep up my courage and inquired how they could help me; they would do everything in their power to save me. I reread the note countless times, unable to believe that it was real. Projects of various kinds flitted through my head.

Long past midnight, I stealthily left my bunk and searched the attendant's desk for a pencil and a piece of paper to answer Sarah's note. I wrote that the woman who carried the note should be paid, since she was taking a great risk in doing so. Then I suggested that if it was at all possible, she should be bribed to change places with me so that I would have an opportunity to go into the field. When we met we could discuss details. In the morning I gave the note to the woman and arranged to see her in the evening.

All day I kept turning Sarah's words over in my mind. "We will do everything we can for you," she had written. "Zivia sent a man well supplied with money to save you, if at all possible." What gave me the greatest comfort was the knowledge that the remaining comrades were out of the ghetto and accommodated in Polish homes.

In the evening I received the reply: "Everything will be all right. The woman agreed to change places with you. She will receive adequate compensation. She is poor and was glad to agree to the arrangement."

The following morning, I exchanged clothes with the woman. It was a cold November day. My face was wrapped in whatever ragged remnants I could find, and none of the guards recognized me. We were taken outside the prison compound. Many prisoners worked there: Russians, French, Italians. We too started to work, loading bricks onto freight cars. The work was not too hard, but I had grown very clumsy with weakness and the bricks kept falling from my hands. I grew apprehensive lest I attract attention by my clumsiness before Sarah arrived.

The minutes dragged like hours. Then I saw two elegantly dressed ladies approaching from a distance; I recognized Sarah as one of them. She stopped and looked around, but did not recognize me. I explained to the other women that they were acquaintances of one of my cellmates and approached the two ladies. The guard followed me, but despite his presence Sarah and I could not refrain from weeping.

Sarah offered him some pastries; meanwhile I began to talk in a low voice to the other girl. Her name was Halina. She informed me that she had been sent from Warsaw by Zivia. We set a day the following week when she would bring me other clothes; meanwhile I was to work out the details of my escape.

We could not linger for long and they started to walk away. I followed them with my eyes until they disappeared. My plan entailed great hazard. But the words of the girl sent from Warsaw rang in my ears: "Even though you may fail, you must make the attempt. Your life is in great danger in any case."

CHAPTER FIVE

Rescue

The Escape

When I returned from work a great weakness came over me. The meeting with Sarah had a strange effect on me; I felt as one does after a serious illness. My headache, which had been bothering me for some time now, increased in intensity. For a few days I was hardly able to stand up. My mind was a wild confusion of memories. I developed a high temperature and babbled deliriously. Some of the women pitied my state, not knowing what was its cause, and offered me the slices of bread they received for breakfast. But I could not swallow anything.

In a few days my fever subsided. On Sunday the women arranged a thanksgiving service. I, too, knelt down to pray. Suddenly a mist seemed to come before my eyes and I fainted. The doors were locked and there was no way of getting water; the women therefore used the dirty water in which our bowls had been rinsed to revive me. Again I lay on my bunk for two days, unable to move. But I was compelled to get up. The appointed day, the day of escape, was approaching.

Thursday, November 12, 1943, was the date set for my escape. After a sleepless night I was the first to leap out of the bunk when the morning bell rang. The attendant reluctantly consented to let me change clothes with the other woman and go out to work once more. She had more easily agreed to it the first time, but was afraid to risk it again.

Once again I went out, bundled up in shawls and rags, and escaped recognition by the guards. We were fifteen women prisoners, working under the supervision of five guards. I began loading the bricks onto the freight cars, anxiously looking about me to see whether Sarah and Halina were anywhere in sight.

They arrived about ten o'clock. I slipped away from my work. I was certain no one had noticed it, but before I could say a word to them, the chief guard came running and shouting: "Why did you leave your work without permission?" Sarah appeased him with a few words. I whispered to Halina that they should return at two in the afternoon and bring along some cigarettes and whiskey.

The other women, too, were angry with me. My leaving the work without permission could have resulted in trouble for all of them. A few minutes before lunchtime, one of the guards called me over and told me he had learned that I was from the political section of the prison. My heart sank within me. But he reassured me and promised not to report the matter, out of pity for my youth. "But no silly ideas," he said shaking a warning finger at me. "Don't you try to escape. You'll surely be caught, and then they'll tear you to pieces." I disowned any such intentions. "How could I even think of such a thing?' I said. "Don't you think I know what's good for me? I am under arrest only for crossing the border, and I'll probably be released any day. You won't find me trying to escape and spoiling all my chances for release."

I could not understand who possibly could have informed the guards that I was from the political section. The logical conclusion was that the women who worked with me had denounced me to them. It was a reasonable conclusion, too; everyone lived in dread. Since the two men had been spirited away by the partisans, everyone tried to protect himself, often at the expense of the others.

This complicated matters. Now I would be watched still more carefully and escape would be more difficult. And yet, now I had to flee. Since the guards knew that I was a political offender, I would never get another chance. It was today or never.

My anxiety mounted. The minutes dragged. Would Sarah and Halina ever show up? I had no watch and it seemed to me that endless hours had passed. After countless eternities two figures appeared in the distance. "It's them," my heart pounded.

I asked the guard to walk over with me to them. We stood behind a brick wall. They gave him cigarettes and a few bottles of whiskey. He stuffed the cigarettes into his pockets and downed a bottle of whiskey on the spot. I offered some bottles to the other guards and asked them to keep the women away from the back of the wall. My friends had brought me some food, I said, and I wanted to eat it alone without sharing with the others. It seemed a plausible enough reason to them. Besides, they knew there was a guard with us. In a little while that guard became somewhat hazy from the effects of the liquor. I begged him to go and see if any of the other women were coming. He went. Now was the opportune moment. In an instant, aided by the two girls, I put on another coat, shawl, and shoes and we broke into a run. Sarah and I ran in one direction, Halina in another.

We thought it was best that way: in case we were caught, she might escape.

We reached a hill, and in my weakened condition I could not climb it. An Italian prisoner who happened to be nearby helped me up. With difficulty we surmounted the barbed-wire fence. Now we were on the road. We didn't know our way, and decided to walk straight ahead. My coat was caked with mud from climbing the hill. The decisive moment in our lives had come. We ran faster and faster, trying to put as much distance as possible between ourselves and the prison yard. We were bathed in perspiration, the wind beating against our flaming faces.

I kept looking back to see whether anyone was chasing us. It seemed to me as if my father and mother were by my side, protecting me from evil. Suddenly a car came down the road. Sarah grasped her head in panic. But the car passed without taking notice of us. "Hurry, Renia, hurry," she urged me on. I tried to run as fast as I could.

I grew fainter from minute to minute. Try to run as I might, my feet would not obey me. Another step and another, and I collapsed on the road. Sarah lifted me up.

"Please, Renia," she implored, "try to go on a little more or we'll both be lost. You're the only one left to me of our entire family; I will not lose you now. I will not." Tears ran down her cheeks and dripped onto my face.

Making another effort I rose and we proceeded, though not as fast as before. Now and then a car would approach and we froze in our tracks. Then we would resume our pace. My mouth opened wide and my lips were dry. Pedestrians stopped to look at us in surprise. It did not seem possible that we would reach our destination unreported. Our appearance was strange enough: we were covered with enough mud to arouse anyone's suspicion.

Sarah preceded me by about thirty meters. I followed along at a snail's pace. After covering seven kilometers [four miles], we approached Katowice. Sarah took me inside a gate and wiped my face and clothes as best she could. Her face now glowed with joy. Not far away there lived a German acquaintance. Nacha, Meyer Shulman's wife, disguised as a Catholic, was employed by her as a seamstress. That was our destination. Six kilometers [three and a half miles] still lay ahead of us. We could have taken a trolley but dared not, for fear of encountering some policeman familiar with our faces.

Slowly we resumed our walk. We left the road and took to a path through the fields. In the distance some policemen appeared, walking in our direction. It was too late to retrace our steps. They passed us without incident.

I became feverish. After every few steps we had to stop and rest. Sarah kept up my spirits; for her sake I drove myself onward. I had lost all interest in the matter; I swayed as if drunk. Sarah held my arm to support me and gently pulled me along. If she could have, I am sure she gladly would have carried me in her arms.

The first houses of the outskirts of Siemianowice appeared. I staggered along, oblivious of everybody. There was a haze before my eyes, broken by blurred lines and occasional stares. We entered a courtyard. I washed my face with some cold well water and felt somewhat refreshed. Passing through the town, Sarah walked ahead and I followed, trying to attract as little attention as possible.

We turned into a side street and approached a two-story house. "This is it," Sarah said. I was taken upstairs. As if in a dream I saw a door open before me. I felt someone supporting me in his arms, then I lost consciousness.

When I revived, the stench and rags had been removed from my body and I was lying in a clean bed. My body shook with fever, the pillow swayed beneath my head, and my teeth chattered. Sarah and Nacha were at my side trying to make me comfortable. We were beginning to feel some concern for Halina. She was to have joined us in this house and was long overdue. However, we felt quite confident that no harm had befallen her.

Our German hostess did not know who I was or where I had come from. Sarah told her that I was a friend and that I would stay in her house until I felt a little better.

Late in the evening Sarah and Nacha took me to Michalkowice, a distance of four kilometers [two and a half miles]. We went on foot and encountered no difficulties until we reached the house of a Mr. Kubylec, a Polish farmer in whose home a bunker had been built. He and his wife were expecting my arrival and knew who I was. They met us with great joy and friendliness. But it was out of the question to stay in the room with them very long; through a concealed opening, they led me into the bunker.

The bunker was quite cleverly contrived. It was built under the cellar and was entered through a small window underneath the stairs leading to the cellar. Twenty other people were already hiding in it. They all welcomed us and impatiently asked for news from the outside.

Halina arrived after midnight. She told us the manner of her escape:

> As soon as I left you, I turned my coat inside out and took off my kerchief. A laborer was walking ahead of me. I caught up with him and asked him whether he would like to go for a stroll. He glanced at me briefly and readily agreed. I took his arm and began chattering whatever silly nonsense came into my head. He must have thought that I was a streetwalker. About ten minutes later, I saw two guards running madly in the direction of the camp [adjacent to the prison] and questioning all passersby whether they had seen three fleeing women. They asked us too, and described the three in considerable detail. They seemed terribly upset and I enjoyed their discomfiture. From their frantic questions I realized that you had not been caught. And I was quite safe. My companion escorted me as far as the trolley, where we agreed on a date for tomorrow.

The next morning Halina left for Warsaw happy and warmhearted, and a week later we received a letter from her saying she had crossed the border on foot and completed her journey safely. She was very happy that she was able to help me and to participate in my escape. Afterward we received a letter from Zivia, Yitzhak, and Rivka Moskowitz. They were evidently joyous about my escape as well. The letter was very touching and, incredibly, I received it through M. P.'s mother who lived in the Aryan part of Warsaw.

The Story of a Shelter

Mieczyslaw, the eldest son of the Kubylec family, was wanted by the Gestapo.[1] He was a very young man, not yet twenty, and had worked for the Gestapo in Krakow for a time. Simultaneously he was secretly in contact with the ghetto. Mieczyslaw knew Meyer Shulman and for compensation helped find hiding places at his acquaintances in Bielsk for a few Jews who had escaped the ghetto. However, these people's lives were difficult there, and danger awaited them at every moment. One of his friends unintentionally blurted out the story when drunk, and Mieczyslaw had to flee for his life. He went into hiding but continued to maintain contact with Meyer Shulman and his own family. Shulman urged the elder Kubylec to construct a secret bunker under his house, where his son as well as Jews fleeing from ghettos could hide out. At first Kubylec was reluctant, but he was promised monetary compensation and finally consented.

The work was done at night, with great secrecy and caution. The bunker was finally completed. Though at first it had been agreed that only two or three persons should be harbored in it, eventually as many as twenty found refuge there.

Food presented a serious problem, for it could only be bought on ration cards. It was necessary to obtain forged cards. Arranging for the cards and going out into the open to get them were matters involving the greatest risk. Money to pay for the food as well as for the services of Mr. and Mrs. Kubylec was not too difficult to arrange. At first everyone still had some money or valuables brought from the ghetto; later money was sent by Zivia from Warsaw, through Halina.

Existence in the bunker was very difficult. Overcrowding and lack of fresh air contributed to the general spirit of depression. Then there was the constant fear that, despite all precautions, some of the neighbors might get wind of us. The Kubylec family also lived in constant dread of discovery. Their fears were quite genuine and well-founded, but they also utilized these reasonable fears to extort more and more money from the people they were sheltering.

In addition to those hiding in the Kubylec bunker, a number of persons also hid at the home of their daughter, Banasikowa. Her husband served in the army, and the meager allowance she received was not enough to make ends meet. Now Banasikowa as well as her parents became fairly affluent from the income they derived from the Jews in hiding.

After resting in the Kubylec bunker for a few days, I was transferred one night from Michalkowice to the home of Banasikowa in Little Dombrowka. Chavka[2] and Eliza[3] were also hiding there. Gradually my spirits began to revive after the experiences I had undergone, and I began to take an active interest in events outside.[4] Obviously, none of the neighbors knew that Banasikowa was hiding anybody. The door was always locked; whenever somebody knocked, we would immediately hide in a wardrobe that was in the same room. We did not go out in the street; Banasikowa would bring us everything we needed. Deportations from the neighboring ghettos were still going on, and some of our girls who could pass as Aryans—Sarah,

Chavka, Kasia, and Dorka—still managed to enter the ghetto from time to time and save a few of the survivors. The number increased as days went by, and the problem of hiding them in the Aryan quarters of the towns became more severe. Some way out of the dilemma had to be found soon.

We began to think seriously of Slovakia as a way out. If only we could organize an underground railroad to Slovakia, our rescue activities could be accelerated without increasing the risk. Slovakia was the only neighboring country not completely occupied by the Germans. We knew that Joseph K. was there but we did not have his address.[5] We got in touch with Warsaw, and after a long time we obtained his address through underground channels. So devious were the ways in which the underground worked that his address was finally obtained via The Hague. Mieczyslaw Kubylec was commissioned to establish contact with smugglers who would get people across the border. This was not an easy matter, for we could never be sure of the smugglers' integrity. We well remembered our experiences in Bendzin in the attempt to join the partisans, when the guide led our comrades into a German trap. In the meantime, smugglers were found only by Hanoar Hatzioni. They had been traveling with their smugglers to the Slovakian border for several weeks. However, they kept this secret and there was no way that we could find out from them who these smugglers were. Nevertheless we had to take this risk again; our situation was becoming daily more intolerable and it would not be possible much longer to keep the Gestapo from learning of the growing numbers in hiding.

We Find a Way Out

Though the Kubylec family was receiving lavish compensation for harboring us, they too were becoming more apprehensive daily and constantly urged us to try to make the run to Slovakia. Finally Mieczyslaw arrived one day with the news that he had established contact with smugglers. We were to send a first group, and if their trip was successful, others would follow. From Warsaw Zivia and Itzhak constantly prompted us in the same direction. As for me, they suggested that it might be best to return to Warsaw, and Zivia offered to arrange for my passage. But I was determined to stay with the comrades.

The first group left at the beginning of December. They all went disguised as Poles and carried forged passports and working papers. Early in the morning they left by train from Katowice to Jelesnia, a village on the Slovakian border.

We waited in dread anticipation for the return of the guide. A week later he came back with the report that all had gone well: the group had crossed the border safely. As proof he brought notes from all the members of the first group urging us to follow in their footsteps.

In the meantime, only a small handful of Jews, who could be murdered any day, remained in the camp inside the ghetto. The severities multiplied and it became more difficult to move into the Aryan part of the city; nevertheless, anyone who could escape would do so. People snuck out with great difficulty, like a bird from its almost closed cage.

On the twentieth of December, Eliza and I waited impatiently for Chavka or Sarah to return from the bunker. The second group was being organized and on that day it was to be decided who would be in it. About midnight Chavka knocked on the door. Rather unexpectedly, she told us that I was to prepare to go with the second group, which was to consist of eight people.

I was somewhat reluctant. I had not seen Sarah in a fortnight and did not wish to leave without first discussing the matter with her. She had risked her life to save me from the Myslowice prison; how could I leave now without seeing her first and talking the matter over with her?

Chavka and Eliza tried to persuade me not to tarry. The Gestapo was still searching for me; no time should be lost, and I must leave at once. Sarah would understand. Besides, if everything turned out well, she too would go with an early group. For the present, Sarah and Eliza had to remain behind to look after the children of Kibbutz Atid, who were scattered among German farms. They would leave only when all the children could be taken along.

The discussion lasted all night. Eliza promised that they would try to take the children with the following group. I agreed to go.

We made some hasty preparations, taking hardly anything along besides our clothing. Banasikowa parted from us feelingly, with real motherly compassion, and begged that we remember her after the war. It was difficult to take leave of Eliza. Who could tell what might happen before she had a chance to cross the border?

We Cross the Border

It was half past five on a late December morning. The fields were still enveloped in darkness. Chavka and I walked on, groping through the darkness. I had put on different clothes and changed my coiffeur. But my face was still unchanged; I prayed that no one should recognize me. We went on foot from Little Dombrowka to Michalkowice. On the way we talked in German in subdued voices, trying to attract as little attention as possible.

At the Michalkowice station, we met the other six persons who were to make up our party. Mieczyslaw Kubylec arrived; he was to accompany us part of the way to Bielsk. From Michalkowice we went by train to Katowice. Though it was early in the morning the Katowice station was astir with life. I walked back and forth on the platform with Mieczyslaw, and the rest of our group walked behind us. Mieczyslaw was in a gay mood, joking about what would happen if he and I were to be apprehended, he a fugitive from the Gestapo and I a suspected spy who had escaped from a prison.

Whenever anyone in uniform appeared, we would disappear into the crowd. We had something of a scare when three Gestapo men whom I recognized as being from the Myslowice prison suddenly appeared. I hastily pulled my hat down low and pressed a handkerchief to my face, as if I were suffering from a toothache. It all went off well.

The train trip as far as Bielsk also passed without incident. Even our documents were not examined. The most dangerous part of the trip for me was over: until now Gestapo men and police had been liable to recognize me every step of the way.

At Bielsk the smugglers awaited us. We bought tickets to Jelesnia, which is close to the border and which we reached the same day. From that point on, the trip had to be made on foot. Mieczyslaw parted from us like a relative, as a family member. He reminded us not to forget their kindness. Before leaving, he said that after a while he would also come to Slovakia, but first he wanted to get the rest of the Jews out of there. He warned the smugglers to look after us as if we were their nearest and dearest.

We wrote brief notes to those left behind, telling of our safe arrival at the border, and gave them to the returning Mieczyslaw. We waited until night, resting a little at the home of one of our guides.

Stealthily we left the village. There were twelve of us altogether; eight in our group, two guides, and the two smugglers. High, snow-covered mountains could be seen far away. The boundary between the two countries ran through these mountains. But first we had to cross a long stretch of flat ground. On the level ground the snow was not too deep. It was a bright night and we could see for a considerable distance.

We walked for some time before we reached the foothills. Now the going became more difficult. The snow got deeper, turning into drifts. We formed a single file, the stronger ones gradually working up to the head of the line while the weaker ones lagged behind. In spots the wind had blown away the snow, but that only made things worse for then the ground was covered with ice and very slippery.

The guides seemed to be familiar with the path. One of them walked some distance in front as scout. Every now and then he would signal with his hands and we would stop. A strong wind arose, which was in our favor since its whistling among the crags covered the sound of our footsteps. We reached the top of the mountain, 6,400 feet high. Once in a while we rested, lying down on the snow as if on soft feathers.

Now the mountains were partly covered with forest and new terrors arose.

Each sound, each moving branch frightened us and loomed in our imagination as frontier patrols. We would then drop to the ground until we were reassured, or if there really were patrols, until they vanished among the trees. Despite the cold our bodies were covered with perspiration, and as the hours drew by some of us began slipping at each step. We got some comfort from little Monish of Kibbutz Atid.[6] Small as he was, the trip proved to be no hardship for him. He walked lightly at the head of the line poking fun at the stragglers.

I was still very weak from my experiences during the preceding weeks and required assistance. The cold did not bother me, though I was coatless, but I felt exhaustion overpower me. Breathing became more difficult. The familiar apathy that goes with exhaustion began to manifest itself. I kept thinking of my escape from Myslowice. If I could do it then, I must exert all my powers and go on now.

We approached some buildings of the border patrol and cautiously gave them a wide berth. We began to descend. We were in Slovakia. A bonfire blazed in the distance; we stopped to rest in the forest and also lit a fire. This was the designated spot where the Slovakian guides would take over our group and lead us to our destination. Now that we had stopped, we were afflicted by the intense cold. Our clothes and shoes were damp, and we tried to dry them by the fire as well as we could. Steps were heard among the trees.

The Slovakian guides arrived and brought with them some wine to refresh us.

After resting for an hour, we parted from our Polish guides and proceeded. More mountains, hills, valleys, and forests. Then we approached a little village and were greeted by the barking of dogs. Our guides led us into a stable. Utterly exhausted, we dropped on the straw. A small kerosene lamp lit the stable. Cattle and chickens were peacefully sleeping. The ammoniac stench was suffocating, but we dared not leave the stable. Besides, it was warm inside. Our exhaustion got the best of us and we all fell asleep.

At noon the mistress of the house brought us some food. It was Sunday and she was dressed in colorful Slovakian attire. She warned us to remain quiet; the villagers were going to church and we must not betray our presence.

We spent the day in the stable. The sense of relief at having crossed the border successfully was dimmed by fears of the future. It was now the end of 1943, and each of us silently recalled the loved ones lost during that year. Now that we were on the threshold of safety, the full awareness of our losses assailed us in all its sharpness.

At night a sleigh arrived and took us to another village farther away from the border. Here we were quartered in a house and spent the day waiting for the next lap of our journey, which was to be made by car. Our host treated us very kindly, showing great sympathy for our misfortunes.

The car came in the evening exactly on time. It waited for us on the outskirts of the village. We were going to a town called Miklas,[7] the driver informed us. There was a Jewish community in that town, and we would be taken care of. We were all amazed at the efficiency with which every step of the trip had been planned. Each detail had been attended to.

We entered Miklas and stopped in front of what been the Jewish community offices. Max F. waited for us. The other members of the first group had already left for Hungary. Here we were advised that Joseph K. was already in Hungary.

There might be an opportunity for legal emigration from Hungary to Palestine, we were told. We were overjoyed. We still talked in whispers, as we used to do in the bunker. We were just like birds liberated from a cage. We spread our wings as only those who are free can do. The dread of immediate pursuit and death had left us. We felt like new people.

A Short Stay in Slovakia

The Slovakian Jews were glad to see us but would not take us into their homes. The dread of the police was upon them. We met many others who had escaped from Poland. Some were registered with the police, others had no documents at all. But with the aid of money it was possible to arrange such matters.

We remained in Miklas for a few days before departing for the Hungarian border, awaiting the next group from our bunker. On the second day we met B.,[8] a member of Hashomer Hatzair in Slovakia, who was very active in the rescue endeavor. He told us a little about the Slovakian Jews. Most of them had been deported to Poland. Out of approximately sixty thousand Jews in Slovakia, only ten thousand remained, and these too were uncertain of their future. They were compelled to wear the Star of David on their clothes. Most of those who were allowed to remain were so far relatively unmolested—either because they paid lavish bribes or embraced Christianity.

Each day new refugees arrived. Some of these were brought in by the border patrols. There were men and women, children and old people. Hardly any of them had surviving relatives. Many wished to live only in the hope of seeing vengeance wreaked on Germany. The ones arriving from Krakow related that there was still a ghetto there, but not a day passed without hundreds of Jews being killed. For every Jew who escaped the ghetto, twenty were put to death. Jews seized in the Aryan section of the city were publicly shot. Reports of small ghettos still existing in other Polish cities reached us from the fugitives arriving daily.

There was also a Jewish camp at Majdanek to which people from all over Poland were brought and put to arduous and punishing work. Every day they expected to be exterminated. There were still small camps within the ghettos of Radom, Lublin, and Lodz. It appeared that a few thousand Jews were working in military plants in Skarzysko-Kamienna. They lived there in unbearable conditions, working like horses and receiving meager rations. They fell like flies at the end of autumn from exhaustion and hunger. We learned from people in refugee housing that thousands of Jews were living in each of the big cities, hiding in cellars to that very day.

A few days later another group of eight arrived from our bunker. We began making arrangements to leave for the Hungarian border. Police had been bribed to accompany our convoy to it. Those of us joining the convoy declared that we were Hungarian nationals and that, this being the case, the police needed to accompany us to the border.[9]

News about Paul Banasik's Death in the Bunker

The convoy got underway. Chajka Klinger[10] and I remained behind; we were awaiting the arrival of other groups. Another group arrived after a week.

The people were very terrified because of what had recently taken place at the Kubylec bunker.

Banasikowa's husband, Paul Banasik (the Kubylecs' son-in-law), had taken leave from the army to spend the holiday at home, and the visitor and his wife had gone to visit the Kubylecs. Paul always pretended to be unaware that his mother-in-law was sheltering Jews in her house.

During the visit, Meyer Shulman happened to walk past the room. Banasik was already slightly tipsy. He approached Meyer and while talking to him let slip that he knew the location of the bunker where the Jews were hiding. Meyer was shocked to hear this. Banasik went on to say that there was nothing to be afraid of; he would never do the Jews any harm; "live and let live" while they were there. He then went to the camouflaged entrance and entered the bunker. Apparently someone had shown him the exact location and how to get inside since, despite the good camouflage, he knew how to open the door easily. It was possible to conclude from the conversation that he had received all that information from Roman, Mieczyslaw Kubylec's friend. This man knew all the secrets; he had helped many of those who had left the ghetto.

Banasik went down into the bunker; he wanted to see for himself how it was built and what it looked like from the inside. He was so drunk that he could hardly stand on his own two legs. Meyer followed him down. There were only four or five people in the bunker; the others had already left for Slovakia. There were a number of people in Novak's house in Bendzin.

Meyer took out his gun, which he had made himself, and gave it to Banasik to look at. (Those who tell this story say they don't really know why he did that.) Banasik looked the gun over with great curiosity. Out of the blue, there was a disaster. Without thinking, he pressed the trigger and the gun went off. Banasik fell to the ground; the bullets had wounded him. He was immediately removed from the bunker. He was lucid despite the pain. Meyer asked him not to reveal the secret of the bunker; Banasik replied that he knew what to tell the police when they came.

The incident was reported to the nearest Police Guard. When the police arrived, Banasik gave his statement. He showed the gun with which he had shot himself and said that he had originally taken it from some partisans. Lately, while in the army, he had been engaged in discovering partisan bands. He was about to clean the gun, but apparently hadn't known how to handle it and the gun had gone off. The police wrote down his statement; the rescue wagon that had been called in from Katowice transferred the wounded patient to the hospital (the whole time Banasik told the doctors that he wanted to get better, since he had to return to the army).

However, all the doctors' efforts were in vain. After two days of unendurable suffering, Banasik passed away. Even after the disaster, the Kubylecs didn't dare to turn the comrades out of the bunker.

Once the route to Slovakia had been opened, the comrades immediately left the bunker; they were worried that their hiding place would eventually be discovered. Meyer Shulman was left alone in the bunker. There were a few dozen Jews still in the ghetto who were expected to be expelled in January.

One of the comrades, who had recently arrived, remembered that in Zivia's last letter, she had written that she was sending someone special to bring me to Warsaw. Zivia still wasn't aware that I was already in Slovakia.

Before we could leave, another incident occurred. The house in which we stayed was raided and we were all placed under arrest. The Slovakian police threatened to deport us to Germany, but it was evident that the arrest as well as the threat were merely another method of extortion. We communicated with our contacts outside, and efforts were at once begun to get us out of the prison and the country.

One day we learned that Chajka Klinger and I were scheduled to leave for Palestine as soon as we reached Hungary. Our joy was boundless. Our dreams of so many years were going to be fulfilled. My excitement was so great that I could not fall asleep even for a moment the whole night. I at once dispatched a letter to Poland, informing Sarah and Eliza that there were possibilities of going to Palestine from Hungary and that they should come, together with the children, as soon as possible. But on the day we were to leave for Hungary we received a report from one of the runners that it would be impossible to bring them, since the mountain passes were blocked by snow.

The Road to Hungary: On the Verge of Immigration

Early in January Chajka Klinger, B., and I left Mikulas for Prešov.[11] We preceded the others because we had to arrive at a definite time to be included in the group departing for Palestine. Our photographs had already been sent to Hungary. Police who had been bribed accompanied our convoy to the border. In Prešov arrangements were made by comrades from Hashomer Hatzair for our crossing the border. The engineer and the fireman of the train were bribed to take a few of us in the cab of the engine, which was seldom searched at the border; many had previously crossed in this manner. We, too, made the crossing safely near Košice. We left the engine cab, on the other side of the border, under the cover of heavy steam from the engine. The engineer had bought tickets to Budapest for us. We sat in the car avoiding conversation but we felt reassured. Hungarians resemble Jews in appearance, and there seemed to be little danger of being singled out.

We reached Budapest. Here the Jews wore no distinctive armbands, but hardly any of them spoke Yiddish. On the train there was no check of documents; evidently nobody suspected where we came from. At the station all the passengers' baggage was examined. We hurried off to the address we had been given. It was fortunate that Moshe, who spoke Hungarian fluently, was with us.

By trolley we reached the Palestine Bureau. There many people were mingling about speaking all languages—Slovakian, German, Hungarian, Polish, Yiddish. We encountered many familiar faces. We had not succeeded to forward our photographs and it seemed there would be some delay about our passports. But we were promised that the matter would be attended to as soon as possible.

The place was humming like a country fair. Everyone wanted to be first to leave, everyone pressed his case, pointing out the special circumstances that made it imperative for him to leave soon. Indeed, the circumstances of all were pressing, but only a small number could be taken care of. Those coming from Poland, who had undergone the worst ordeals, were given the highest priority.

We waited impatiently for the day of departure, which was constantly postponed.

Then the passports were ready, but the Turkish visas had not yet been obtained. The uncertainty was depressing, uncertainty and fear that something might happen at the last moment to cancel the trip. Perhaps all our efforts of escaping and crossing the various borders had been in vain. The situation in Hungary was still tolerable but there were ill omens for the future: the thunderbolt might strike any day. Even during our short stay in Hungary, we had to have some certificate in hand.

Occasionally identification papers were checked in the streets. Those who had no satisfactory documents were arrested and held until their status was clarified. I, as well as the others in our group, had registered at the Polish consulate as refugees from Poland. I received twenty-four pengö,[12] food and lodging allowance for a few days, and a temporary certificate, according to which I could walk legally in the city. The Polish official working in the consulate questioned us at length on whether we belonged to the PPR; we had to convince him that we were adherents of Sikorski. "Is the lady really a Catholic?" one of the officials asked me. I assured him that I was indeed a Catholic. He felt relieved. "Thank God," he said. "Until now only Jews pretending to be Poles came to us." I pretended surprised indignation: "What? Jews pretending to be Poles?" "Much to our regret, this is so," he admitted sadly.

At the consulate I was told to report a few days later with some passport photographs. They would then provide me with documents that would permit me to stay at a village where Polish refugees lived in considerable comfort.

Returning to my comrades, I learned that all Jews arriving from Poland registered with the consulate as Gentile Poles. In most cases they did not fool the officials and were given only a certificate of identification to be used for the police. For this service the Polish consulate was well paid by the Joint Distribution Committee.

I did not return to the consulate. Wouldn't I be leaving in a few days in any case?

But the few days dragged out into a monthlong wait. Meanwhile there were daily debates at the Palestine Bureau, with everyone trying to obtain a larger number of visas for members of their own group. Zvi G. and Elia-Yeshaya suggested the name "Union" for our group (which included the Dror, Maccabi, Hashomer Hatzair, and Habonim movements). Through W.[13] we were in constant contact with Turkey and were cheered by the reports reaching us from Palestine. This was the final, ultimate dream of our lives, the most fervent dream of each of us. There we would be received with open arms, like a mother who receives her children. Palestine lived in our dreams and excited imaginations. We had never seen it, yet it seemed so warmly familiar to us. Night and day we thought of it, our impatience growing with each succeeding hour. There we would find the cure for our wounds, there we would find peace and solace, there we would be rid of the fear that had filled our lives until now with a feeling that the earth was breaking under our feet and that we were going down the drain. Occasionally a vague shadow of a doubt would cross our minds: Would they in Palestine, who had not undergone our tribulations and had not seen all these horrors, understand us? Would we ever become accustomed to a simple everyday life after what we had lived through?

We Go to Palestine

The longed-for day finally arrived. One group had set out a few days earlier. I was leaving in three days. Everyone envied me, but my heart was sad. The memory of the millions who had been exterminated, the memory of comrades who had devoted their lives to the Land of Israel and who had dreamed the same dream but had not lived to see its realization, haunted me with redoubled force on this day. Nor did I imagine how I could bring to the Land of Israel the terrible news I had.

We came to the station. The platform was black with people. Most of those who were going had become acquainted only a few days before, yet we felt we knew each other well, so much akin were we in spirit and in common experiences. If no political change was forthcoming, most of these people would surely follow us.

On the adjoining track stood a German troop train. Evidently the troops knew we were Jews and looked at us malevolently; some jeered. They would gladly have attacked us if they could have. We stared at them, and the fury of hatred that welled up in our hearts was almost intolerable. I too, if I could have, would have exterminated them.

There was a strong impulse to go over and to tease them: "See, we have fled from the Gestapo and are going to Palestine."

Weeping, laughter, noisy exclamations filled the air as the train was about to depart. "Do not forget us here" was heard on all sides from those remaining behind. They were beseeching us to knock on all the doors: that each one of us should hasten, wherever he was and whenever he could, to help the small handful of people still alive. As the train started moving, there was one picture I could not erase from before my eyes: the picture of the mass of deported Jews being thrown into the railway cars that were to take them to their death. A shiver was running up and down my spine. At last the platform and the crowd were out of sight. For a long time I still bore the impression of those last moments. I wanted to rejoice so much, but my heart was heavy and nothing pleased me. I kept thinking of Sarah, Eliza, and the children who remained in Poland. I felt stunned. The pleasant weather did not appeal to my heart, not even the nice scenery.

There were more than ten persons in our group. Most of them had photographs in their passports. Some traveled with assumed surnames. Each married couple took along some children whose parents had been killed or had remained behind in Hungary The children were happy and proudly repeated the name "Eretz Israel."

The following night we arrived at the border and our baggage was examined. We were now in Romanian territory. There was a noticeable difference in the people. The conductors tried every trick to swindle us; for money it was possible to obtain almost anything from them. When the train became overcrowded, it was possible, for a fee, to arrange for extra cars. In Romania we found out that all the people in the Palestine Bureau had been arrested there.

We crossed the Bulgarian border without incident and stopped overnight at the first station within the country. Next to this border we were joined by a few people from Romania. Here we could make ourselves understood by speaking Polish or Slovakian. We were impressed by the Bulgarians, who were friendly, serious, and did not try to swindle everyone. The Bulgarian soldiers and civilians alike showed us much consideration and offered their assistance whenever it was needed. At one point the track was blocked by a landslide and we were forced to walk about a kilometer to the nearest station. Everyone showed great courtesy to all the passengers. The Bulgarians—military men, railway workers, and citizens—all helped us willingly.

At the Stara-Zagora station we lingered again. Here, for some reason, a German officer became interested in us, trying to help us find rooms in a hostel. I suppose he did not know we were Jews. In the evening he came to the hostel to raise a glass for his enjoyment and to talk with the men among us. We were accompanied by two German gendarmes up until we reached the Turkish border.

We crossed into Turkey. Europe was behind us. A heavy weight of fear was lifted from us.

In Istanbul we were met by W. and Menachem B.[14] They did not know themselves to what extent it would bring them joy to see us. W. was impatient and asked a lot of questions about the people he knew or had heard of. W. and B. put us up in a hotel and spent whatever leisure time they had with us, though that was little enough. W. told us about how happy he had been when he bathed little Monish, who had arrived here with the first group. However, he did not have much free time for conversations with us; he was always busy and there was always work to be done. His aim was to reach out to the Jews who remained in various countries and to arrange passage for other groups. When W. talked with us about people who had been killed, he cried like a child.

With amazement we saw the Jews of Istanbul walking about freely without distinctive armbands, without fear. We were surprised. We had forgotten that such things were possible.

At the end of a week, W. and B. accompanied us by boat to the railway station on the other side of the Bosporus. We boarded a train for Palestine via Syria.

We arrived in Haifa on the sixth of March, 1944. Our wanderings were finally at an end. But the burden of our experiences weighed heavily upon us, and the memory of those who had perished was in our minds and gave us no peace. We felt somehow smaller and weaker than the people about us, as though we had less right to live than they.

Figure 1. Renia Kukielka, after her escape from Poland to Palestine, c. 1944–45. *Source*: Courtesy of the Ghetto Fighters' House Museum (Beit Lohamei Hagetaot), Israel/Photo Archive.

Figure 2. Renia's group that escaped from Poland: in Budapest, Hungary, February 1944. Left to right—sitting: Chavka Lenchner, Monia (Monish/Moshe) Hofenberg, Renia Kukielka; standing: Max Fisher, Yitzhak Ben-Nun, (unknown), Zvi Goldfarb. Because the Germans were still searching for Renia after her escape from a Gestapo prison in Poland, the Hungarian Zionist Youth movement gave her a false document with a photo of a Hungarian woman. The woman had black hair and glasses, so they dyed Renia's hair black and she wore glasses all along her route to Turkey. *Source*: Courtesy of Yifat Barkan-Pinto, Israel/private archive.

Figure 3. A street in Bendzin, Poland, during the war. The Jews were forced to wear Star of David armbands. *Source*: United States Holocaust Memorial Museum, courtesy of Yad Vashem Photo and Film Archives.

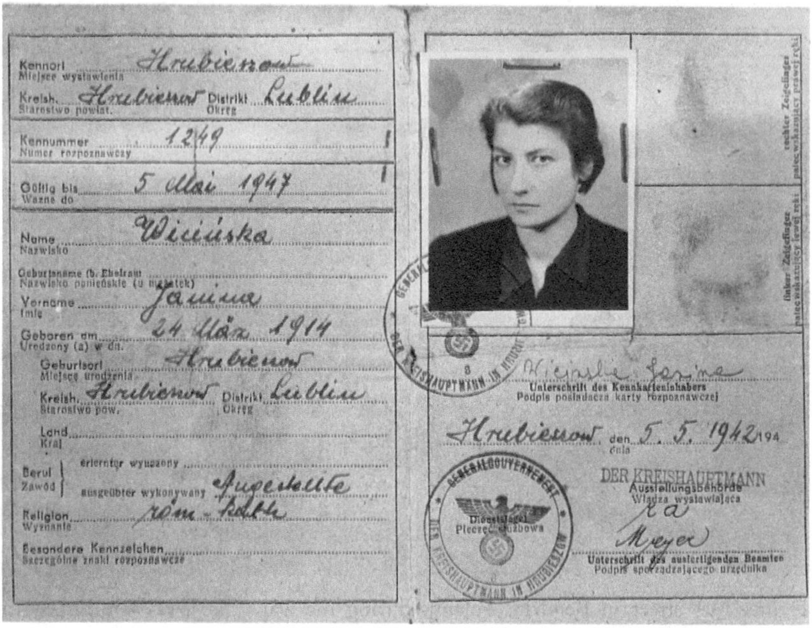

Kennort Hrubieszow
Miejsce wystawienia
Kreish. Hrubieszow Distrikt Lublin
Starostwo powiat. Okręg
Kennummer 1249
Numer rozpoznawczy
Gültig bis 5 Mai 1947
Ważne do
Name Wicińska
Nazwisko
Geburtsname (b. Ehefrau)
Nazwisko panieńskie (u mężatek)
Vorname Janina
Imię
Geboren am 24 März 1914
Urodzony (a) w dn.
Geburtsort Hrubieszow
Miejsce urodzenia
Kreish. Hrubieszow Distrikt Lublin
Starostwo pow. Okręg
Land
Kraj
Beruf erlernter wyuczony
Zawód ausgeübter wykonywany Angestellte
Religion röm.-kath.
Wyznanie
Besondere Kennzeichen
Szczególne znaki rozpoznawcze
rechter Zeigefinger
palec wskazujący prawej ręki
linker Zeigefinger
palec wskazujący lewej ręki
Wicinska Janina
Unterschrift des Kennkarteninhabers
Podpis posiadacza karty rozpoznawczej
Hrubieszow den 5. 5. 1942 194
dnia
DER KREISHAUPTMANN
Ausstellungsbehörde
Władza wystawiająca
i.a.
Meyer
Unterschrift des ausfertigenden Beamten
Podpis sporządzającego urzędnika
GENERALGOUVERNEMENT
Dienstsiegel
Pieczęć służbowa
DER KREISHAUPTMANN IN HRUBIESZOW

Figure 4. Zivia Lubetkin's false papers during WWII in Poland. Lubetkin was one of the founders of the Hechalutz Dror youth movement; she participated in the founding of the Jewish Combat Organization (ZOB) in the Warsaw Ghetto and in the Warsaw Ghetto Uprising. *Source*: United States Holocaust Memorial Museum, courtesy of the Ghetto Fighters' House Museum.

Figure 5. Frumka Plotnicka, c. 1939, was an exemplary member of Hechalutz Dror. She traveled throughout occupied Poland to gather together dispersed members of the youth movement. Frumka organized the defense activities of the Zionist youth-movement groups in Bendzin and Sosnowiec. She was killed defending the bunker in Bendzin on August 3, 1943, aged twenty-nine. *Source*: Courtesy of the Ghetto Fighters' House Museum, Israel/Photo Archive.

Figure 6. Baruch Gaftek, c. 1939, a founder of the Dror Zionist youth movement, one of the founders of the Zionist youth underground in Bendzin, and was also the commander of the Jewish Combat Organization there. He was killed in defense of the bunker in Bendzin Ghetto on August 3, 1943, aged thirty. *Source*: Courtesy of the Ghetto Fighters' House Museum, Israel/Photo Archive.

Figure 7. Zvi Brandes, c. 1939, was a prominent activist in the Hashomer Hatzair Zionist youth movement in Poland; organized defense activities in the Zaglembie region of Poland; member of the Jewish Combat Organization in Bendzin; participated in the defense of the bunkers and was killed at the beginning of August 1943, aged twenty-six. *Source*: Courtesy of the Ghetto Fighters' House Museum, Israel/Photo Archive.

Figure 8. Sarah Kukielka, c. 1943; Renia's older sister, active in Hechalutz Dror as a courier; killed in January 1944, aged twenty-nine. *Source*: Courtesy of the Ghetto Fighters' House Museum, Israel/Photo Archive.

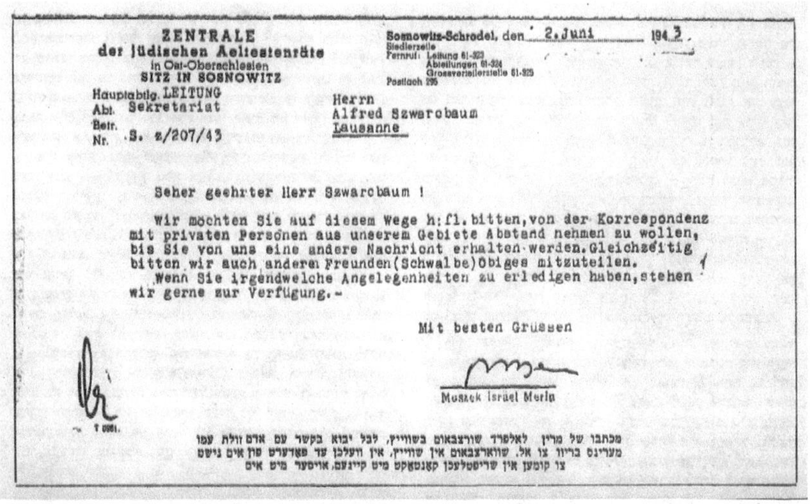

ZENTRALE
der jüdischen Aeltestenräte
in Ost-Oberschlesien
SITZ IN SOSNOWITZ

Sosnowitz-Schrodel, den 2. Juni 1943.
Siedlerzelle
Fernruf: Leitung 61-323
Abteilungen 61-324
Grossverteilerstelle 61-325
Postfach 295

Hauptabtlg. LEITUNG
Abt. Sekretariat
Betr.
Nr. .S. z/207/43

Herrn
Alfred Szwarcbaum
Lausanne

Seher geehrter Herr Szwarcbaum !

Wir möchten Sie auf diesem Wege h: fl. bitten, von der Korrespondenz mit privaten Personen aus unserem Gebiete Abstand nehmen zu wollen, bis Sie von uns eine andere Nachricht erhalten werden. Gleichzeitig bitten wir auch anderen Freunden (Schwalbe) Obiges mitzuteilen.

Wenn Sie irgendwelche Angelegenheiten zu erledigen haben, stehen wir gerne zur Verfügung. -

Mit besten Grussen

Moszek Israel Merin

מכתבו של מרין לאלפרד שורצבאום בשוייץ, לבל יבוא בקשר עם אדם זולת עמו
מערינס בריוו צו אל. שווארצבאום אין שווייץ, אין וועלכן ער פאדערט פון אים נישט
צו קומען אין שריפטלעכן קאנטאקט מיט קיינעם, אויסער מיט אים

Figure 9. Letter from Moshe (Moszek) Merin, chairman of the Judenrat (Jewish Council) in Eastern Upper Silesia, Poland. Zionist youth-group members opposed Merin's policies and branded him a collaborator. The letter (in German) is to Alfred (Alf) Schwarzbaum, a Jewish merchant from Bendzin, Poland, who fled to Switzerland after the German occupation. In Switzerland he set up a relief enterprise that provided aid and relief to Jews in Poland by sending out food, papers and passports, and money. He sent hundreds of parcels to German-occupied areas via Portugal, Sweden, and Turkey. The letter (translated from German) reads as follows:

> June 2, 1943
>
> Deeply respected Mr. Schwarzbaum!
> We would therefore like to ask you to refrain from correspondence with individuals in our area until you receive a new message.
> At the same time, we ask you to tell this to your other friends (acquaintances). If you have any other questions, we will be happy to help you.
>
> Best wishes,
> Moszek Israel Merin

Source: Courtesy of United States Holocaust Memorial Museum, courtesy of Arnold Shay (Abram Szyjewicz).

Figure 10. A postwar Zionist collective, in Poland, c. 1945: Zivia Lubetkin (in the second row, center) and Yitzhak Zukerman (first row, center), both from Hechalutz Dror. The collective consisted of different Zionist parties and Zionist youth movements. Zionist activities in the liberated regions of Poland began as early as the end of 1944. Close to two hundred Zionist collectives were formed in Poland in 1945 and 1946. *Source*: Courtesy of United States Holocaust Memorial Museum, courtesy of Ghetto Fighters' House Museum.

Figure 11. Renia Kukielka (on the left) in Palestine, c. 1944–45. *Source*: Courtesy of Yifat Barkan-Pinto, Israel/private archive.

Figure 12. Renia Kukielka (second from right); Chavka Lenchner (center); Joseph Kornianski (first on the left) in Kibbutz Dafna, Palestine, c. 1944. *Source*: Courtesy of Yifat Barkan-Pinto, Israel/private archive.

Figure 13. Title page of Renia Kukielka's 1944 Hebrew memoir *Bindudim Uvamachteret: 1939–1943 B'Polin,* which translates to "While Wandering and in the Underground: 1939–1943 in Poland," published by Hakibbutz Hameuchad Ein Harod, Palestine. *Source*: Courtesy of Asya Kovnat, Canada/private archive.

Figure 14. Yitzhak Zuckerman, one of the leaders of the Warsaw Ghetto Uprising, testifying at the trial of leading Nazi criminal Adolf Eichmann for his role in the genocide of European Jewry, Israel, 1961. Zuckerman stated: "We [the youth movements] deliberately chose to revolt. And not only in Warsaw [but also in other ghettos] . . . in order to rescue what could be saved: if not life itself, at least our honor." *Source*: Courtesy of the Ghetto Fighters' House Museum, Israel/the Photo Archive.

Figure 15. Zivia Lubetkin testifying at the trial of one of the principal organizers of the Holocaust, leading Nazi criminal Adolf Eichmann, in Israel, 1961. *Source*: Courtesy of United States Holocaust Memorial Museum, courtesy of the Israel Government Press Office.

Figure 16. Renia with her husband, Akiva Hershkovitz, c. 1985–90, Israel. *Source*: Courtesy of Merav Waldman, Israel, private archive.

Figure 17. Renia Kukielka-Hershkovitz with her brother, Aaron Kleiman, 2008, Israel. *Source*: Courtesy of Merav Waldman, Israel/private archive.

Figure 18. Renia with her children and grandchildren at granddaughter Michal's wedding, 2008, Israel. Left to right—standing: Renia's daughter, Leah Waldman; Renia Kukielka-Hershkovitz; granddaughter, Michal Waldman-Gino; Tzahi Gino (Michal's husband); granddaughter, Tal Harel; Renia's son, Jacob (Koby) Harel; Ilana Harel (Jacob's wife). First row: granddaughter, Merav Waldman, a lawyer, who assisted Renia with this publication; grandson, Roie Waldman; grandson, Liran Harel. *Source*: Courtesy of Merav Waldman, Israel/private archive.

Figure 19. Renia Kukielka with Dr. Asya Kovnat, her literary agent, in Renia's apartment, Haifa, Israel, May 2009. *Source*: Courtesy of Asya Kovnat, Canada/private archive.

Afterword: Life after Escape

ASYA KOVNAT, WITH PAULINA EZER

In his autobiographical novel *Ha-Sefer Ha-Meshugah* (The Crazy Book), Haim Gouri, a famous Israeli poet laureate, writes about meeting Renia Kukielka soon after her arrival in British Mandate Palestine in March 1944.[1] At the time Gouri was one of the young members of the Palmach, a Jewish paramilitary force. One night that spring or summer, as was the custom in the Palmach, Gouri gathered around the bonfire with his comrades and their famous commander Yitzhak Sadeh, whom they called "the Old Man." Also present at this informal meeting were two important guests whom Sadeh had invited to speak.

The bonfire began with everyone singing favorite tunes. Beside the Old Man sat the strangers, their faces illuminated in the firelight. Their appearance alone gave Gouri the impression they had come from far away.

Later on, the Old Man announced that it was the turn of one of the newcomers, Joseph, to speak.

They waited.

"Friends," Joseph finally began slowly, speaking in very refined, foreign-accented Hebrew, "I would like to tell you. I would like . . ."

A terrible silence followed, writes Gouri, during which the woman, sitting next to Joseph, "stared at the bare, red soil, taking refuge in the Old Man's shadow, invisible." Eventually Joseph began again. As they listened to his story, those present became "something they were not." They emerged unable to recognize themselves or each other.

And when the man finished his story after years, after cities, after rivers, after fire, after trains, the silence lasted longer than expected, and only the flames were heard, and only the dogs and the frogs in the nearby orchard could be heard. . . .

The "Old Man's" face appeared to be on loan from someone else.

One of the young Palmach members left his seat to feed the fire. Several others rushed up to help him, unable to bear the silence. The rest remained still as stone.

Someone asked the young woman to tell them what she had to say. "I can't," she whispered apologetically. They pleaded with her, but she remained silent. One man, who had known her abroad many years before, when they were children, recalled that she had been a good singer. He asked whether she could sing something.

Her reluctance was palpable. When she finally gave in, she began singing a Yiddish tune, "a song left over from the world that was no more," writes Gouri. But after a line or two she began to cry, like a child, in the arms of the Old Man.

The young woman was Renia Kukielka, and the other visitor was Joseph Kornianski, whom Renia refers to in her memoir as Joseph K.[2] Many years later, Renia Kukielka's and Haim Gouri's paths would cross in a significant way again, as will be related below.

Renia's memoir ends with her arriving in Haifa on March 6, 1944, with a group of over ten Jews who had miraculously escaped Nazi-occupied Poland, where the war was still raging. They were among the first Holocaust survivors to reach the safe shores of the Land of Israel. Renia was the second representative (after Joseph Kornianski) of the surviving Polish underground fighters of the Hechalutz Dror (Freedom Pioneers) Zionist youth organization[3] to arrive in the Land of Israel. This Zionist youth organization helped her to flee Poland because the Germans were hunting for her there after she escaped the Gestapo prison. The same organization chose Renia to be their representative, tasked with informing the Jews in the Land of Israel about the tragic fate of Polish Jews during the war and about the fate of Hechalutz Dror in particular. Renia was just nineteen years old at that time.[4]

Soon after her arrival Renia settled in Kibbutz Dafna, in the northern part of modern-day Israel, where she lived for five years. She was immediately invited to many kibbutzim and other Jewish communities to recount her experiences during the war and to inform them about the gas chambers, the Jewish uprisings, and, in general, the tragic mass annihilation of the Polish Jews at the hands of the Nazis. (Three million Jews—about 90 percent of the Polish Jewish population—were murdered in Poland by the end of the war.) This new testimony was shocking and incomprehensible to her audience, many of whom could not imagine the extent of German brutality and could not bear to hear about it. Other survivors and Renia's comrades in arms attested to similar experiences.[5] Renia's premonition at the end of her book—"Would they in Palestine, who had not undergone our tribulations and had not seen all these horrors, understand us?"—was proving to be well-founded.[6]

The Hechalutz Dror movement in Poland was aligned with Hakibbutz Hameuchad (the United Kibbutz Movement). The headquarters of this organization was located in the Land of Israel. A month after Renia's arrival, the secretariat of Hakibbutz Hameuchad, recognizing the importance of recording and publicizing news about the death camps and other German atrocities, tried to convince her to write down an account of what had happened to her during the war: "They asked me to agree to write a book that would be translated into Hebrew. They said that the book would be published because nobody had written about the war yet and they wanted to publicize this book urgently. They told me to write without delay because otherwise I would forget."

Although at first Renia was reluctant to relive the horrors she had so recently endured, she eventually agreed. However, while she was writing her account in April and May 1944, the members of Kibbutz Dafna noticed her exhaustion from her traumatic experiences during the war, and they sent her to a sanatorium to rest. "I rested for two, three weeks," Renia told me, "and then I returned to Dafna, and I continued and finished the book. I wrote it in an authentic way, without philosophy."

Kibbutz Dafna gave Renia a room in which to write. Renia recounted that she cried so much while writing that many pages became illegible from her tears and had to be thrown out. She wrote in Polish because she, like many Jewish girls in prewar Poland, had been educated predominantly in a Polish public school and, therefore, had an excellent knowledge of the Polish language. (She knew Yiddish from home and minimal Hebrew from Hebrew grammar school.)

Renia told me that she finished writing sometime in the summer of 1944, after only a few months. She gave her manuscript to the editors of Hakibbutz Hameuchad's publishing house and told them that she wanted nothing more to do with her memoir and that they should continue the publication process without her. "I didn't even know that the publishing house should have paid me," Renia explained many years later. "But in any case, did I write for money? I wrote for the world to know."

Renia never participated in any negotiations with the original publisher. Instead they were handled by the Hakibbutz Hameuchad publishing house's administration, which hired H. Sh. Ben-Avram, who seems to have been one of the main translators of the time, to translate the memoir into Hebrew, and his name was mentioned at the end of the book. Renia told me that, years later, when she knew Hebrew well, she read the Hebrew translation of her original Polish manuscript and found it faithful and that her original Polish manuscript had not been tampered with. She recounted repeatedly that "it was written that it was the first book about the war. At that time no books had been published at all in Mandate Palestine [about the war and Holocaust]."

The only decision that Renia took part in after she finished writing concerned the title of her memoir. The Hebrew title of her book, *Bindudim Uvamachteret: 1939–1943 B'Polin*, translates to *While Wandering and in the Underground: 1939–1943 in Poland.*

A large portion of the book describes her wanderings and travels in wartime Poland: trying for three years to escape from the German onslaught on the Jews and later, serving for almost a year as a courier between ghettos for the Zionist-youth-movement underground cell in Bendzin[7] that they called Kibbutz Bendzin.[8] Renia explained to me:

> The title meant to survive and to fight. "Wandering" because I really wandered all the time, I hid in the cornfields, and I drank dew and I ate seeds . . . I did everything in order to survive. And "in the underground" because I worked for a secret underground organization, I would deliver weapons, forged documents and American dollars, and I traveled to Warsaw to buy weapons. And in that way I was caught. It is an individual fight for the good of all—and for the Jewish people. To be active, to fight [the Nazis] and not just give ourselves up like someone taken to slaughter. There was constant fighting and people fought until they couldn't withstand it.

While the title *Escape from the Pit* did not appear until the first English edition in 1947, for simplicity I refer to Renia's book by this title throughout this text.

Because Renia wrote about her experiences so soon after her escape from war-torn Poland, she was able to describe her four-year ordeal in minute detail, showing the reader the different stages of the Nazis' "Final Solution" for the genocide of Jews. Her account is an immediate testimony of the war from within Poland—in the communities of southwestern Poland, which had been annexed by Nazi Germany, and in the General Government ruled by a German-run administration in Krakow.[9] Her account is unique because she describes life and activities outside of the ghettos and concentration camps. Even though she was an inexperienced writer, it is a balanced narrative expressed in a matter-of-fact manner, which adds to its credibility. While it is a personal story, her account is both panoramic and accurate.[10] Renia described the effects of this terrible war on different communities and organizations that she had been part of, giving her own analysis and important insights. At the same time, she did not shy away from criticizing the conduct of Poles and Jews.

Renia's account appears to be the first one to mention Jewish slave labor in Nazi labor camps and workshops.[11] Renia was also the first to describe in detail the escape route from Poland to Palestine via Slovakia, Hungary, Romania, Bulgaria, and Turkey.[12] Renia's is also the earliest description of the inner workings of the two high-security Gestapo prisons where, remarkably, she was held as a Polish spy. She described the severe torture she endured and how she organized her daring escape. Her consistent courage and survival ingenuity during the three years of her wandering and later, while a courier and during her incarceration, evokes a great deal of admiration.

Renia's memoir became the continuation of her heroism. At only nineteen years old, just six months after her deeply traumatic experience in the Gestapo prison, she wrote what is most probably the first comprehensive eyewitness account published by a Holocaust survivor. *Escape from the Pit* allows us to see the life and resistance of Jews not en masse, observing from a distance, but up close, bringing our focus to individuals. This is what most affects the reader. The language of her memoir, while simple, is powerful and nuanced. And while her prose is subdued, it has a great emotional impact. In addition, it presents the first female voice in Holocaust literature. Uniquely, Renia's book is written by a female survivor and underground fighter who was not interned in the concentration camps.

Escape from the Pit was published in Hebrew sometime in early fall 1944, less than a year before the end of World War II.[13] Renia recalled that it was around the time that Chavka Lenchner, her comrade in arms with whom she escaped from Poland, arrived in Palestine.[14]

According to Renia, the book was soon reprinted twice. It was published under the name Renia, with no surname. The only other option her publisher gave her was to change her surname to Zamir (which means "nightingale"), an approximate Hebrew translation of her Polish surname (*kukielka* means either "cuckoo bird" or "small doll"). At the time, that was common practice in the Land of Israel. However, because Renia worried that a new surname would conceal her identity and make it harder for her family to find her after the war, she chose to use only her first name. Recalling this decision, Renia explained, "I was very sad and overwhelmed by writing this story, and the issue of changing my family name saddened me even more. It is enough that the Gentiles [in Poland] changed my name all the time and my antisemitic teachers in the Polish school twisted my name because it was a very Gentile name [for a Jew]." At home she was called by her Jewish first name, Rivka (Rywka in Polish spelling), but she was mostly known by her Polish name, Renia. It turned out that Renia was right to be concerned that her family might not find her if she changed her surname, as we shall see below.

A few months after the first publication of *Escape from the Pit*, in response to another request by the Hakibbutz Hameuchad publishing house, Renia wrote two short accounts about Hancia and Frumka Plotnicka, heroic female resistance fighters, activists of the Jewish Fighting Organization, and members of Hechalutz Dror, both of whom she had met in Kibbutz Bendzin during the war. *Hantze VeFrumka* (Hantze and Frumka), the volume in which these accounts appeared, was published in 1945 (and is referenced in two recent English publications).[15] Renia writes about the Plotnicka sisters in her memoir, and her short accounts carry the same strong literary and emotional impact.[16] Her contributions to the book are also among the earliest Holocaust writings. This time the author was identified as Renia K.

Renia's writing appeared in a third book in 1954, a decade after *Escape from the Pit* was published. One chapter of her memoir, "In the Toils of the Gestapo," was included in the Holocaust anthology *The Book of Ghetto Wars: Between the Walls, in the Camps, and in the Forests*.[17] The author's name remained simply Renia.

After she finished *Escape from the Pit*, Renia studied Hebrew and finished high school at Kibbutz Dafna. Although she had been an outstanding student in Poland, she was not allowed to attend high school in 1938, a year before the war, because Jewish students were barred. Instead, at the age of fourteen, she had learned shorthand and found work as a lawyer's secretary until the war began.

Renia loved living in the kibbutz: "It was a paradise!" she told me. In 1946 she became a naturalized citizen in British Mandate Palestine. Meanwhile she started working for the Sochnut (Jewish Agency), an organization responsible for Jewish immigration to the Land of Israel. "We would meet the newly illegally[18] arrived Jewish immigrants at Atlit [a coastal town on the Mediterranean, south of Haifa]. We would go to the ship in which they arrived and which was still anchored in the water. We would board the ship and issue a citizenship certificate to the immigrants."

She worked there until 1950, when her first child was born.

What markedly stands out in *Escape from the Pit* is the dichotomy between the small, organized Jewish youth movement's resistance and the disorganized and overwhelmed masses of Jews who were left dehumanized by Nazi actions and unable to resist physical extermination by the Germans. In the beginning of Renia Kukielka's memoir we see how the Jews who tried to hide from the Nazis, including Renia's family, were quickly stripped of their ability to resist the deportations and killings. In her private conversations with me, Renia would repeatedly say that descriptions of Jews who "went like sheep to their slaughter" made her very angry, because German actions had dehumanized the Jews profoundly and rendered them powerless. Slave labor, poisoned spirit, and starvation further destroyed the human dignity of Jews. However, as illustrated in Renia's account, the Polish Jewish youth groups were more organized and more prepared for the German assault than the wider Jewish community because they had better anticipated German intentions to annihilate the Jewish people. Nevertheless, many in the youth movements were critical of themselves after the war for not organizing resistance earlier.[19]

Renia wrote in her memoir: "Nothing was left for us but to continue to struggle against fate. Who could know what it held for us in the future? But this I did say to myself: If it were destined that I, too, should fall—I would not fall like a hunted animal."

We learn from Renia's account that, although the connections with their organizations in Palestine were severed during the war, each of the Jewish youth movements in Poland adjusted to war conditions. Many of the youth groups began to shift their activities to self-defense and, ultimately, to armed struggle. Renia's Hechalutz Dror was led in Warsaw by Yitzhak Zuckerman and Zivia Lubetkin, who are mentioned throughout Renia's memoir. By July 1942, during the "Great Deportation" of 250,000 Jews from the Warsaw Ghetto to the Treblinka death camp, they established the underground Jewish Combat Organization (in Polish, Żydowska Organizacja Bojowar, or ZOB) in total isolation from the outside world.[20] Shortly afterward, a number of fighters were dispatched from Warsaw to different Polish cities to set up ZOB cells in the ghettos and provide the framework and initiative for armed resistance. The general Jewish leadership in Poland did not support ZOB's activities, and the two main underground Polish military organizations[21] almost totally ignored them at that time.

By September 1942, after a mass deportation of Jews from the Zaglembie area of Poland (where Bendzin was located) to the nearby Auschwitz death camp,[22] an armed local chapter of ZOB was established in Bendzin-Sosnowiec, organized by ZOB fighters Frumka Plotnicka and Zvi Brandes. It included all the active Zionist pioneer movements and had ties to ZOB in Warsaw. Hershel Springer, a leader of Hechalutz Dror, and Baruch Gaftek, an educator and one of the founders of Dror who was appointed commander of ZOB, were already active there.[23]

The Warsaw Ghetto Uprising in April 1943 further strengthened this new idea, which had been unthinkable during the previous years of terror: that the Jews could kill the Germans. Part of this uprising was heartbreakingly described by Renia, who witnessed the valiant battle against the overwhelming German force and the burning of the ghetto while standing among the incredulous—but also indifferent or hateful—Poles outside the ghetto, where life went on as usual.

Each of the Jewish youth movements functioned autonomously while maintaining cooperative ties with one another, as was the case in Renia's Kibbutz Bendzin.[24] As described by Renia, its Jewish Combat Organization activities culminated in the armed uprising against the Germans in early August 1943 during the final deportation of Jews from the Bendzin Ghetto to extermination camps. The revolt was defeated by the Germans and most of Kibbutz Bendzin's members were killed, meeting the same fate as the simultaneous Sosnowiec Ghetto uprising nearby.[25]

At the time of the revolt, Renia was in Warsaw obtaining information, forged travel certificates, and several thousand marks for her comrades. On her return to Bendzin in early August, after the failed armed revolt in the ghetto and during the final deportations of the remnants of Jews to death camps, Renia describes how, devastated, she tried to rescue her surviving comrades from the ghetto by finding a way for them to escape to the Aryan part of the city.[26]

In her memoir, Renia describes a disappointing incident of noncooperation from a Hanoar Hatzioni youth-group member whom she refers to as "B." Just a few days before her own arrest, she tried to persuade B. to help her comrades escape the ghetto. He agreed after she promised him a large sum of money, but he did not appear at a prearranged meeting with her two days later. However, according to Israeli historian Avihu Ronen, it was attested after the war that B. (Bolesław Kożuch) did fulfill his promise, despite not receiving the money, which Renia must not have known while writing her account.[27]

Ronen states that Renia was the first person to organize an escape to the Aryan part of the city for her comrades who remained in the Bendzin Ghetto. These were members from Dror and Hashomer Hatzair and included, among others, Chajka Klinger,[28] Chavka Lenchner,[29] and Renia's sister Sarah.

The surviving members of Dror and Hashomer Hatzair, while hiding in Kubylec's shelter, which was getting overcrowded with Jews who escaped the ghetto, frantically looked for escape routes from Poland and for smugglers to take them to the border with Slovakia. Renia writes that smugglers were found only by Hanoar Hatzioni, but they kept this a secret.[30] Renia explains that to find smugglers "was not an easy matter, for we could never be sure of the smugglers' integrity. We well remembered our experiences in Bendzin in the attempt to join the partisans, when the guide led our comrades into a German trap. . . . Nevertheless we had to take this risk again."

It was the young Mieczyslaw Kubylec who, at last, established contact with smugglers. Unfortunately, after the successful escape of Renia's group to Slovakia, Mieczyslaw himself was betrayed by a smuggler. He was caught and arrested together with his father, Piotr, and both were sent to a concentration camp where they were murdered.[31]

By mid-October 1943, about forty Jews from Hanoar Hatzioni had escaped to Slovakia. They recounted in detail what was happening in Bendzin and Sosnowiec, which was the first time the Slovakian Jews got a full picture of the annihilation of Polish Jews and the ghetto uprisings. They also related news about the fifteen survivors from Dror and Hashomer Hatzair who were still in hiding. This information was sent to Jewish emissaries from Palestine in Istanbul. After Renia's escape to Slovakia in late December, another letter was sent to Istanbul with the list of names of the eight Polish refugees in Renia's group.[32]

Renia's detailed account of her escape from Poland is the earliest description of the escape route Jewish refugees followed to Palestine via Slovakia, Hungary, Romania, Bulgaria, and neutral Turkey (see attached map). It became possible to travel to Turkey at the end of 1943, after the youth movements' leadership received Turkish permission documents.[33] This is how Joseph Kornianski made it to Palestine in January 1944. He had been commissioned to relay to the leadership in the Land of Israel what had been learned from Jewish refugees from Poland, with the aim of preparing a speedy Jewish migration to Palestine while it was still possible to save the remaining Jews.[34] While in Budapest in February 1944, before Hungary had been occupied by the Germans, Renia writes that she witnessed arguments among the representatives of the different youth movements about who should be given the few immigration permits to enter Palestine.[35]

In Hungary, the Zionist youth movement was well organized to receive the Polish refugees. They gave Renia a false document with a photo of a Hungarian woman. The woman had black hair and glasses, so they dyed Renia's hair black and she wore glasses all along her route to Turkey. At the end of February, the youth movements decided that Renia Kukielka would be the representative of Hechalutz Dror. Renia received special consideration not only because she was hunted by the Gestapo but also because she had new information about Zivia Lubetkin for the Land of Israel's leadership. Lubetkin, who had been erroneously presumed dead, was one of the leaders of the Jewish underground in Nazi-occupied Warsaw, the only woman on the High Command of ZOB in Warsaw, and also one of the leaders of the April 1943 Warsaw Ghetto Uprising.[36] Two more representatives were chosen, one from Hashomer Hatzair and one from Hanoar Hatzioni. All were to bring firsthand news of the Holocaust to their respective youth-movement leaders and the Jewish settlements in Palestine.[37] Renia told me that she left Hungary on February 22, 1944. German forces occupied Hungary four weeks later, on March 19.

After arriving in Palestine in March 1944, the three representatives did their best to relay the terrible plight of Jews in Poland. Although the leaders of the Land of Israel gradually learned about the mass murders of European Jewry, it appeared that there was little they could do beyond participating in the Allied war effort.[38] Yet, at the beginning of 1943, a clandestine rescue operation of Jews from Poland via Hungary, the Lishkat Hakesher (Liaison Office), had been established in Istanbul by the Palestinian Jewish leaders.[39]

Renia writes that "in Istanbul we were met by W. and Menachem B." These were the clandestine emissaries Wenya Pomerantz (the representative of Dror and Kibbutz Hameuchad) and Menachem Bader (the representative of Hashomer Hatzair), who made contact with Jewish organizations and movement leaders and transferred money, letters, and instructions to and from Jews captive in the German-occupied countries.[40] They were part of a very small group of illegal-immigration emissaries to have any contact with the Jewish movements in Poland during "their most tragic hours."[41] Renia could not reveal their names and the clandestine operation in her memoir because she was writing in the middle of the war while the activities were still ongoing. Dina Porat quotes Wenya Pomerantz, according to whom "the Yishuv [the community of Jews living in the Land of Israel] in fact did more [for Jewish rescue] than it was ever given credit for—either then or now."[42] In the spring of 1944, Pomerantz and Bader obtained Turkish transit visas to Palestine for the refugees.[43] They also provided the refugees with clothing. In fact, Renia told me in an interview that she arrived in Istanbul without shoes, and Wenya Pomerantz took her shopping for shoes and clothes.

By the summer of 1944, "tidbits of news [about the mass murder of Jews in Europe] arrived one by one, mounting up as they penetrated the hearts of the Jews [in Palestine]," writes Zvi Dror, an Israeli author of important books about the Holocaust. He continues: "Gradually, fragmentary newspaper headlines started reporting the existence of ghettos, death camps, mass murders as well as Jewish resistance and steadfastness."[44]

The impact of *Escape from the Pit* was immediate in the Land of Israel, especially on the members of the Palmach, the paramilitary organization to which Renia had been invited to speak in the spring of 1944. The Palmach, consisting of young Jewish men and women volunteers, was an elite strike force of the Haganah, the chief Jewish paramilitary organization in the Land of Israel.

Yitzhak Sadeh, their commander, connected the Israeli-born sabras with the old Diaspora that was no more.[45] He brought the surviving partisans and ghetto fighters, including Renia, to each and every Palmach campfire meeting "because we must hear this, in order to transform our suffering to strength."[46]

At the start of 1945, Sadeh brought Renia Kukielka and Joseph Kornianski to the most senior command gathering of the entire brigade, which took place in Kalmaniya near Tel Aviv. Kornianski spoke, as did Renia.[47] That same year, when Renia told Sadeh that she had brought with her a flag of the Jewish youth underground organization in Poland that she had carried throughout her entire journey to Palestine, he brought her to another Palmach convention in Mishmar HaEmek where she ceremoniously handed over this flag to Palmach members.[48]

The secretariat of Hakibbutz Hameuchad distributed *Escape from the Pit* among members of this pioneering underground. In his interview with me in 2014, Zvi Dror explained, "The book became required reading for Palmach members because Sadeh viewed it as one of their important weapons: 'A word is a weapon, as speech is also a weapon.' " Dror related that Renia's book was published very quickly. "It was the first book [about the Holocaust]. It was a small book and it was distributed among the people of the Haganah, and especially among the people of the Palmach." He also explained that

> Renia became the symbol of a fighter for Palmach members. Most Palmach fighters knew Renia's [first] name[49] and there is a picture of Palmach fighters with Renia's book in their side bags.[50] In other words, it was as though her book accompanied the fighters. One could read it very fast. And it influenced those girls, especially the girls [of the Palmach]. But it also had an effect on the male fighters. I remember this definitely, the effect of this book.[51]

Haim Gouri told me in an interview that he was forever changed when he first learned about the horrors of the Holocaust from Renia and that this affected his future career.[52] Renia was able to express the profound need for justice and dignity that drove her and her comrades in arms to fight the cruel Nazi regime. As she related to me in an interview: "I wanted to do something to take revenge on the Germans. Even the smallest revenge: to have revenge so that I would have a feeling that I did something. This I wanted very much, otherwise it didn't matter to me if they [the Germans] would catch me, and they did catch me. Many people had perished, I thought, so I will perish too."

Escape from the Pit made its way outside the Land of Israel. The Palmach was active in the illegal immigration of Jews to Palestine from countries such as Iraq, where there was a large Hechalutz underground during the war.[53] Young girls in the Jewish underground in Baghdad were deeply touched by Renia's book, as Zvi Dror explains: "They felt deep sorrow about the dead, the Jews murdered by Nazis in Poland; and about this young girl [Renia]; and about what she had done. One of the young women said, 'If I could only shake Renia's hand in encouragement!' "[54]

Many of the emissaries dispatched from Israel to aid Holocaust survivors in Europe after the war were aware of Renia's memoir. Renia told me, "One emissary from Kibbutz Dafna [where Renia lived] traveled to a DP [displaced persons] camp in Germany and spoke of a girl who was a fighter in the Polish underground, and that she lived in his kibbutz now, and that she wrote a book about her struggles during the war, and told them the title of the book." One of Renia's two surviving brothers, Hirshe (Tzvi), was at this same DP camp and heard the emissary speak. He wondered if the author was one of his sisters and asked the emissary if he could read her book. Renia said that "when my brother started reading the book, he fainted. He fainted at the moment when he read about who my father and mother were. They immediately sent me a notice that I had two surviving brothers." Tzvi had married after the war and had a two-year-old son. The emissary had ensured the legal immigration of Tzvi and his family to the Land of Israel. Renia's other surviving brother, Aaron, arrived later, after the establishment of the State of Israel in 1948.

Renia also told me that in 1945 Tzvi and Aaron, who met after the war in a DP camp, went to their hometown, Jędrzejów in southern Poland, to see if their family was still alive: "They arrived in Jędrzejów and they slept there one night. Some Polish Gentiles from the area came to the apartment where they stayed, together with a few other Jews, and the Gentiles told them, 'You should escape immediately from here because tomorrow night they [the Poles] will come to kill you.' So, they escaped."[55]

Renia's memoir even reached as far as the United States. In 1946 excerpts from *Escape from the Pit* appeared in Yiddish translation there.[56] Renia's book was also translated into English and published on November 1, 1947, without Renia's knowledge, by Sharon Books, a publishing company that no longer exists. The English edition made no mention of the original Hebrew publication of the book. Renia learned about this edition by chance a few years later: "Somebody who knew my sister Sarah found me in Israel and told me: 'Do you know that your book came out in English in the United States?' I wondered: Who gave them the permission to publish the book?"

It is not known how Renia's memoir ended up in the United States. It was registered in the Library of Congress as an original English publication under the new title *Escape from the Pit,* and it had a misspelling of Renia's family name ("Kulkielko"). An autobiographical note was attributed to Renia, and Ludwig Lewisohn wrote the introduction.

Renia had never seen the English edition until I sent her some photocopied excerpts in 2009. She knew English, and after reading the text she told me, "It was written the same way as the book in Hebrew. The impression is that the book was 'born' in English and the title means fighting by oneself. This sounds very similar to the original book's title. It is both fighting and also a fight to survive. The English editors wanted to show that we went through so much and even then we remained human beings. One would want it to be written this way."

When Holocaust survivors, mostly from Jewish underground resistance movements, started to arrive in the Land of Israel in the middle of the war, the process of archiving their oral testimonies began immediately. Renia's early memoir and later oral and written accounts of other survivors, mostly describing resistance to the Nazis, did a great deal to educate the public.

The Jewish resistance to the Nazis was not limited to youth organizations. In Europe, evidence shows that, although targeted for total annihilation, Jews engaged in open armed resistance more frequently than other oppressed groups during World War II (which included revolts in death camps and organizing rescue and escape networks as well).[57]

In *Escape from the Pit,* Renia also records instances of personal responsibility and spiritual resistance. One poignant story concerns the attempts of the Kibbutz Bendzin underground fighters to save the orphaned children in the Bendzin Ghetto in late May 1943. The story plays out in the wake of the terrifying and unforgettable scene that Renia had witnessed a few weeks earlier during the Warsaw Ghetto Uprising, which took place from April 19 to May 16, 1943, and the brutal reprisal of the Germans, who burned the ghetto and "tore the children out of their mothers' arms, dropped them to the ground, trampled upon them with heavy boots, split them with their bayonets."[58] About a year earlier than that, in 1942, the Kibbutz Bendzin fighters had selflessly organized the care of Jewish orphans whose parents had been sent to extermination camps by forming a children's kibbutz, Atid, on their premises.[59] Renia writes that by June 1943, the fighters managed—by bribing Polish officials—to send young girls from Atid disguised as Gentile laborers to villages in Germany and Austria.

In August 1943, after the armed revolt in the Bendzin Ghetto and during the final deportation of Jews to death camps, the surviving members of Kibbutz Bendzin smuggled some of the remaining children from Atid, one by one, as they escaped to the Aryan side of the city. Chavka Lenchner brought with her three little children, including Monia (Monish) Hofenberg, whom Renia mentioned in the memoir when describing her escape from Poland.[60]

Most of the children from Atid survived as farm laborers in Germany until January 1944, when Sarah Kukielka and Eliza Sittenfeld decided not to escape to Slovakia with Renia's group but to remain behind to gather these children and bring them with the next group of escapees from Poland. They were able to collect and bring most of the girls from Kibbutz Atid from farms in Germany to the Slovakian border in another escape group that followed the same route as Renia's a few weeks later. Tragically, they were betrayed by one of the smugglers, and according to what Renia later heard, Gestapo SS men stopped them in the forest on the Slovakian border and shot everyone in Sarah's group.[61]

Three years later, Renia would search for her sister among Holocaust survivors. She felt that, like her brothers, Sarah could still be in a DP camp in Europe. Zivia Lubetkin and Chavka Lenchner, Renia's comrades in arms in Bendzin, knew that Sarah had been killed but chose to withhold this information from Renia after the war, knowing how fragile she was following her incarceration and torture in the Gestapo prisons. In a 2010 interview, Chavka recalled, "Renia came to the Michalkowice bunker after her escape from the Gestapo prison. What can I say? It wasn't the same Renia. She was able to survive, but even now she is broken in her body and soul."[62]

Renia found out about Sarah only when Yitzhak Zuckerman arrived in the Land of Israel in 1947.[63] Shortly after his arrival, Yitzhak, whom Renia vividly describes in her book, visited Renia in Kibbutz Dafna with Zivia Lubetkin. During this encounter, Renia remembered telling them, "Look, it's strange—I got to Israel and Sarah didn't." Yitzhak, who wasn't aware of Renia's fragile emotional state, was surprised that Renia didn't know about Sarah. Renia recalled:

> He was an open kind of a person, so I asked again what he knew about Sarah. At this moment, Zivia said to him, "Never mind, not now." She wanted him not to tell me. But he told me the whole story. You can imagine what happened afterward. Yitzhak was very sorry that he told me about Sarah. I went through a very difficult time after that. I stopped functioning; I was in a real depression. Even many years later, I refused to travel to Poland and Germany because I believed that I would not return from there alive.

Renia told me in an interview that her younger brother Aaron visited their hometown, Jędrzejów, in Poland many years after the war. He and many other Jewish families from various countries went to dedicate a tombstone to the memory of all of the Jędrzejów Jews who had been killed during the war, so that their families could visit a symbolic communal grave. Many people, including non-Jewish Americans, donated funds for this tombstone. Aaron, who was a cantor, said the general kaddish (mourner's prayer) for all the fallen Jews of Jędrzejów. The mourned ones included, of course, four of his and Renia's siblings—Sarah, Bella, Esther, and the youngest, Yaakov—and their parents, Leah (Kleiman) and Moshe Leib Kukielka.[64]

Renia met her future husband, Akiva Hershkovitz, soon after she settled in Kibbutz Dafna. He, too, was from Jędrzejów. They knew each other from before the war because she was friends with his younger sister. His family had been able to send him to Palestine to study at the Technion

(Institute of Technology) in 1938. When the war broke out in Poland the next year, he stayed on in Palestine.

Renia and Akiva planned to marry, but their plans were delayed because of political developments in Palestine. Immediately after the declaration of Israeli statehood on May 14, 1948, the Israeli War of Independence broke out when Israel was attacked by a military coalition of four neighboring Arab states. Akiva was enlisted to the Israeli army, as was Renia's older brother Tzvi.

Renia and Akiva were married after the end of the war, in February 1949, and they settled in Haifa. Renia changed her surname to Hershkovitz. Their son, Jacob (Koby), who was named after her youngest brother, was born in 1950. Renia stopped working after the birth of her first child because they wanted to raise him in a traditional family environment. Their daughter, Leah, whom Renia named after her mother, was born in 1955. Renia went back to work in 1964 as a secretary at a large health care center, where she worked for twenty-eight years until her retirement. Renia was known among her friends as a very intelligent, enthusiastic, and passionate person.

In the mid-1950s, ten years after her arrival in Israel, the Hakibbutz Hameuchad publishing house approached Renia again, this time about publishing a revised Hebrew edition of her 1944 memoir. (By this time Renia was fluent in Hebrew.) After considering the matter and discussing it with her husband, she decided to refuse the offer. One reason was that she did not think the information in her original Polish manuscript had been tampered with when translated and first published and, therefore, she did not see the need to revisit it. She also wanted the authentic Hebrew of the 1940s left untouched: "It was a memory of a tumultuous time—it was wartime." Renia would never write again after the 1940s.

The increased interest, during the early postwar years, in the Holocaust and the heroes of the Jewish resistance subsided a few years after their arrival in Palestine. It was only in the late 1970s that Renia was asked to share her war experiences again. She gave an extensive interview to Haim Gouri for his upcoming Israeli Holocaust documentary film, *Flames in the Ashes*, about the Jewish resistance and its activities during the Nazi occupation. Gouri described the film: "The Jewish story includes those who rebelled at the extermination camps, the forest fighters, and those who revolted at the Warsaw Ghetto and other ghettos, when the hopes for salvage vanished, in the loneliest and most desperate revolt ever known."[65]

In his 2015 interview with me, Gouri confirmed that he used parts of Renia's interview as one of the voice-overs for this movie. Her name appeared in the credits as Renia Hershkovitz. In the audio recording of that interview, Renia seems to be collected and very engaged, with strong opinions and a good, consistent memory. She also reveals some additional details about her incarceration that did not appear in her memoir.[66] It's important to mention that Renia's recollections during interviews were consistent throughout her life.

The first time Renia's full last name appeared in a publication was in Zivia Lubetkin's 1979 memoir *In the Days of Destruction and Revolt*.[67]

Following an increased interest in the Holocaust among Israeli scholars, Renia was interviewed in the early 1980s by Holocaust historians Rivka Perlis[68] and Naomi Shimshi.[69] In their publications, they also acknowledged her book and used both of her family names, Renia Kukielka-Hershkovitz. By this time, however, Renia's name was no longer known to the wider public, and her book had already been out of print for many years. Renia and her story became less visible and were gradually forgotten.

In 2002 Renia was interviewed on video by the Yad Vashem Holocaust Remembrance Center for what was supposed to be a two-part testimony. However, she sometimes had strong emotional reactions after reminiscing about her war experiences, and, in this case she was unable to continue with the second part. Renia said of herself during my interview with her: "I am very strong. That's how I am also in life. If I want to get something in life, I will give my every effort to get what I want. And if I don't get it, it means that I really couldn't do it." This, in fact, was the reason why Renia could not testify at the trial of leading Nazi criminal Adolf Eichmann in Israel in 1961.

Renia's family and friends were protective of her, and they avoided talking with her about her traumatic war experiences, especially in the later years, "because they [the prison and Sarah] were very, very sensitive issues for Renia."[70] Yet, despite her emotional vulnerability when talking about her wartime experiences, Renia was always willing to participate in important initiatives for the preservation of Holocaust history.[71]

After retirement, Renia continued to lead an active life and became involved in many activities: Torah study, lectures at the Open University, exercise classes, and a community choir in which she sang for many years (she had a strong and beautiful voice). At this choir she met and befriended my mother, Sonia Lion (Kovnat), who later became instrumental in the republication of *Escape from the Pit*.

After her husband's death in 1995, Renia went through a difficult period of depression and adjustment to a new phase of life, but she was able to recover and remain active. "My children were sure that I would live with them, but I would never in my life agree to that," she told me. "They should have their own lives and not take upon themselves such a burden—for what?" In 2007 Renia moved into a retirement home in the same area of Haifa (Neve Sha'anan) where she had been living.

Since her book was no longer available in bookstores, Renia's family—her children and her five grandchildren, with whom she was close—gave her a special gift at the turn of the new millennium. They found her book in the archives of Kibbutz Lohamei Hagetaot, photocopied it, bound a dozen copies, and presented them to Renia as a family memory. Renia gave these copies to her friends to read, and many people commented to her that while so many books had been published on the Holocaust, hers stood apart.

One of these readers was my mother, who later told me about Renia's story and mentioned that Renia was interested in republishing her memoir. With this idea in mind, I began interviewing Renia by phone from Canada at the end of 2007. A year later, I met her when I visited Israel. Renia, who was eighty-three years old at that time, was an attractive woman who looked younger than her age. She was energetic, spoke with a strong voice, and held strong opinions. She spoke Hebrew very well and enunciated clearly. She was active in her retirement home, spent much of her time outside her apartment, and kept busy with friends, lectures, exercise, entertainment, and visits to her children's homes on the weekends.

Renia was eager to talk to me about her life, family, and memoir. I also needed this information for archival research in Poland as part of this republication project, and she was keen to hear the results. In Polish archives I was able to find Renia's, her parents', and some of her siblings' vital statistics, as well as those of her relatives going back a few generations. I also learned that after September 16, 1942, Renia's father, Moshe Kukielka, was moved from the Wodzisław Ghetto to the Sandomierz Ghetto and from there, sometime later, to Treblinka.[72]

Renia expressed pride about her experience during the war. She was able to share with me her memories of her family in Poland, her life, and her book without obvious emotional disturbance. Perhaps this was because our conversations were shorter, more frequent, and more relaxed than the long, intense, and strenuous interviews she had given earlier. However, she did sometimes express some anxiety when discussing her wartime suffering. For example, on more than one occasion, without being prompted, she spontaneously brought up the terrible event of her capture by the Gestapo in 1943. At this point, as in her other interviews, Renia repeatedly expressed feelings of grief for the death of young Ilsa Hansdorf, whom she tried to rescue during the liquidation of the Bendzin Ghetto. In her memoir she describes Ilsa's torture and hanging after both of them were incarcerated. I suppose she still carried feelings of responsibility for Ilsa's death.

Renia's health began to decline in 2012, and she passed away on August 4, 2014, several weeks shy of her ninetieth birthday.

A unique aspect of *Escape from the Pit* is that it was written by a female survivor who described in detail the equal roles of women and men in the Zionist pioneer youth movements. Gender equality was part of the socialist youth movements' ideology and contrasted with the socially defined prewar roles of Jewish men and women.[73] In general, before the war, like Renia, Polish Jewish women were more often educated in Polish schools. Compared to men, they knew the Polish language better, assumed greater responsibility for their households, and were more involved in secular activities.[74] From the very beginning of the war Jewish women began to assume unprecedented responsibilities.[75] Women made up a third of fighters in ZOB.

Renia describes in great detail the role of a courier who traveled illegally between isolated ghettos. This dangerous job was delegated specifically to young Jewish women instead of Jewish men, who were more easily identified with the "circumcision test" instituted at German checkpoints.[76] The couriers collected intelligence and spread the word about the mass murders, which enabled Jewish leaders of the youth movements to realize that the German plan was to kill all the Jews of Europe. In parallel, the couriers delivered money and also helped smuggle Jews out of the ghettos, which was often the only way to save lives.[77] The couriers' roles were so dangerous that most couriers, especially those sent on missions to buy and smuggle guns, did not survive.[78] Renia describes the perilous road she traveled as a courier from Bendzin to Warsaw and back and how at the end, on a train, she and her young friend, Ilsa, fell into the hands of the Gestapo. After the Warsaw Ghetto Uprising, Renia was only one of the two couriers left who continued the liaison with Warsaw.[79]

Gender inequality in the Land of Israel was discussed as early as spring 1945 in a newspaper article by Chajka Klinger, one of the Bendzin underground resistance leaders who escaped Poland with Renia. Writing a year after her arrival, she compared the unique role of women in Poland's underground to that of women in the Land of Israel. She challenged the "man's world" of the latter, writing that, in wartime Poland, women had "equality with men in their life and death."[80]

The double standard with regard to gender and age in Israel also manifested itself in the greater attention resistance leaders received compared to young, rank-and-file women like Renia. Thus, Joseph Kornianski has been better remembered than Renia (his memoir was written many years after hers).[81]

Historian Avihu Ronen points out that many women leaders in the Jewish underground played a crucial role in the ghettos' "dual leadership." This was a unique model of leadership composed of one man and one woman who were often romantically involved. As depicted in *Escape from the Pit*, Hershel Springer and Frumka Plotnicka co-led Dror in Bendzin, but in that particular case, while they had a very good rapport with each other, they were not lovers.[82]

After the war, in Israel, these women wrote the first history of the Jewish uprising, but they tended to minimize their own role in the events and emphasize that of their partner (usually their dead lover-leader). The stories were sometimes edited to conform to party lines; however, Renia's account was not altered. The later historiography was written by men, and again the role of women was reduced. As Ronen observes, the time has come to give the women their due.

Historians began to reevaluate the roles and contributions of women during the war many years after its end. Yehuda Bauer, for example, stated in 1982 that acknowledging gender issues adds to study of the Holocaust.[83] Recently the inequality issue affecting female Holocaust survivors has been brought more into focus in Israel.[84]

The status of the Holocaust in early postwar Israeli literature differs from its status in Western writing of the same period.[85] The Holocaust was memorialized in Israel as early as the middle of World War II. Renia Kukielka's memoir was published during the war, in early fall 1944, and more Holocaust memoirs—by male and female resistance fighters alike—started to appear the following year. Over the next decade, these publications influenced early postwar society and gradually shaped the early historical awareness in Israel.

However, the attention to the small groups of survivors, former underground fighters, and their literary works diminished after the establishment of the state in 1948, when Israel focused on its new priorities as a nation: the War of Independence, mass immigration (including Holocaust survivors), further external security threats and wars, and the challenges of building a modern state. This atmosphere didn't encourage reflections about the past, although the survivors did speak to each other and to their local organizations.

In the United States, despite reviews in *Jewish Book Annual* in 1948 that recommended *Escape from the Pit* and a few other books for special attention, and in the *Journal of Jewish Education* the same year that recommended Kukielka's book for Holocaust education at schools,[86] the book appears to have gone largely unnoticed in subsequent years. In general, the period from 1948 to 1961 came to be known as the (relative) "Years of Silence" about the Holocaust among both the media and survivors[87] and contributed to the fading public memory of *Escape from the Pit* and its author.

This period of relative silence about the Holocaust ended with the trial of one of the principal organizers of the Holocaust, Adolf Eichmann, in Jerusalem in 1961, which sparked renewed public and academic interest in the Holocaust worldwide and a "changed attitude towards the Holocaust and towards the behaviour of Diaspora Jewry."[88] In the words of historian Dalia Ofer, "For the first time, survivors were prominent, present and publicly vocal."[89] Renia was among them. As noted above, she retold her story when Haim Gouri interviewed her in the late 1970s for *Flames in the Ashes*. She was also interviewed at length by three Israeli Holocaust historians, Rivka Perlis, Naomi Shimshi, Avihu Ronen, and the politician Moshe Arens, who drew from *Escape from the Pit* in their extensive academic publications in the 1980s, 1990s, and 2010s.[90]

Escape from the Pit was released in the United States in November 1947 as an original text in English and received a favorable mention in the *New York Times Book Review* the following year.[91] Its mysterious publication puzzled Renia for the rest of her life. It remains unknown who commissioned and translated the English version. The English publication registered in the Library of Congress makes no mention of the Hebrew original. While the translation was accurate, the book was slightly shorter than the Hebrew edition and omitted some of the original poetic language.[92]

Until very recently, *Escape from the Pit* was still unknown in the United States except for citations of the book in a few obscure bibliographies.[93] Renia Kukielka's name and book did not even appear in influential turn-of-the-century summaries of English-language Holocaust publications that contain extensive bibliographies.[94] One of the reasons for the obscurity of the memoir's US edition, as historian Dan Michman notes, is that during the first decades after the war, academics in the West paid little attention to the resistance activities of Jewish youth movements.[95] However, interest in *Escape from the Pit* is building in North America. References to Renia Kukielka and her memoir appeared in English publications of Dina Porat's 2008 essay on the first Holocaust testimonies,[96] as well as in the 2016 edition of Doris Bergen's *War and Genocide: A Concise History of the Holocaust.*[97] In a 2017 essay Bergen noted: "Kulkielko's [*sic*] account provides a valuable glimpse into the heavy burden of bearing responsibility for others in deadly circumstances. It also anticipates accusations of failure leveled after the war by Jews against Jewish leaders."[98] And, very recently, Renia plays a significant role in Judy Batalion's *The Light of Days*.[99]

As Katalin Pécsi notes, historian Saul Friedländer was the first, in 1976, to point out that the "master narrative" that emerged from the many early postwar Holocaust stories was primarily male: "Men's experiences and memories became the norm."[100] More recently, in 2014, Stefania Lucamante reiterated the sentiment that no attention was paid to the totality of women's war experiences.[101] Women's contributions to the war effort were overlooked and their heroism unrecognized in postwar society.

"In the early Holocaust canon, women are mostly powerless victims or the emblematic remains of an older Jewish world," writes Friedländer.[102] Most of the renowned authors of the early European Holocaust canon were male concentration-camp survivors writing about their experiences in the camps.[103] There are very few Jewish-female narratives among these authors that became well-known, although women wrote already during the war years.[104] "Literary critics, much like other researchers of the Holocaust, have been slow to distinguish the experiences and writing of women from those of men," notes historian Sara Horowitz.[105] It is no wonder, therefore, that *Escape from the Pit* went unremarked during this time.

The mainstream early postwar European narrative was, by and large, "a black-and-white vision of the events, with occupiers and resisters, villains and heroes";[106] women were mostly relegated to the confines of "female victims or seductresses."[107] Transcending these fixed categories, *Escape from the Pit* is a wartime account of Jewish persecution, annihilation, and fighting spirit written by an underground female fighter who was never interned in a concentration camp. Furthermore, it encompasses a whole spectrum of human behavior: it is balanced and fair in describing the Jews, Poles, and Germans, as well as the perpetrators, victims, resisters, collaborators, and bystanders. It includes descriptions of male and female characters, many of whom actively resist, fight, and respond to their oppression; and it is full of emotional and descriptive detail. Above all, Renia Kukielka's book shows us the very worst of human behavior, but it also shows the capacity for choosing life (even if that means losing one's own) and accepting responsibility for others no matter how dark, oppressive, helpless, or unfair the present may seem.

In their last letter, written in December 1942, Renia Kukielka's parents implored Renia and her sister Sarah: "If we are not found worthy of remaining alive, you, at any rate, keep on fighting for your lives with everything you possess, so that you may be witnesses to the world; so that you may testify by what cruel means your own dearest ones, and your whole people, have been robbed of their lives. May God protect you always."[108]

Renia fulfilled her parents' wishes with her memoir. *Escape from the Pit* is a testament to the spirit of hope: in the midst of their suffering, Renia Kukielka and her comrades were able to conceive of and strive together toward a positive, life-affirming vision of the future. This memoir is as important a "witness to the world" now as it was when it was first published in 1944.

"The pits were wide; the earth swallows all. But the secret of this frightful deed was not swallowed up by the earth. The fact must be proclaimed. Some Jew who escaped those bloodstained hands will surely make the abomination known in full detail."[109]

Notes

Introduction

1. In her later years, Renia disclaimed having composed this note.

2. Jędrzejów was located in southwestern Poland, twenty-two miles southwest of Kielce. In 1939 it had fourteen thousand inhabitants, 32 percent of them Jews. German Army units captured the town on September 4, and a ghetto was established in the spring of 1940. In the Aktion of September 16, 1942, almost all of the Jews of the town and nearby villages were deported to Treblinka.

3. For an account of the German attack on southern Poland, see Alexander B. Rossino, *Hitler Strikes Poland* (Lawrence: University Press of Kansas, 2003), 75–92.

4. For a balanced discussion of Polish–Jewish relations in the region as recalled by survivors from Bendzin, see Mary Fulbrook, *A Small Town near Auschwitz* (Oxford: Oxford University Press, 2012), 37–40, 180–85.

5. Renia Kukielka, *Escape from the Pit* (current edition).

6. Renia belonged to the Dror (Freedom) group, one of several Zionist youth groups in the Bendzin Ghetto. Other groups included the better-known Marxist Hashomer Hatzair and the more centrist Gordonia and Hanoar Hatzioni. Dror's membership was more working-class than Hashomer Hatzair and less fond of the Soviet Union. There were also religious and right-wing Zionist youth groups, although it is not clear how much, if at all, the "kibbutz" coordinated its activities with them.

7. Kukielka, *Escape* (current edition); see also Dina Porat, *The Blue and Yellow Stars of David* (Cambridge, MA: Harvard University Press, 1990), 239–42, for a discussion of the choices of the youth groups from the standpoint of Yishuv leaders and their failure to understand the psychology of the resisters; Asher Cohen in Asher Cohen and Yehoyakim Cochavi, eds., *Zionist Youth Movements during the Shoah* (New York: Peter Lang, 1995), 127–31, about the youth movements in Poland and the possibility of escape to Slovakia.

8. "Halina" was the assumed name of Irena Gelblum (1923–2009), a Hashomer Hatzair courier for ZOB and a heroic participant in the Warsaw Ghetto

Uprising. She later took part in the (Polish) Warsaw Uprising in August 1944, went to Palestine in 1946, and eventually converted to Catholicism in Italy, where (under the name Irena Conti) she became a well-known poet.

9. For a discussion of the moral dilemmas, rescue plans, and actions taken by Ben-Gurion and the Yishuv leadership during the Holocaust, see Tuvia Frilling, *Arrows in the Dark*, vol. 2 (Madison: University of Wisconsin Press, 2003), 139–218.

10. Certain other individuals were involved in helping smuggle Polish Jews to Slovakia. Among these were Alfred Schwarzbaum (1896–1990), an industrialist based in Lausanne, originally from Bendzin; Abraham Silberschein (1882–1952), based in Geneva and affiliated with the World Jewish Congress; and BenZion Kolb (1910–1973), who was assisted by the Working Group in Slovakia.

11. Dalia Ofer, *Escaping the Holocaust* (Oxford: Oxford University Press, 1991), appendix D, 320. According to Ofer, 282 individuals escaped from Poland along the same route as Renia Kukielka and received certificates to enter Palestine. The number of unauthorized entries via this route is difficult to estimate, but perhaps as many as five thousand went over the mountains and by land to Palestine during the years 1939–45.

12. Kukielka, *Escape from the Pit* (current edition).

Chapter One

1. Chmielnik is located on the road between Kielce and Buska, and in 1939 it had twelve thousand inhabitants, 82 percent of them Jews.

2. Volksdeutsche were ethnic Germans. This was the Nazi term for German minority groups in other countries. Poles who claimed German descent were permitted to inscribe themselves on a register of such "ethnic Germans" without close examination of the claim.

3. This was based on the November 23, 1939, decree by Hans Frank, governor general of much of German-occupied Poland. It was required of all Jews over the age of ten.

4. Ten decagrams—about a quarter of a pound.

5. Fifty zlotys, at the fixed (occupation) rate of two zlotys to one Reichsmark (RM), was a considerable sum, perhaps $250 in 2023 dollars.

6. Wodzisław is a town in Silesia thirty-two miles southwest of Katowice. There were four thousand Jews there when the ghetto was established in 1940. Three thousand were sent to Treblinka, three hundred to the Sandomierz labor camp. The last 318 Jews were killed when the ghetto was liquidated in November 1942.

7. "Black Dogs" refers to members of SS units, probably Allgemeine SS.

8. The reference is to the ammunition factory located in Skarzysko-Kamienna, twenty-two miles northeast of Kielce. Controlled after 1940 by the Hugo Schneider AG firm as subcontractor for the German Army, this facility utilized Polish and Jewish slave labor. Eighteen thousand died there or in Treblinka.

Chapter Two

1. This may be a reference to Sedziszow-Malopolski, near the large slave-labor camp complex at Pustkow.

2. Translation from the German: "Stand still, damn Jew . . . Rexl, go and bite him."

3. This was a territory of Poland with its own administration, created by the Nazis on October 26, 1939, after the German invasion. Poland was divided into three parts: the western part, where Bendzin was located, was annexed to the Third Reich; the eastern part was occupied by the Soviet Union; and the central part was named the General Government, which was a semi-independent unit (with Krakow as its administrative center) that was intended by the Nazis for the concentration of slave labor and the mass extermination of European Jewry.

4. The town of Bendzin was located in the Dabrowa Basin near the German border in southwestern Poland, which is an industrial area rich in coal. At the start of the war, Bendzin became part of the Polish territories that were annexed to Germany. Persecution and mass murder of Jews began immediately after annexation and the Bendzin synagogue and surrounding buildings were burned with Jews inside them. During 1940–41 about twenty thousand Jews lived in Bendzin and the neighboring city of Sosnowiec; the Jewish population was over half of these two cities' populations. At that time these were the only large cities in Poland that did not have a ghetto, so about ten thousand Jews from neighboring communities fled to them. The underground Jewish youth resistance in Bendzin and Sosnowiec began its activities in early 1940 by circulating illegal papers and establishing contact with the underground in the Warsaw Ghetto. It eventually became one of the underground Jewish centers in Poland and attracted about two thousand young Jews.

5. "Kibbutz," literally "group," refers in this context to a group of young Zionist pioneers training for immigration to Palestine and life in a collective settlement there.

6. Sarah Kukielka became a member of Hechalutz Dror (Freedom Pioneers), a Zionist pioneer youth movement, prior to the war and moved with her Hechalutz Dror group to Bendzin. She was a courier and was killed by the Germans in January 1944.

7. The young Zionist pioneers in the group Kibbutz Bendzin and later in the Bendzin Ghetto belonged to different Jewish youth movements. These movements were established in the interwar period and had different (sometimes overlapping) motivations: social, cultural, religious, or political. One of their ideological goals was to send members to settle in Palestine. Right before the war there were a hundred thousand young Jewish members of these movements in Poland. The main movements that existed in the Bendzin Ghetto were: Hashomer Hatzair (the Young Guards), which combined Zionism and Marxism in its ideology; Hechalutz Dror (Freedom Pioneers), which was similar to Hashomer Hatzair but less socialist, radical, and with more working-class members; Gordonia, which promoted a

more moderate Zionist-socialist platform; the religious-Zionist Bnei Akiva, which advocated Zionism and Hebrew culture; and the centrist Hanoar Hatzioni (Zionist Youth) movement, which encouraged Zionism, pluralism, and Jewish culture. Renia's Kibbutz Bendzin members were mostly from Hechalutz Dror and Hashomer Hatzair. Other regions of Poland also had right-wing Zionist and religious non-Zionist youth movements. Despite the fact that the Nazis outlawed Jewish youth movements, they reorganized their activities soon after the war began and continued as secret underground organizations.

8. Sandomierz is a town on the Vistula River, fifty-six miles southeast of Kielce. The Germans carried out two deportations. In the first Aktion, on October 29, 1942, 5,200 Jews were sent to Belzec. In the second, in January 1943, 6,300 were sent to Treblinka and 500 were murdered in the town itself; Renia's family likely was among them.

9. As noted in the previous chapter, Skarzysko-Kamienna.

Chapter Three

1. *Sonder*: special work certificates that permitted bearers to work and could provide exemption from deportation.

2. Kibbutz Bendzin operated a laundry service for the Jewish community.

3. Several such accounts appeared in 1944, notably a clandestine booklet by Yankel Wiernik, *One Year in Treblinka* (in Yiddish). The Hebrew edition was printed in Palestine in December 1944.

4. Frumka Plotnicka (1914–1943) was an exemplary member of the Hechalutz Dror youth movement. She organized the first kibbutz in German-occupied territory (in Warsaw) and was sent as a courier by Dror to clandestinely visit many Jewish communities in divided Poland and gather together the dispersed movement's members. From September 1942 Frumka was a resistance fighter and a ZOB (Zydowska Organizacja Bojowa, the Jewish Combat Organization) leader in the Bendzin-Sosnowiec Ghetto. She maintained contact with Zionist representatives in Geneva and Istanbul. She was killed in the Bendzin uprising on August 3, 1943. Some of her letters are assembled in the book *Hancia and Frumka* (1945, in Hebrew), which also included a chapter about Frumka by Renia Kukielka.

5. A worldwide Zionist pioneer youth organization, engaged in preparing and training young Jews for pioneering in Palestine.

6. Zvi Brandes (1917–1943), a prominent activist in Hashomer Hatzair, was one of the original organizers of ZOB in the Zaglembie region. He was active in Bendzin from the beginning of January 1943, organizing defense activities. He participated in the defense of the bunkers and was killed early in August 1943.

7. Hancia Plotnicka (1918–1943), a member of Hechalutz Dror, was active in the organization, guidance, and development of the underground in Grochov

and from the beginning of 1942, in Bendzin. She encouraged the members to keep Kibbutz Bendzin running and to prepare to defend themselves in battle. In March 1943 Plotnicka was called to Warsaw, where a decision had been made to try to smuggle her out of Europe so that she might record the history of the movement during the war years. However, she was killed by Germans during the Warsaw Ghetto Uprising on April 20, 1943. Some of her letters and articles are assembled in *Hancia and Frumka* (1945, in Hebrew), which also included a chapter about Hancia by Renia Kukielka.

8. The Bendzin Ghetto was established in the suburb of Kamionka. Its area was defined by the neighborhoods of Kamionka and Mala Shrodula and it bordered the Sosnowiec Ghetto. The Jewish police was stationed by the SS along the perimeter of the ghetto.

9. Baruch Gaftek (1913–1943), one of the founders of Hechalutz Dror, was the commander of the Jewish Combat Organization (ZOB) in Bendzin. Gaftek engaged in the education of orphaned Jewish children rescued from the Germans and was the main combat instructor for all youth movements in the ghetto. He fell in a bunker in defense of the Bendzin ZOB on August 3, 1943.

10. Their house was located on Podsiadly Street.

11. Oswiecim (Polish) or Auschwitz (German) was Nazi Germany's largest concentration and extermination camp, located in the town of Auschwitz in Eastern Upper Silesia, close to the German border. The Jews who lived in Auschwitz were expelled from the town in 1940, prior to the construction of the concentration and death camps. They fled thirty miles north to nearby Bendzin and Sosnowiec, the only two cities where at that time there was no ghetto. The construction of the concentration camp began in May 1940. The first transport of prisoners to Auschwitz arrived in June 1940. The first deportation of Bendzin Jews to the Auschwitz death camp took place in May and June 1942. Altogether, more than 1.1 million people were murdered in Auschwitz, of whom one million were Jews. By the end of the war, it was considered the most lethal death camp.

12. The reference is to trumped-up foreign passports, the holders of which were kept in special camps by the Germans for exchange against German nationals.

13. Three bunkers were built in different places underneath or adjacent to the building. The first, the "coal" bunker, was built in the backyard of the house under a pile of coal. The second bunker was built a few yards from the first one, near the kibbutz's kitchen. It was located under the stove that was not in use and the entrance to it was through the door of the stove. The third, the "laundry" bunker, was about a hundred yards away from the second one and was built under the laundry of the kibbutz. In addition to preparation for the uprising, the bunkers were also used as a hideout for the youth-movement members at the times of an *Aktzia*—roundups of Jews by the Germans to be transported from the ghettos to death camps.

14. Zivia Lubetkin (1914–1976), whose nom de guerre was Celina, was a Warsaw Ghetto underground organizer and the only woman in the ZOB high

command. She was also one of the leaders of the 1943 Warsaw Ghetto Uprising, and she took part in the Polish Warsaw Uprising in 1944 as well. Following World War II, Lubetkin was active in the Holocaust survivors' community in Europe and helped organize the Bricha, the smuggling of Jews to Palestine where she settled in 1946. She later became the wife of Isaac (Yitzhak) Zuckerman (1915–1981), whose nom de guerre was Antek and who was deputy commander of the ZOB and a participant/chronicler of the Warsaw Uprising. After the war he worked with Bricha and reached Palestine in 1947. Both were members of Hechalutz Dror.

15. Polska Partja Robotnicza (the Polish Workers Party), the communist underground organization in occupied Poland.

16. Tosia (Taube) Altman (1918–1943), born in Lipno, was youth leader of Hashomer Hatzair in Warsaw, organizer of resistance in the ghettos, and participant in the Warsaw Ghetto Uprising, in which she was killed.

17. During the war the leadership of Polish youth movements had some communication with Jewish clandestine organizations in Geneva and Istanbul. In 1943–44 the American Jewish Joint Distribution Committee managed to transfer $300,000 to the Jewish underground in Poland. Some private individuals, such as Alfred (Alf) Schwarzbaum, a Jewish merchant from Bendzin, set up in Switzerland a relief effort that provided aid to Jews in Poland by sending food, papers, passports, and money.

18. Kazik was the nom de guerre of Simha Rotem (born Warsaw 1924), member of the Hanoar Hatzioni youth movement and subsequently of ZOB. He took part in the Warsaw Ghetto Uprising, leading surviving fighters to safety; he also took part in the (Polish) Warsaw Uprising in August 1944.

19. Ina Gelbart (1921–943) was a member of Hashomer Hatzair, a leader of ZOB in Sosnowiec, and a liaison between Zaglembie, Częstochowa, and Warsaw. Caught by Germans, she was executed on August 1, 1943.

20. Alfred Rossner (1906–1944) was born in Oelsnitz, Germany. He managed the largest clothing factory in the Bendzin Ghetto under the auspices of the SS, manufacturing uniforms for the German Army. According to survivor testimony, he treated the Jews humanely and tried to save as many as possible during the 1943 deportation. He was executed by the Germans in January 1944 and honored as Righteous Among the Nations by Yad Vashem in 1995.

21. Hershel Springer was one of the prominent figures of the Hechalutz underground in Upper Silesia and one of the leaders of Dror. He was killed on August 10, 1943.

22. Marek Folman (1916–1943), born in Miechow, was leader of Hechalutz Dror in Warsaw and escaped from a train to Treblinka in January 1943. He took part in the Warsaw Ghetto Uprising and joined the underground in Częstochowa and Bendzin. Betrayed by his Polish liaison, he was executed sometime in 1943.

23. The members chosen to go to the partisans were from Dror, Hashomer Hatzair, and Gordonia.

24. Moshe (Moszek) Merin (1905–1943). In 1940 the Germans appointed him chairman of the Jewish Council in Eastern Upper Silesia, which included Sosnowiec, Bendzin, and more than thirty other communities. Despite a high degree of cooperation with the Germans (somewhat similar to that of Mordechai Chaim Rumkowski in Lodz), he was arrested in June 1943 and is assumed to have died in Auschwitz. Renia's description of him as "our instructor" either is a translation error, as he bitterly opposed the youth organizations and the resistance, or, if accurate, is highly intriguing.

25. Rivka Glanz (1915–1943) in 1940 fled Lodz where she was secretary to Mordechai Chaim Rumkowski, head of the Judenrat in the Lodz Ghetto, who tried to coerce her to marry him. One of the founders of the Hechalutz Dror underground, she became a leading figure in the Warsaw and Lublin undergrounds and commander of ZOB in Częstochowa. She rejected the idea of renouncing the ghetto uprising in May–June 1943 and set up a partisan base for the fighters of Częstochowa instead. On June 26, 1943, Glanz, head of a unit of six ghetto fighters in the Częstochowa Ghetto, was killed in a bunker together with her comrades while fighting the Germans.

26. Nechama (Nacha) and Meyer Shulman testified about these events in Israel in 1986.

27. Boleslaw (Bolek) Kozuch was one of the leaders of Hanoar Hatzioni. He organized the escape of his group's comrades from the Bendzin Ghetto liquidation camp to a hiding place in the Aryan part of Bendzin with Novak's family. This was the first hiding place found by Meyer Shulman.

28. Evidently the two Polish women saw B. with Ilsa and Renia, took his features to be Jewish, and assumed the two women were Jewish as well.

29. Although Boleslaw Kozuch did not show up for his meeting with Renia Kukielka and did not receive the money from her, he did help the Hechalutz Dror and Hashomer Hatzair members to escape to Novak's apartment in the Aryan part of Bendzin. Kukielka was not aware of this when writing her memoir in the summer of 1944, in the middle of the war. Kozuch was later caught by the Germans and killed.

Chapter Four

1. Władysław Sikorski was then premier of the Polish government-in-exile.

2. The Myslowice (Myslowitz) provisional police prison was located on the Przemsza River, nine miles southeast of Katowice, and supervised by the Katowice Gestapo. The jail opened in February 1941 and closed on January 16, 1945. During this period twenty thousand persons, including three thousand women and children, mostly Poles, were imprisoned there. The facility was used especially for interrogation of those arrested by the Gestapo and as a transit camp to Auschwitz, Gross-Rosen, and Ravensbrück. Many were tortured and executed within the prison itself.

Chapter Five

1. The Kubylec family, Piotr and Karolina and their children Mieczyslaw, Alojzy, Wiktor, and Klara, were coal miners from Michalkowice, near Katowice, who provided a hiding place in a bunker that became a transit point en route to Slovakia and Hungary and helped rescue as many as eighty-four Jews. In 1964 and 1992, family members were named "Righteous Among the Nations" by Yad Vashem.

2. Chavka Lenchner (Robinovitz) (1913–2015), a member of Hechalutz Dror, was a resistance fighter in Kibbutz Bendzin. She escaped Poland in December 1943; her memoir *I Was Ordered to Live* was published in 2010.

3. Eliza Sittenfeld.

4. Chavka Lenchner recalled: "And Renia came to the bunker after her escape from the Gestapo prison . . . it wasn't the same Renia. She certainly doesn't remember how I brought her back to health, because the Christian woman I stayed with bought for me Vitamin B12 for injections. . . . I was a nurse from the time I lived in Vilna. . . . I injected [Renia] and I brought her health back. Somehow she recuperated" (Lenchner interview with Dorit and Chaim Koren, November 2, 2010).

5. Refers to Joseph (Yosef) Kornianski (born Bialystok 1901). Kornianski facilitated communication between the Bendzin underground and Warsaw; he organized the Hechalutz Dror underground in Warsaw and spent much of the 1941–44 period in Slovakia and Budapest with Hashomer Hatzair. He was a central figure in maintaining contacts between the leaders of the Bendzin and Warsaw Jewish underground youth groups until summer 1943. He was among the first to convey news of the mass murder of Polish Jews to the leadership of the Land of Israel. He reached Palestine in January 1944.

6. Monia (Monish) Hofenberg.

7. "Miklas" refers to the town of Liptovsky Svaty/Mikulaitis in northern Slovakia on the Vah River near the Low Tatra Mountains. Three hundred Jews, exempted from the deportations, were there when Renia arrived. They had to flee and hide for a few weeks after August 29, 1944, when Germany invaded Slovakia following the Slovak uprising.

8. Benito Rozenberg.

9. Slovakia's Jewish Council had two sections. The legal "Working Group" section organized shelters for Polish Jewish refugees in the summer and fall of 1943, met the refugees at the border with Poland, and helped to take them to the Hungarian border. The second section performed illegal activities, which involved bribing officials. It later developed into "Europa Plan," a failed attempt to rescue large numbers of European Jews from the Nazi murderers.

10. Chajka Klinger (1917–1958) was a Bendzin-born member of Hashomer Hatzair and a leader of the resistance there. She arrived in Palestine in March 1944 and joined the community that would become Kibbutz HaOgen. She committed suicide in 1958. Her book *A Diary from the Ghetto* (*Mi-Yoman ba-Ghetto*) was based

on 1942–44 diary notes describing events in Bendzin and was published posthumously (1959). It was heavily edited and censored because it was harshly critical of, among others, the Zionist leadership in Palestine with regard to events in Poland.

11. Prešov is a city in eastern Slovakia.

12. Hungarian currency between 1927 and 1946.

13. "W." refers to Wenya Pomeranz (Ze'ev Hadari) (1916–2001) of the Lishkat Hakesher (the Liaison Office) based in Istanbul.

14. There were two organizations in Istanbul from the Land of Israel. One was the Jewish Agency, which was there from before 1943 and was accepted by the Turkish authorities. The other one, Lishkat Hakesher (the Liaison Office), was established early in 1943 in response to requests by emissaries from the kibbutz movement and the clandestine immigration agency (Aliyah Bet) in the Land of Israel. It was not subject to the control of the Jewish Agency. One of the leaders of Hechalutz Dror in Poland, Pomeranz (Hadari) was subsequently deputy head of Aliyah Bet, and during World War II he represented Hakibbutz Hameuchad on the Rescue Committee of the Jewish Agency, which attempted, clandestinely, to help Eastern European Jews under Nazi occupation. He reported directly to Ben-Gurion via Teddy Kollek and was especially involved in attempting to help the Jews of Hungary. After the war Hadari, a nuclear physicist, helped create the Dimona nuclear reactor and helped establish Ben-Gurion University, where he was a professor of nuclear physics. "Menachem B." refers to Menachem Bader (1895–1985), a Ukrainian-born member of Hashomer Hatzair. Based in Istanbul, as a treasurer and secretary of the Rescue Committee he engaged in clandestine efforts on behalf of the Jewish Agency to help Jews trapped in German-occupied Eastern Europe. He later was a member of the first Knesset (1949–51) representing the Mapam Party and held various Israeli government positions.

Afterword

1. Haim Gouri, *Ha-Sefer Ha-Meshugah* (The Crazy Book) (Tel Aviv: Am Oved, 1971) 215–16 (Hebrew).

2. Gouri confirmed Renia's identity in an interview with me on May 15, 2015. Yosef (Joseph) Kornianski (see chapter 5 above) was a member of the Hechalutz Dror Zionist youth organization and was a member of Kibbutz Dafna in the Land of Israel since 1944. According to Yitzhak Zuckerman, Kornianski was "active in He-Halutz . . . in Poland. Went to Slovakia in spring 1941 and helped establish He-Halutz underground in Hungary; reached Eretz Israel in January 1944" (*A Surplus of Memory: Chronicle of the Warsaw Ghetto Uprising* [Berkeley: University of California Press, 1993], 41).

3. Yehuda Bauer, *A History of the Holocaust* (New York: Franklin Watts, 1982), 145.

4. Renia was born on October 7, 1924. Details of her biography and quotes are taken from interviews that Asya Kovnat conducted with her between 2007 and 2010, and from the audiotaped interview she gave to Haim Gouri in the late 1970s. The interviews were conducted in Hebrew and translated into English by Asya Kovnat.

5. See, for example, Chavka Robinovitz (Lenchner), *I Was Ordered to Live* (Jerusalem: Yad Vashem, Azrieli group, 2010), 122 (Hebrew); and Zivia Lubetkin, *In the Days of Destruction and Revolt* (Tel Aviv: Hakibbutz Hameuchad and Am Oved, 1981), 282 (translated to English from 1979 Hebrew edition): "I have heard that when Yosef [Joseph] Konianski and other comrades arrived in 1944, there were many in Eretz Israel who didn't want to believe what these comrades told."

6. *Escape from the Pit* (current edition).

7. Bendzin is a town in the Zaglembie-Dabrowskie area, Kielce district, in southwestern Poland. About a hundred thousand Jews lived in this area before the Second World War. The largest communities were in Bendzin and in nearby Sosnowiec. The Zaglembie region was annexed to the German Reich. No ghetto was established there until the beginning of 1943, which gave the youth movements in Bendzin a better opportunity to function. Starting from October 1942 till March 1943, all the Zaglembie Jews were concentrated in two large ghettos that bordered each other: the Sosnowiec Ghetto in the Srodula district and the Bendzin Ghetto in the Kamionka district. Zaglembie became one of the centers of Jewish youth movements all over occupied Poland, attracting about two thousand youngsters to Bendzin and Sosnowiec. Several leaders of Hashomer Hatzair in Warsaw, including Tosia Altman and Mordechai Anielewicz, stayed in Bendzin for long periods during these years. See "Bendzin (Będzin-Polish)," *Encyclopaedia Judaica* (Jewish Virtual Library: A Project of AICE), https://www.jewishvirtuallibrary.org/bedzin (accessed February 20, 2023); and Avihu Ronen, "Chajka Klinger: 1917–1958," Jewish Women's Archive, *Shalvi/Hyman Encyclopedia of Jewish Women*, https://jwa.org/encyclopedia/article/klinger-chajka (accessed February 20, 2023).

8. This was a community of thirty-seven young people in Bendzin led by Hershel Springer. Renia writes about how she and her young comrades in arms lived and fought in "a kibbutz" in the town of Bendzin. This may be surprising for the modern reader who associates "kibbutz" with the intentional collective communities in Israel. This, therefore, calls for an explanation and some historical background: Renia's sisters, Sarah and Bella Kukielka, had participated in Hechalutz Dror before the war. They called their community "Kibbutz Bendzin" to identify themselves with the kibbutz movement in Palestine at that time. The members of her "kibbutz" group in Bendzin had known each other since before the war, which allowed them to continue their activities and reorganize themselves into a resistance group during the war. After daily work, the kibbutz operated a laundry service for the Jewish community. By January 1943 the kibbutz had to move to the Kamionka neighborhood, to the quarters of the Bendzin Ghetto, which by that time had been

emptied of its Aryan habitants, shut, barred, and guarded. Approximately twenty-five thousand Jews lived in the ghetto. Kibbutz Bendzin moved into a two-story house on Podsiadly Street that they shared with the nineteen children of Kibbutz Atid. Renia was not a member of a youth movement before the war.

9. Following Germany's invasion of Poland on September 1, 1939, the country was split into three zones, with the General Government (German, *Generalgouvernement*) in its center, Polish areas annexed by Nazi Germany in the west, and Polish areas annexed by the Soviet Union in the east. The territory was expanded substantially in 1941 to include the new District of Galicia. The General Government was to serve as a "racial dumping ground," an endless supply of slave labor, and ultimately as a site for the mass extermination of European Jewry. See "Generalgouvernement," Shoah Resource Center, Yad Vashem, https://www.yadvashem.org/odot_pdf/Microsoft%20Word%20-%206246.pdf (accessed February 20, 2023).

10. Kukielka's account was confirmed by later accounts by Zivia Lubetkin, Chajka Klinger, Chavka Robinovitz (Lenchner), Rivka Perles, Avihu Ronen, and others.

11. Kukielka writes that in December 1942 her brother Aaron was transferred to a "Skorzysk munition plant" and describes the slave labor there. This was the ammunition factory located in Skarzysko-Kamienna, twenty-two miles northeast of Kielce. See also Wolf Gruner, *Jewish Forced Labor under the Nazis: Economic Needs and Racial Aims, 1938–1944* (Cambridge: Cambridge University Press and USHMM, 2006).

12. Chajka Klinger, who escaped from Poland in the same group as Renia, kept a diary in 1943 recording the history of the Jewish underground in the Zaglembie region and in Warsaw. However, her diary was published only in 1959 and didn't contain information on the escape route from Poland to Palestine. See Avihu Ronen, *Condemned to Life: The Diaries and Life of Chajka Klinger* (Haifa: University of Haifa Press, 2011, 382) (Hebrew).

13. Even though some sources mention 1945 as the year of the Hebrew publication of *Escape from the Pit*, the year appears to be 1944. According to the Hebrew edition of Kukielka's book, it was published by Hakibbutz Hameuchad in Ein Harod and printed in Palestine in the Hebrew year 5705. This year covers the period from autumn of 1944 to autumn of 1945. The archive of Kibbutz Lohamei Hagetaot contains an entry about Kukielka's book indicating January 1, 1945, which in library terms indicates that the date of publication was not clear and that the book could have been published in the fall of 1944.

A recent mention of the 1944 publication of *Escape from the Pit* in an Israeli newspaper in relation to a book on the Holocaust substantiates Renia's claim that her book was published in the fall of 1944. The book, *Prohibited in a New Land* by Ruth Glick (Haifa: Pardes, 2013 [Hebrew]), reveals chapters in the life story of Hannah Szenes. This book is mentioned in a 2013 article in the Israeli *Haaretz* newspaper that states: "The friendly format [of the book] as a pocket book corresponds with early books on the Holocaust, such as 'Wandering and in the

Underground,' by Renia Kukielka Hershkovitz, published in the year of Hannah Szenes's death [November 7, 1944]." In other words, the book by Renia Kukielka was (according to this article) published in 1944—the same year in which Hannah Szenes died (the years mentioned in the article are *not* Hebrew years, as in Renia's memoir, but calendar years). See Sharon Geva, "Hannah Szenes, the Israeli Joan of Arc," *Haaretz,* April 4, 2013 (Hebrew), https://www.haaretz.co.il/literature/study/.premium-1.1978375 (accessed February 20, 2023).

14. Chavka Lenchner (Robinovitz) arrived in Palestine in August 1944 (Robinovitz [Lenchner], *Ordered to Live,* 110).

15. Renia K., "The Last Days of Hantze Plotnicka's Life" and "The Last Days of Frumka Plotnicka's Life," in *Hantze VeFrumka* (Hantze and Frumka) (Tel Aviv: Hakibbutz Hameuchad, 1945), 100–102, 144–48 (Hebrew). Kukielka's original manuscript of Hancia's story in Polish and its unedited Hebrew translation are housed in the archive of Kibbutz Lohamei Hagetaot (Department of Central Registry, #01061). The English citation of Kukielka's chapters can be found in Naomi Shimshi's online articles: https://jwa.org/encyclopedia/article/Plotniczki-Hantze; https://jwa.org/encyclopedia/article/plotniczki-frumka (accessed February 20, 2023).

16. Renia Kukielka, *Escape from the Pit* (New York: Sharon Books, 1947); Frumka Plotnicka: 65, 74, 124–25; Hancia Plotnicka: 82–84.

17. Renia, "In the Toils of the Gestapo," in *The Book of the Ghetto Wars: Between the Walls, in the Camps, and in the Forests*, ed. Yitzhak Zuckerman and Moshe Basok (Tel Aviv: Hakibbutz Hameuchad, 1954), 349–57 (Hebrew). The next edition of this book came out under the title *The Wars of the Ghettos.*

18. The British imposed severe limits on Jewish immigration from Nazi-occupied Europe to Palestine in the 1939 White Paper.

19. See "Jewish Youth Movements in Wartime Poland: From Minority to Leadership," *Holocaust Encyclopedia*, United States Holocaust Memorial Museum, https://encyclopedia.ushmm.org/content/en/article/jewish-youth-movements-in-wartime-poland-from-minority-to-leadership (accessed February 20, 2023). See also Zivia Lubetkin's speech printed in the *Yagur Conference* volume (1947) under the title "The Last on the Wall" and later incorporated in Lubetkin, *Days of Destruction*:

> The legendary Zivia Lubetkin, one of the Jewish underground resistance leaders in wartime Poland, in her famous speech on June 7, 1946, in the Land of Israel, addressed the issue of the so-called passivity of the Jews in the face of German brutality in Poland: Lubetkin strongly underscored her view that there was utter futility for Polish Jews in bringing the world's attention to their annihilation. Lubetkin also spoke about what gave the Hechalutz youth movement the moral strength to resist:
>
> We knew that we were a collective, a movement. Each of us knew that he wasn't alone. Every other Jew faced his fate alone. The movement took on the responsibility of all Jewish public life, a bit too late perhaps,

> during the most difficult days. . . . The greatest tragedy was that the Jews did not know what to do. . . . Although it may not help, nor does it make it any easier, but I doubt whether any other nation would have reacted against the well-oiled, highly perfected German machine under those same conditions of dreadful isolation. . . . We know very well how the Poles and Russian prisoners went off to slaughter, and how entire European nations surrendered to the Nazis. . . . But the [Jewish] people did resist. *The Jewish people stood the test.*

20. Lubetkin, *Days of Destruction*, 111. The ZOB was established on July 28, 1942, and consisted of Zionist and non-Zionist parties. The Revisionist Zionist youth movement, Betar, organized its own Jewish Military Organization (ZZW) and also participated in the Warsaw Ghetto resistance and uprising.

21. Armia Krajowa (the Home Army) and Armia Ludowa (the People's Army); see Yitzhak Zuckerman, *A Surplus of Memory: Chronicle of the Warsaw Ghetto Uprising*, trans. and ed. Barbara Harshav (Berkeley: University of California Press, 1993), 76.

22. Martin Gilbert, *The Holocaust: The Jewish Tragedy* (New York: HarperCollins, 1986), 862. In addition to being an extermination camp, Auschwitz had fifty subcamps for slave labor.

23. Ronen, "Chajka Klinger," https://jwa.org/encyclopedia/article/klinger-chajka. The armed underground that was established in Bendzin included all the active Hechalutz movements (Dror, Hashomer Hatzair, Hashomer Hadati, Gordonia, and Hanoar Hatzioni), with altogether about two hundred members. In addition to learning fighting skills, ZOB also built bunkers for themselves and other Jews in the ghetto, with food and radios (the bunkers were hidden in the closets, walls, and chimneys; in Dror's house the three bunkers were in the oven, under the laundry room, and under a pile of coal in the yard).

24. Dina Porat, *Blue and Yellow Stars: The Zionist Leadership in Palestine and the Holocaust* (Cambridge, MA: Harvard University Press, 1990), 240: "The pioneering youth movements in 1943 decided to ignore all ideological political differences, as they decided to take up arms together. . . . They also established a common treasury."

25. Renia Kukielka, personal interview with Haim Gouri in the 1970s (unpublished). The interview was audiotaped and is housed in the Ghetto Fighters Museum, Israel. The interview was translated from Hebrew to English by Asya Kovnat. As Renia stated:

> I was told that on August 3, 1943, in the very beginning of their resistance, two Germans were killed near the bunker by a resistance fighter, and afterward more Germans were summoned. When the Germans found an opening into the bunker (the "laundry" bunker) they could hear shots being fired from there (the resistance fighters had guns, a few grenades, and Molotov cocktails), so they knew that the

> people underneath, in the bunker, were resisting. The Germans released a poisonous gas into the bunker. Some of the resistance fighters died from gunfire wounds and some died from the gas. The survivors—my sister Sarah, Eliza Sittenfeld, Chavka Lenchner, and Max Fisher—were in the third, furthest, and most isolated "coal" bunker, and were not aware of their comrades' fate.

26. This text was omitted from the 1947 English edition of *Escape from the Pit* and was restored from the original Hebrew in the current edition. Renia's account about returning to Bendzin for the last time was confirmed by the postwar testimony of Nechama and Meyer Shulman (Tel Aviv, 1986, Hebrew). See Ronen, *Condemned to Life*, 430–31.

27. Ronen, *Condemned to Life*, 362, 378. Bolesław (Bolek) Kożuch, or "B" in Kukielka's book (130–33 in the Hebrew edition), was one of the leaders of the Hanoar Hatzioni youth group. According to Aharon Brandes, he organized the connection between the Bendzin liquidation camp and the hiding place with Novak's family in the Aryan part of the city for the Dror and Hashomer Hatzair members. Kożuch was caught by the Germans and later killed.

28. Ronen, *Condemned to Life*, 266, 349, 362. Meyer Shulman, who was active in Kibbutz Bendzin (although he did not belong to any youth movement), escaped to the Aryan side of Bendzin with his wife after the uprising and found a temporary hiding place in an apartment on 12 Belbanski Street that belonged to the Novaks, a Polish family who helped to hide some surviving Jews. At that time Meyer Shulman started to share a leadership position with Dror's and Hashomer Hatzair's surviving members.

29. Robinovitz (Lenchner), *Ordered to Live*, 75–76.

30. Ronen, *Condemned to Life*, 361. Yaakov Rosenberg of Hanoar Hatzioni found Polish smugglers and organized the first crossings to Slovakia already at the end of August or beginning of September 1943. They found that the road to Hungary was free.

31. Ronen, *Condemned to Life*, 363, 388. The Kubylecs were a family of miners from the Michalkowice village whom the Germans for some reason considered unreliable elements and whose documents were stamped "Stateless." They expected to be deported and they felt an affinity with persecuted Jews.

32. Ronen, *Condemned to Life*, 375–76, 392. At the time of Renia's escape, there was a period of calm in the deportation of Slovakian Jews to concentration camps in Poland.

33. Porat, *Blue and Yellow Stars*, 230: "An avenue of rescue opened at the end of 1943: the Turkish government instructed its consuls in Rumania, Hungary, Slovakia, and Bulgaria to issue each of the nine transit visas permitted each week, to families, rather than individuals." See also Ira Hirschmann, Shoah Resource Center,

Yad Vashem, https://www.yadvashem.org/odot_pdf/Microsoft%20Word%20-%20 6413.pdf (accessed February 20, 2023).

34. Ronen, *Condemned to Life*, 382, 400, 409. Three thousand stunned people listened to Yoseph Kornianski's and to Eliezer Ungar's first presentations in the Land of Israel.

35. The severe limits the British imposed on Jewish immigration to Palestine in the 1939 White Paper made these decisions especially difficult. However, in March 1944, the British temporarily mitigated the restrictions.

36. "Zivia Lubetkin: 1914–1976," Jewish Virtual Library: A Project of AICE, https://www.jewishvirtuallibrary.org/zivia-lubetkin (accessed February 20, 2023). During Lubetkin's years of underground activities, her name in Polish, Cywia, became the code word for Poland in letters sent by various resistance groups both within and outside the Warsaw Ghetto.

37. Ronen, *Condemned to Life*, 400. Chajka Klinger, who was one of the leaders of Hashomer Hatzair in Bendzin and who escaped from Poland with a diary documenting the history of the underground and its resistance in Zaglembie and Warsaw, represented her organization; and from Noar Hatzioni, Fridka Oksen-hedler-Kozhuch, who had a lot of information about the war, was chosen.

38. Alan Mintz, "Foreword," in Haim Gouri, *Facing the Glass Booth: The Jerusalem Trial of Adolf Eichmann* (Detroit: Wayne State University Press, 2004), x.

39. Tuvia Friling, *Arrows in the Dark: David Ben-Gurion, the Yishuv Leadership, and Rescue Attempts during the Holocaust*, vol. 1 (Madison: University of Wisconsin Press, 2005), 134, 156. A branch of Lishkat Hakesher was also established in Geneva, in neutral Switzerland.

40. Friling, *Arrows in the Dark*, 1:156: "[Lishkat Hakesher] received its covert instruction directly from Ben-Gurion, Sharett, Kaplan and Meirov (Avigur), the leaders of Israel." See also Rivka Perlis, *The Pioneering Zionist Youth Movements in Nazi-Occupied Poland* (Ghetto Fighters' House, 1987), 2:271 (Hebrew).

41. Hanna Yablonka, *Survivors of the Holocaust: Israel after the War* (New York: Palgrave Macmillan, 1999), 43.

42. Porat, *Blue and Yellow Stars*, 251: "Ben-Gurion was far more involved in rescue work than has generally been assumed"—from Porat's interview with Venya (Wenya) Pomerantz (Hadari) on November 3, 1984. Also p. 262: "[The Yishuv] was a minority in a country ruled by foreigners. It was a social-national experiment in its early stages. Its resources—in manpower, money and arms—were small . . . for all its limitations—and in face of the efficiency of the German death machine and the interference of the Allies—the Yishuv, in fact, did more than it was ever given credit for—either then or now."

43. Porat, *Blue and Yellow Stars*, 230–31.

44. Zvi Dror, *The Life and Times of Yitzhak Sadeh* (Tel Aviv: Hakibbutz Hameuchad, 1996), 272 (Hebrew); also Zvi Dror, personal video interview with

Asya Kovnat, March 19, 2014 (unpublished). See also Ronen, *Condemned to Life*, 404; and Dina Porat, "First Testimonies on the Holocaust: The Problematic Nature of Conveying and Absorbing Them and the Reaction of the Yishuv," in *Holocaust Historiography in Context: Emergence, Challenges, Polemics and Achievements*, ed. David Bankier and Dan Michman (Jerusalem: Yad Vashem/New York: Berghahn Books, 2008), 455.

45. Dror, *Life and Times*, 271.

46. Dror, *Life and Times*, 273.

47. Dror, *Life and Times*, 272. This date is also mentioned by Dror in a March 19, 2014, personal video interview with Asya Kovnat (unpublished); Dorit Koren, videographer. The interview was conducted in Kibbutz Lohamei Hagetaot, where Dror lived, and was translated from Hebrew to English by Asya Kovnat.

48. Dror, *Life and Times*, 272–73.

49. Renia's surname wasn't known among her readers for a long time, until the publication of Zivia Lubetkin's book *In the Days of Destruction and Revolt* (Hebrew) in 1979.

50. Every Palmach soldier had two bags: one knapsack on the back and one knapsack on the side. In the backpack they kept the military equipment they needed; in the side bag, simpler things such as a first-aid kit and books. The Palmach was very proud of the fact that there was no military unit in the world that included so many literary members who also wrote. Zvi Dror, personal video interview with Asya Kovnat, March 19, 2014.

51. Zvi Dror, personal video interview with Asya Kovnat, March 19, 2014.

52. Haim Gouri, in discussion with Asya Kovnat, May 15, 2015.

53. Mordechai Bibi, *The Pioneering Zionist Underground in Iraq: 1944–1945*, vol. 2 (Jerusalem: Ben Tzvi Institute, Yad Tabenkin, 1988), 573–74, 578 (Hebrew).

54. Personal video interview with Asya Kovnat, March 19, 2014.

55. This happened about a year before the infamous Kielce pogrom of Jews in Poland on July 4, 1946. See Bauer, *History of the Holocaust*, 373–75.

56. See Leib Spizman, ed., *Freuen in di Ghettos* [Women in the Ghettos] (New York: Pioneer Women's Organization, 1946); cited in Judy Batalion, *The Light of Days: The Untold Story of Women Resistance Fighters in Hitler's Ghettos* (New York: William Morrow, 2021), 424.

57. See, for example, Nechama Tec, *Jewish Resistance: Facts, Omissions, and Distortions* (Washington, DC: United States Holocaust Memorial Museum, Research Institute, Miles Lerman Center for the Study of Jewish Resistance, 1997), 22; Gilbert, *The Holocaust*, 726, 828; and Mordecai Paldiel, *Saving One's Own: Jewish Rescuers during the Holocaust* (Philadelphia: Jewish Publication Society, 2017).

58. *Escape from the Pit* (1947 edition), 88.

59. *Escape from the Pit* (1947 edition), 63. See also Lubetkin, *Days of Destruction*, 332: "After the closing of the orphanage in the city [Bendzin] Hershel Springer and Baruch Gaftek saved the forsaken children and set up a Movement house for them."

60. *Escape from the Pit* (current edition); Ronen, *Condemned to Life*, 362. The other two children were Esterka and Bronia Leser. In Renia's Hebrew edition (p. 130) the names are Esterka and Moishele. (The fighters and the children who survived hid in the bunker under the coal in the yard near their house.)

61. Ronen, *Condemned to Life*, 388. The smuggler's name was Roman Bzhokowski.

62. Chavka Robinovitz (Lenchner), personal video interview with Haim and Dorit Koren, November 2, 2010, Hebrew (unpublished). The interview was translated from Hebrew to English by Asya Kovnat.

63. Porat, "First Testimonies," 437. Yitzhak Zuckerman arrived in the Land of Israel on April 29, 1947.

64. Renia's extended family was also, presumably, murdered. Renia's father's family lived in nearby Chmielnic: his parents, Abram Alter Kukielka and Estera Malka (née Glajt), and his seven siblings. Renia's mother was born in Pinczow, Poland, in 1895 to Leibish and Rakhel Kleiman. Data are from Jewish Records Indexing–Poland (www.jri-poland.org) and from Page of Testimony of Yad Vashem.

65. Translated from Hebrew by Avi Shoenberg.

66. This tape and its transcription in Hebrew of Renia's interview with Haim Gouri are housed in the archive of Kibbutz Lohamei Hagetaot. I translated the tape into English in 2014, and it is housed at the United States Holocaust Memorial Museum.

67. Lubetkin, *Days of Destruction*, 282, 315.

68. Perlis, *Pioneering Zionist Youth Movements*, part 2, 279n.144 (Hebrew).

69. Naomi Shimshi, "Communication Networks and the Couriers of the Pioneering Youth Movements in Occupied Poland" (master's thesis, University of Haifa, 1990), 328–29 (Hebrew).

70. Robinovitz (Lenchner), *Ordered to Live*, 50. Also the video interview with Chavka Robinovitz-Lenchner on November 2, 2010; Haim and Dorit Koren, interviewers and videographers.

71. These included interviews with Haim Gouri in the late 1970s and early 1980s (archive of Kibbutz Lohamei Hagetaot); her interview with Yad Vashem, 2002; her interviews with various historians; and her interviews with Asya Kovnat from 2007 to 2010.

72. Startseite / 1933–1945 Lager / 1933–1945 Lager W [Home / 1933–1945 Camp /1933–1945], Camp W, Ghetto Area: Poland, Heiligkreuz Province, Jędrzejów District, Wodzisławia Commune. According to the information from the Wodzisław Ghetto, Moshe (Leib) Kukielka (or Moszek Lejb, in Polish) was held in this ghetto. Deportations from there started on September 16, 1942. The Jews were deported to the Sandomierz Ghetto and to Treblinka. The Wodzisław Ghetto was liquidated on November 1, 1942. Renia writes in her memoir that in December 1942 "a letter arrived from Sandomierz. My parents had been there for some days" (*Escape from the Pit*, current edition). See http://www.tenhumbergreinhard.de/1933-1945-

lager-1/1933-1945-lager-w/wodzislaw.html and http://www.tenhumbergreinhard.de/19331945opfer/1933-1945-opfer-k/index.html (both accessed February 20, 2023). The archival work was partially aided by Jewish Records Indexing–Poland (www.jri-poland.org).

73. Yehuda Bauer, "Gisi Fleischmann," in *Women in the Holocaust*, ed. Dalia Ofer and Leonore J. Weitzman (New Haven, CT: Yale University Press, 1998), 253.

74. Dalia Ofer and Lenore J. Weitzman, "Introduction," in Ofer and Weitzman, eds., *Women in the Holocaust*, 4.

75. Samuel D. Kassow, *Who Will Write Our History?: Emmanuel Ringelblum, the Warsaw Ghetto, and the Oyneg Shabes Archive* (Bloomington: Indiana University Press, 2007), 241.

76. Bauer, "Gisi Fleischmann," 254.

77. Sheryl Silver Ochayon, "The Female Couriers during the Holocaust," Yad Vashem, https://www.yadvashem.org/articles/general/couriers.html (accessed February 20, 2023). In addition, coded postcards with information about ZOB's activity and its desperate need for money and other support were mailed by Zivia Lubetkin and a few other couriers to the American Jewish Joint Distribution Committee (JDC or "Joint") in Switzerland. The JDC clandestinely funneled funds into ghettos. See https://encyclopedia.ushmm.org/content/en/article/american-jewish-joint-distribution-committee-and-refugee-aid (accessed February 20, 2023).

78. Lenore J. Weitzman, "Kashariyot (Couriers) in the Jewish Resistance during the Holocaust," Jewish Women's Archive, *Shalvi/Hyman Encyclopedia of Jewish Women*, https://jwa.org/encyclopedia/article/kashariyot-couriers-in-jewish-resistance-during-holocaust (accessed February 20, 2023).

79. Ronen, *Condemned to Life*, 258, 266. After the Warsaw Ghetto Uprising, it was only Renia Kukielka (Hechalutz Dror) in Bendzin and Ina Gelbard (Hashomer Hatzair) from Sosnowiec who continued the liaison with Warsaw.

80. Ronen, *Condemned to Life*, 432.

81. Joseph Kornianski, *On a Pioneering Mission* (Tel Aviv: Hakibbutz Hameuchad, 1979) (Hebrew).

82. Avihu Ronen, "Poland: Women Leaders in the Jewish Underground during the Holocaust," Jewish Women's Archive, *Shalvi/Hyman Encyclopedia of Jewish Women*, https://jwa.org/encyclopedia/article/poland-women-leaders-in-jewish-underground-during-holocaust (accessed February 20, 2023). Love affairs between the youth-movement leaders were quite common in the Polish ghettos. The most famous couples were Yitzhak (Antek) Zuckerman and Zivia Lubetkin; Gusta Dawidson and Shimshon Draenger; Haika Grosman and Adek Buraks; Vitka Kempner and Abba Kovner; and Chajka Klinger and David Kozlowski. These couples supported each other on both the collective and personal levels. Single women also became leaders among the surrounding men, such as Mire Gola, Tosia Altman, and Rivka Glanz.

83. Bauer, *History of the Holocaust*, 246.

84. Sharon Geva, *To the Unknown Sister: The Heroines of the Holocaust in Israeli Society*, Migdarim (Genders) Series (Tel Aviv: Hakibbutz Hameuchad–Sifriat Poalim, 2010) (Hebrew).

85. Dan Michman, *Holocaust Historiography: A Jewish Perspective: Conceptualizations, Terminology, Approaches and Fundamental Issues* (Portland, OR: Vallentine Mitchell, 2003), 337.

86. See Hasia R. Diner, *We Remember with Reverence and Love: American Jews and the Myth of Silence after the Holocaust, 1945–1962* (New York: NYU Press, 2009), 101, 134.

87. See Idit Gil, "The Shoah in Israeli Collective Memory: Changes in Meaning and Protagonists," *Modern Judaism* 32, no. 1 (2012): 76–101. However, in the United States the notion of the postwar "years of silence" about the Holocaust that ostensibly lasted over two decades was recently challenged by the historian Hasia Diner. See Diner, *We Remember*, 134.

88. Michman, *Holocaust Historiography*, 338–39.

89. Dalia Ofer, "Israel," in *The World Reacts to the Holocaust*, ed. David S. Wyman (Baltimore: Johns Hopkins University Press, 1996), 864ff.

90. Moshe Arens, *Flags over the Warsaw Ghetto: The Untold Story of the Warsaw Ghetto Uprising* (Springfield, NJ: Gefen, 2011), 302.

91. "Engross[ing]. . . . Its artlessness is its own recommendation" (Gertrude Samuels, review of *Escape from the Pit*, February 28, 1948).

92. In this new edition the text of *Escape from the Pit* has been expanded.

93. See Judith A. Scheffler, *Wall Tappings: An International Anthology of Women's Prison Writings, 200 A.D. to the Present* (Boston: Northeastern University Press, 1989); and *Bibliography, Archival Sources and Other Resources for Research on the Jewish Communities of Zaglembia (Bedzin, Czeladz, Dabrowa Gornicza, Slawkow, Sosnowiec, and Vicinity)*, http://www.shtetlinks.jewishgen.org/zaglembie/Zag001.html (accessed February 20, 2023).

94. See, for instance, Ofer and Weitzman, *Women in the Holocaust*; Martin Gilbert, "Holocaust Writing and Research since 1945," Joseph and Rebecca Meyerhoff Annual Lecture, September 26, 2001, United States Holocaust Memorial Museum, Washington, DC, https://www.ushmm.org/m/pdfs/20050726-gilbert.pdf (accessed February 20, 2023); S. Lilian Kramer, *Holocaust Literature: An Encyclopaedia of Writers and Their Work* (London: Routledge, 2003); Weitzman, "Kashariyot (Couriers) in the Jewish Resistance"; *Jewish Resistance: A Working Bibliography*, 3rd ed. (Center for Advanced Holocaust Studies, United States Holocaust Memorial Museum, 2003), https://www.ushmm.org/m/pdfs/20100920-jewish-resistance-bibliography.pdf (accessed February 20, 2023); Hanna Yablonka, *Survivors of the Holocaust: Israel after the War* (New York: Palgrave Macmillan, 1999). Yablonka incorrectly states that Rozka Korchak, who arrived in the Land of Israel in December 1944, wrote the first Holocaust memoir. Korchak's *Lehavot be-Afar* (Flames in Ash) was published in Tel Aviv in 1946.

95. Michman, *Holocaust Historiography*, 374, 380.

96. See Porat, "First Testimonies," 440, 445, 455.

97. Doris L. Bergen, *War and Genocide: A Concise History of the Holocaust*, 3rd ed. (Lanham, MD: Rowman & Littlefield, 2016), 131.

98. Doris Bergen, "I Am (Not) to Blame: Intent and Agency in Personal Accounts of the Holocaust," in *Lessons and Legacies*, vol. 12, New *Directions in Holocaust Research and Education*, ed. Wendy Lower and Lauren Faulkner Rossi (Evanston, IL: Northwestern University Press, 2017), 87–107.

99. Batalion, *Light of Days*.

100. Katalin Pécsi, "Women's Voices in Hungarian Holocaust Literature," https://theverylongview.com/WATH/essays/womensvoices.htm#[i]#[i] (accessed February 20, 2023).

101. Stefania Lucamante, *Forging Shoah Memories: Italian Women Writers, Jewish Identity, and the Holocaust* (New York: Palgrave Macmillan, 2014), 2–4, 10.

102. Saul Friedländer, "The Historical Significance of the Holocaust," *Jerusalem Quarterly*, no. 1 (Fall 1976).

103. With the exception of Primo Levi, who published in 1947, books by Imre Kertész, Jean Améry, Bruno Bettelheim, Jerzy Kosinski, Jorge Semprun, Tadeusz Borowski, and Elie Wiesel were published in the 1950s and later.

104. Better-known early female Holocaust writers—not a full list—include Anne Frank (1946), Olga Lengyel (1946), Rokhl Auerbach (1947), and Gisella Perl (1948). See Sara Horowitz, "Women in Holocaust Literature: Engendering Trauma Memory," in *Women in the Holocaust*, ed. Dalia Ofer and Lenore J. Weitzman (New Haven, CT: Yale University Press, 1998), 364–77.

105. Sara Horowitz, "Holocaust Literature," Jewish Women's Archive, *Shalvi/Hyman Encyclopedia of Jewish Women*, https://jwa.org/encyclopedia/article/holocaust-literature (accessed February 20, 2023).

106. Debórah Dwork and Jan van Pelt, *Holocaust: A History* (New York: W. W. Norton, 2002), 382, 383.

107. Lucamante, *Forging Shoah Memories*, 3, 5.

108. *Escape from the Pit* (current edition).

109. *Escape from the Pit* (current edition).

Index

Note: Photographs appear on unnumbered pages following page 138 and are referenced here by figure number.